Women and the Texas Revolution

Women and the Texas Revolution

Edited by Mary L. Scheer

UNIVERSITY OF NORTH TEXAS PRESS

DENTON, TEXAS

Permissions:
University of North Texas Press
1155 Union Circle #311336
Denton, TX 76203-5017

The paper used in this book meets the minimum requirements of the American National Standard for Permanence of Paper for Printed Library Materials, z39.48.1984. Binding materials have been chosen for durability.

Library of Congress Cataloging-in-Publication Data

Women and the Texas Revolution / edited by Mary L. Scheer. -- 1st ed.
    p. cm.
 Includes bibliographical references and index.
 ISBN 978-1-57441-469-1 (cloth : alk. paper) -- ISBN 978-1-57441-459-2 (ebook)
 1. Texas--History--Revolution, 1835-1836--Women. 2. Women--Texas--History--19th century. I. Scheer, Mary L., 1949-
 F390.W87 2012
 305.40976409'034--dc23
                          2012016309

For Dr. Ben Procter, teacher, mentor, friend.

Contents

Acknowledgments

An edited book necessarily incurs many scholarly and technical debts to individuals who contributed to the volume. Most importantly, I am particularly indebted to the seven fine scholars who lent their skill and expertise to this project. They cheerfully agreed, with some coaxing, to research a specific group of Texas women, write their essays, and accept constructive criticism, all this while on a tight timetable. Their conscientiousness and good humor has contributed to the success of *Women and the Texas Revolution*. In addition, thanks are extended to Ron Chrisman, director of the University of North Texas Press, who suggested this book project following a roundtable discussion at the Texas State Historical Association 2010 meeting. From its inception he has expressed confidence in its promise to contribute to the scholarly literature on women and the Texas Revolution.

I gratefully acknowledge the assistance of Lamar University and especially Patty Renfro, administrative associate in the history department, who makes my life immeasurably easier. Two readers for the University of North Texas Press strengthened the volume. Also, special thanks are due to student assistant Amarienne Williams and two graduate students, especially Cassandre Durso and Sharon Courmier, who provided technical assistance and made many trips to the library to help secure sources for the manuscript.

Finally, I thank my husband Richard, who has always supported my academic endeavors and is an excellent editor himself. Further, I owe a debt of gratitude to the first generation of Texas women, who courageously bore the burdens of frontier life and contributed to the historical development of Texas and the nation. It is upon their shoulders that we all stand.

Introduction

The Texas Revolution, 1835–1836, changed the course of history for the residents of Mexico's northernmost province. Most individuals living on the Texas frontier during the 1820s and 1830s were subjects of a ruling regime thousands of miles away. Hispanic families already living in the region mingled with Anglo newcomers, who had recently immigrated with their black servants to take advantage of a generous immigration policy. Collectively, they cleared the lands, planted their crops, laid out towns, and lived their lives under Spanish and then Mexican rule. Only the declining native-American population retained any autonomy, although temporary, in the face of conflicting claims on the land. Yet despite their land grants, hard work, and allegiance to the Mexican Constitution of 1824, within a fifteen-year time span relations between Mexico and Texas would deteriorate. Although not all Texas residents at the time supported the coming revolution, Anglo, Tejano, and black men and women contributed to the armed resistance that ultimately would lead to independence. As a result these Texians would found a new sovereign nation—the Republic of Texas, 1836–1845.[1]

The Texas Revolution was similar in many respects to other revolutions of the era while retaining its own unique circumstances. At first there was uncertainty about its goal—independence or more democracy under Mexican rule. Crises such as those at San Felipe de Austin (1832) and Anáhuac (1835) preceded the main military actions. But as Mexican troops methodically crushed Texan forces in south Texas and bore down upon the garrison at the Alamo, delegates met at Washington-on-the-Brazos and adopted a formal declaration of independence. As was typical with other revolutions, once they crossed the threshold of independence, there was a need to balance an effective government with military measures to meet the emergency. At the same time the conflict did not occur easily and engendered opposition from various factions of Texans who opposed the insurgency. Although threatened by the move toward centralism, moderates, Tejanos, and others were conflicted about the dangers these political changes posed for Texas. After months of hesitation and indecisiveness, the leaders of the nascent rebellion unified under the banner of constitutional order, a provisional government, and eventual independence through armed resistance. In the end an independent nation emerged, promising more democracy and the blessings of liberty mainly for the Anglo majority.

In terms of military action, the conflict was relatively short, lasting about seven months. The battles generally involved small numbers of Texan soldiers, many untrained with limited experience, and larger numbers of Mexican troops. Most unusual of all, the fighting ended suddenly with a stunning victory at San Jacinto by General Sam Houston over the Mexican troops led by General Antonio López de Santa Anna. The brevity of the war and its abrupt ending, while securing political objectives, prevented any unraveling of the social fabric, leaving intact a patriarchal, gendered society.[2]

Such dramatic events within a relatively short period of time, it could be argued, impinged primarily on men—not women. After all, the Texas Revolution was in large part a manly event. Men drafted the Declaration of Independence at Washington-on-the-Brazos, men enlisted in the army led by Sam Houston, men defended the walls of the Alamo and defeated Santa Anna at San Jacinto, and men voted and held elective office in the new Republic of Texas. For the most part accounts of the revolution have supported this interpretation, relating its history through the lens of politics, economics, and the battlefield, spheres from which women were generally absent. If the events of 1836 affected women and their lives, scholars documented their participation primarily through the impact on their husbands, sons, and fathers.

In the 1970s, with renewed historical interest in the upcoming bicentennial, proponents of the new social history began to question the conventional historical narrative, especially that of another conflict—the American Revolution. Traditional accounts of those pivotal events had routinely featured generals, politicians, armies, and diplomats, rather than ordinary citizens who also contributed to the war effort. Colonial women, it was thought, had little or no impact on that political and military contest. Nevertheless, scholars began to uncover a variety of new perspectives on the war. They posed new and different questions about the American Revolution and its effects on women and other neglected groups. For example, they asked if women contributed to the war effort. How did the revolution affect different racial and ethnic groups of women? What changes did the revolution bring to women's lives? Did the revolution have the same importance and effects on women as on men? In short, they wondered if the American Revolution was "revolutionary" for women and others.

Surprisingly, few historians have asked those same questions of the Texas Revolution. Instead, most scholars of the period have focused on the political, economic, and military aspects of the revolt. They asked whether the revolution was a collision of two cultures, one Anglo and the other Mexican. Was the Texas Revolution a political crisis fostered by the collapse of liberalism and the rise of Santa Anna? Was it the work of pro-slavery interests to preserve and spread slavery? Or was there a conspiracy of complicity between the United States and the Anglo-American immigrants to annex Texas to the union? Recently, some historians also have questioned its status as a "revolution," a term usually reserved for a profound restructuring of society. While each of these viewpoints has some validity, they rarely addressed issues and changes that directly affected Texas women and their lives.[3]

Historically, wars and revolutions have offered the politically and socially disadvantaged opportunities to contribute to the nation (or cause) in exchange for future expanded rights. Such advances occurred in varying degrees for women during and after the American Revolution, the Civil War, World War I, and World War II. In many cases, though, once the crisis was over, women were expected to return to their appropriate sphere. This was also true of the Texas Revolution. When women stepped out of their domestic spheres to support patriotically the revolution and participate in the conflict, they challenged the bonds of domesticity. Yet the brevity of the revolution and its sudden end prevented any gender realignment and the Texas victory re-affirmed the status quo in social relations.

As in the American Revolution, women's experiences in the Texas Revolution varied by class, race, and region. While the majority of immigrants who crossed the Sabine and Red rivers into Texas in the 1820s and 1830s were men—farmers, adventurers, debtors, profit-seekers, and criminals—many were Anglo women who accompanied their husbands and families or, in some instances, braved the dangers and the hardships of the frontier alone. Black and Hispanic women were also present in Mexican Texas. Most black women came as chattel property (or free blacks) and most Tejanas were already living in predominantly Spanish or Mexican communities. The native-American female population, a sizeable but declining segment of the population, was also in the region, inhabiting the prairies and plains, but rarely counted in the various censuses at the time. Whether Mexican loyalist or Texas patriot, elite plantation mistress or subsistence farm wife, free black or slave, Anglo or

Indian, Texas women, as the contributors to this volume point out, were at the center of the revolutionary upheaval.

While there is wide scholarship on the Texas Revolution, there is no comparable volume on the roles of various women and the effects of that conflict on them. Many of the standard works on the Texas Revolution include women briefly in the narrative, such as Emily Austin, Susanna Dickinson, and Emily Morgan West (the Yellow Rose), but not as principal participants. Only the women and children who fled Santa Anna's troops during the Runaway Scrape, which was mainly a female event, have received much in-depth examination.[4]

Previously published books, biographies, and articles about Anglo women and the conditions on the Texas frontier are abundant. They include Neila Petrick, *Jane Long of Texas, 1798–1880* (1995); William Ransom Hogan, "Pamelia Mann: Texas Frontierswoman," *Southwestern Historical Quarterly* (1935); Rebecca Smith, *Mary Austin Holley: A Biography* (1962), William Seale, *Sam Houston's Wife* (1970); Anne Crawford and Crystal Ragsdale, *Women in Texas History: Their Lives, Their Experiences, Their Accomplishments* (1982); Sandra Myres, *Westering Women and the Frontier Experience, 1800–1915* (1982); Anne Patton Malone, *Women on the Texas Frontier* (1983); Fane Downs, "'Tryels and Trubbles,'" *Southwestern Historical Quarterly* (1986); Evelyn Carrington, *Women in Early Texas* (1975; 1995); Annie Doom Pickrell, *Pioneer Women in Texas* (1929; 1991); Paula Mitchell Marks, *Turn Your Eyes Toward Texas* (1989); Angela Boswell, *Her Act and Deed* (2001); Linda Hudson, *Mistress of Manifest Destiny* (2001); and Light Cummins, *Emily Austin of Texas* (2009).

Sources for minority frontier women include: Abigail Curlee, "The History of a Texas Slave Plantation, 1831–1893," *Southwestern Historical Quarterly* (1922), Jane Dysart, "Mexican Women of Texas, 1830–1860," *Western Historical Quarterly* (1976), David Weber, *The*

Mexican Frontier, 1821–1846 (1982), Ruthe Winegarten, *Black Texas Women* (1994), Jean Stuntz, *Hers, His, and Theirs* (2005), L. Lloyd MacDonald, *Tejanos in the 1835 Texas Revolution* (2009), and Juliana Barr, *Peace Came in the Form of a Woman* (2007).

A few edited books contain chapters or portions of chapters on selected groups of women at the time of the Texas Revolution, but none cover in depth all Texas women during that period. Evelyn Carrington edited *Women in Early Texas* (1975). Paula Mitchell Marks wrote "Trials, Tribulations, and Good Times: Westering Women in Frontier Texas, 1821–1870," in *Invisible Texans*, edited by Donald Willett and Stephen Curley. Cary Wintz authored "Women in Texas," and Linda Hudson wrote "Women in Texas: A Pioneer Spirit," in the second and fourth editions of *The Texas Heritage*, edited by Ben Procter and Archie McDonald. And Angela Boswell published "Black Women during Slavery to 1865," in *Black Women in Texas History,* edited by Bruce Glasrud and Merline Pitre.

As valuable as these secondary sources are, the availability of primary sources such as memoirs, reminiscences, and correspondence, many written by women, provided crucial documentation. More primary sources exist for Anglo women, due to their higher literacy rates, than for native, black, or Hispanic women of Texas. Nevertheless, the contributors effectively gathered information on all groups of Texas women from a wide range of materials: the writings of men, historical documents, legal proceedings, newspapers, private papers, diaries, and genealogy records.[5]

With a growing scholarship and numerous first hand accounts, historian Fane Downs, writing about women in early nineteenth-century Texas, suggested in 1986 that "a comprehensive study of women of the 1830–1845 period should include Indian, Hispanic, and Anglo women of all ages, in all classes, in rural areas and towns, who were single, married, or widowed, who worked at home or away from home." While Downs envisioned a broad study including topics on immigration, homebuilding, community life, leadership, education, legal status, church roles, medical practices and others, this anthology will treat only a few of those subjects, with an emphasis on the revolutionary years.[6]

Along with Downs' challenge to create a more comprehensive study of Texas women during the revolutionary and Republic eras, the origins of this book began with a reexamination of the literature published during the bicentennial of the American Revolution. In the months leading up to that two-hundred-year anniversary and beyond, scholars in the 1970s analyzed the causes, experiences, and consequences of that conflict utilizing a broader cross section of the populace—elites and yeomen, native Americans and slaves, apprentices and women. A reconsideration of that scholarship about an earlier revolution led to a re-conceptualization of the political, legal, and social consequences for women during the Texas Revolution.

A roundtable session titled "Did the Texas Revolution Benefit Women?" at the 2010 Texas State Historical Association meeting in Dallas provided the initial forum for a discussion of the topic. Four of the contributors to this volume—Jean A. Stuntz, Lindy Aiken, Angela Boswell, and this editor—participated in the panel and presented our preliminary research and conclusions. Afterwards Ron Chrisman, director of the University of North Texas Press, saw the potential of the topic for a fresh look at the Texas Revolution from the perspective of women. He therefore invited the panelists, as well as future contributors, to submit essays for an edited book on the subject. This volume is the result of that collaboration.

Most of the contributors to this volume are historians, but a few are also archivists and lawyers. They have utilized widely varied sources, primary and secondary, new and old, scarce and abundant. Their essays cover the revolutionary era, broadly defined to encompass the decades before and after the conflict, and may be read separately or part of a comprehensive whole. All have placed women at the center of the Texas Revolution and reframed the historical narrative by asking: What were the social relations between the sexes at the time of the Texas Revolution? Did women participate/contribute to the war effort? Did the events of 1836 affect Anglo, black, Hispanic, and native-American women differently? What changes occurred in women's lives as a result of the revolution? Did the revolution liberate women to any degree from their traditional domestic sphere and threaten the established patriarchy? What benefits, if any, did women gain both in the short and long term? In brief, was the Texas Revolution "revolutionary" for Texas women?

In chapter one "Continuity, Change, and Removal: Native Women and the Texas Revolution," Lindy Eakin utilizes gender, kinship, and age as important elements of analysis of native women's roles before and after the revolution. According to Eakin, native-American women were "key to transmitting culture to the next generation." Despite the westward advance of Anglo Americans, conflicting claims to the land, and harsh Indian policies, they were able to sustain their village way of life and traditional roles. Although the long-term effects of the Texas Revolution were ultimately disastrous on native peoples, leading to removal, loss of hunting territories and buffalo herds, and extermination, women's position and power within those societies remained fairly constant.

Like native-American women's, *Tejanas'* lives revolved around their families, as described by Jean A. Stuntz in chapter two titled "Tejanas: Hispanic Women on the Losing Side of the Texas Revolution." Once the revolution broke out, however, their husbands faced difficult choices between loyalty to Mexico and support for the Texan cause. When the fighting was over, the daily domestic life for *Tejanas* did not change very much. But in the long term, the Texas Revolution had a devastating effect on Hispanic women and their families, resulting in a loss of status, power, and land as the Anglo majority imposed governmental discrimination, anti-Mexican prejudice, and legal restrictions against them.

By the eve of the Texas Revolution Anglo women outnumbered all groups of Texas women with the possible exception of native women, whose numbers cannot be certain. In chapter three, editor Mary L. Scheer argues in "'Joys and Sorrows of Those Dear Old Times': Anglo-American Women during the Era of the Texas Revolution" that white women experienced the revolution in very personal ways, from the death of family members and loss of private possessions to traumatic disruptions to their way of life. At the same time, Anglo women patriotically took an active and direct role in the conflict, contributing to its ultimate victory. But success on the battlefield did not translate to shifts in power or property, and Anglo women's social, legal, and economic status continued to be subordinate to that of men.

If Anglo women failed to improve significantly their lives, black women, mostly slaves, experienced a reversal of fortune. Angela Boswell in "Traveling the Wrong Way Down Freedom's Trail: Black Women and the Texas Revolution," shows in chapter four that as long as Texas remained under Mexican rule, there was hope, even expectation, that the institution of slavery would be abolished or mitigated. But with independence Anglo Texans, many from the southern United States, prevented the disintegration of slavery and established the institution on a firm constitutional basis. For black women, then, the Texas Revolution erased centuries of the promise of freedom and in the long run sentenced them and their families to decades of enforced servitude.

Although the military phase of the Texas Revolution was mainly a male event, women were present on or near the battlefields. For many years the Anglo-centric narrative of the conflict named only Susanna Wilkerson Dickerson and her infant daughter Angelina as the female Alamo survivors. But there were other Bexareña women, many nameless, who remained within the Alamo walls or left during the three-day armistice. In chapter five Dora Elizondo Guerra in "Two Silver Pesos and a Blanket: The Texas Revolution and the Non-Combatant Women Who Survived the Battle of the Alamo" identifies six little-known Hispanic women who survived the battle, only to be socially and economically marginalized afterwards by an increasingly hostile and alien Anglo population.

One of the most difficult episodes of the Texas Revolution for women was the Runaway Scrape, the flight of thousands of Texans eastward, mainly women, children, and slaves, away from the approaching Mexican army. In "'Up Buck! Up Ball! Do Your Duty!': Women and the Runaway Scrape," Light Cummins describes in chapter six the mass exodus as largely a domestic event, as well as a defining moment for women when they had to rely on their own resources for survival. Afterwards, as many women returned to their homes, they found their farms in ruins, their houses looted, and their possessions gone.

In chapter seven, "'To the Devil with your Glorious History!': Women and the Battle of San Jacinto," Jeffrey D. Dunn focuses on the women in the region of Harrisburg and the San Jacinto settlements. Many of these women actively supported the Texan cause, sewed flags for the troops, and evacuated their homes to escape the approaching Mexican army. One woman, Margaret McCormick, returned later to discover hundreds of corpses on her property where the final battle of the revolution was fought—San Jacinto. At the same time Dunn does not neglect the Mexican side of the battle, noting that Mexican women served as camp followers or *soldaderas* and a few were taken prisoner by the Texans. He also analyses the historical evidence concerning Emily D. West, a mulatto female who allegedly was inside Santa Anna's tent at the time of the battle.

Since few women appeared in the early narrative of the Texas Revolution, in chapter eight Laura Lyons McLemore contends that one way women claimed their place in the historical record was by

becoming the memorializers of Texas revolutionary heroes. In her essay "Women and the Texas Revolution in History and Memory" she
focuses on three important women—Mary Jane Briscoe, Adina de
Zavala, and Clara Driscoll—who preserved battle sites such as at San
Jacinto and the Alamo, promoted the memory of Texas veterans, and
shaped public perceptions about the revolution. Further, she argues
that the sentimentalism of the Texas Revolution stemmed from their
personal backgrounds and social needs, which although dissimilar,
allowed them to make common cause and create a public memory.

Overall, the Texas Revolution had a profound effect on all Texas
women. For native and Hispanic women the conflict did not alter their
fundamental roles within their societies, but imposed a new political
entity, which would ultimately lead to their loss of land, power, status,
and even their lives. For black women the Texan victory guaranteed
that the institution of slavery would continue firmly in place, ensuring
future racial antagonisms. And for Anglo women, who were in a position to benefit the most, the Texas Revolution maintained the status
quo in gender relations and failed to improve significantly their legal
or economic status. Nevertheless, Texas women were at the center of
the revolution and contributed, both directly and indirectly, to the
Texan victory in 1836 and the subsequent creation of an independent
nation. Despite the short term, immediate gains of independence
over autocratic rule, on balance the Texas Revolution had long-term
negative consequences, socially, politically, and economically, for
women's lives. For the foreseeable future, the revolutionary experience
of Texas women would be far from "revolutionary."

Endnotes

1   For a discussion of the causes of the Texas Revolution see David J. Weber,
    "Refighting the Alamo: Mythmaking and the Texas Revolution" in *Major
    Problems in Texas History*, ed. Sam W. Haynes and Cary D. Wintz (Boston:
    Houghton Mifflin Co., 2002), 133–139. Also see Gregg Cantrell, *Stephen*

F. Austin: Empresario of Texas (New Haven: Yale University Press, 1999), 115 116, 151–159.

2 Although there were earlier clashes, the Texas Revolution began in October 1835 with the battle of Gonzales and ended with the battle of San Jacinto on April 21, 1836.

3 Scholars disagree on whether the movement for Texas independence was a true revolution with a defined ideology, resulting in profound social, political, and economic change, or a successful separatist movement, similar to others that had broken out all over Mexico at the time. See Crane Britton, *The Anatomy of Revolution* (N.J.: Prentice-Hall, 1952); Paul D. Lack, *The Texas Revolutionary Experience: A Political and Social History, 1835–1836* (College Station: Texas A&M University Press, 1992), xix–xxv; and Weber, "Refighting the Alamo: Mythmaking and the Texas Revolution," 133–139.

4 One of the best volumes is Paul D. Lack, *The Texas Revolutionary Experience: A Political and Social History, 1835–1836* (College Station: Texas A&M University Press, 1992, 1996).

5 In Austin's "Old Three-Hundred" colony, only four could not write.

6 Fane Downs, "'Tryels and Trubbles': Women in Early Nineteenth-Century Texas," *Southwestern Historical Quarterly* (July 1986): 36.

CHAPTER 1

Continuity, Change, and Removal

Native Women and the Texas Revolution

Lindy Eakin

Understanding what impact the Texas Revolution had on Native American women requires an understanding of the experience of Native Americans in Texas from the decline of Spanish influence through Mexican independence in 1821 and eventual Texas statehood in 1845. It is against this backdrop that the period of the revolution can be contextualized for native peoples. In order to ascertain the impact on women, one must look at each native group, understanding the roles and experiences of women within the group to discern change during and following the revolution, and to assess the role the revolution played in creating those changes. However, the Texas Revolution was not the only major factor driving change for native peoples in Texas during the 1830s. The immigration of eastern Indians into Texas and the "Indian territory" during the 1820s and 1830s had a major impact on natives in Texas. Similarly, the political and economic turmoil in Mexico that fed the Texas Revolution was also felt by native peoples on the northern frontier of Mexico and caused a wave of change. Finally, the westward advance of Anglo Americans that spurred the population growth in Texas created pressures and opportunities for natives on the southern plains and in Texas.

Women in most native societies were key to transmitting culture to the next generation. They still provide continuity for their society. This held true if not intensified throughout the period of the Texas Revolution and Republic. Yet the Texas Revolution would set into motion a massive immigration of Euro-Americans into Texas that would soon displace and forcibly remove almost all Indian peoples from Texas. Native women helped provide continuity of culture for their peoples during this wrenching transition.

Why is the experience of native women important? Clearly, the revolution had long-term consequences for all natives living in Texas. A new political entity arose in place of the Spanish and Mexicans whom Indians in Texas had been dealing with for well over a hundred years. Almost all of the written histories of native groups during this period focus on the conflict between natives and the new Anglo Texas (Republic and state). These histories are political and military in nature, not cultural. Some studies focus on resistance, accommodation, survival, and the eventual expulsion or decimation of native groups. While these studies pay close attention to the cultural survival of native peoples, their focus has been a narrative of "disappearance" through removal, dissolution, or death—"genocide" in Gary Anderson's argument. A closer look at the experience of women in selected native groups can help illuminate the experiences of native peoples and the reverberations throughout native society during this period of rapid change and conflict.[1]

Traditionally, gender has not typically been part of the analysis in Native American history. Aside from Pocahontas and Sacajawea, historians ignored native women or portrayed them as "drudge squaws." In the past three decades, however, research on Native American women has allowed us to see more complex versions of native women. Initially, research on native women focused on issues of status and power. The framing question was, did contact with Euro-American colonization cause a decline in native women's position and power within native society? That question caused scholars to look more closely at what power and status meant for women in their cultures. Rather than viewing cultures as predominately matrilineal or patriarchal, gender roles are seen as socially constructed, often from the most basic values of the native society. In some groups, such as the Cherokee, complementarity is an apt description of male and female roles. As opposed to equality, complementarity describes separate cultural roles, without a judgment about power relationships. Gender was part of a set of balanced opposites, not a hierarchal power relationship. Gender roles did change under the pressure of colonization, but a better understanding of those roles in the value system of the culture helps historians frame questions and understand the changes wrought by contact. Gender, along with age and kinship, are key elements in defining a person's status in many native societies. Gender alone did not define a woman's role. Kinship, age, and accomplishments also determined her status and role within society. The impact of the Texas Revolution on native women then, must address gender, kinship, and age as important elements of analysis.[2]

While the Texas Revolution had a profound impact on the native peoples of Texas, it was also part of a larger set of forces affecting native peoples. In Texas the decline of the Spanish empire, the tumultuous experience of the Mexican independence period from Father Hildago's call for revolution until full independence in 1821, and the opening of Texas to Anglo immigration would have far-reaching effects. In addition to those factors, the emergence of a "Comanche Empire" in the nineteenth century was a major factor in the attempts by Mexico to hold on to the far northern frontier inherited from Spain. Indian removal in the eastern United States, beginning as early as the Louisiana Purchase in 1803, also had an impact on the Indians of Texas as immigrant tribes moved west of the Mississippi River in the early nineteenth century. Cherokees were among the earliest Indian groups to move west and into Texas. The creation of the Indian Territory, in what is now Oklahoma, reoriented trade networks, created competition for resources, and created conflict on the southern plains. Shawnees, Delawares, Kickapoos, and others migrated or hunted in what is now Texas as they were displaced from their homelands. All of this activity created a complex and rapidly changing set of circumstances for the Indians of Texas.

Until Anglo settlement began in 1821, Texas was still very much Indian territory. Spanish Texas consisted of three small settlements: San Antonio, nearby La Bahía and its ranching area, and Nacogdoches in East Texas. The total population of Spanish citizens was no more than 2,500, having declined from over 4,000 settlers and soldiers in 1810. San Antonio was the largest settlement; La Bahia had a small garrison of soldiers; and Nacogdoches, founded in 1779 from the remnants of the residents who had been forced to leave their homes and ranches at Los Adaes in 1773, grew from 300 founders to a thriving trading settlement in the early nineteenth century. It also was more oriented to Louisiana and trade than to the northern Mexican frontier. The presence of many non-Spaniards in the borderland region continued to plague Spanish officials. Nacogdoches suffered heavily from the filibusters and expeditions of the revolutionary period, 1810–1821. In effect, it was practically abandoned in 1821 when Stephen F. Austin travelled through on his way to San Antonio. It grew quickly, given its traditional role as the gateway into Texas; yet it would have a history of conflict between the Tejano residents and the newly arriving Anglo immigrants. Infighting among the newly arrived immigrants over land and leadership further divided the town and region. The presence of so many native and immigrant Indians fueled suspicion and conflict between the Indians and the southern Anglos who were coming to dominate the town and region.[3]

Over 20,000 Indians outnumbered these three small Spanish/ Mexican outposts. Most significant to all were the Comanche, whose sheer size and scope in the nineteenth century made them the pre-eminent force on the southern plains. With the Wichita bands as their allies, the Comanche held the Spanish at bay during the last half of the eighteenth century. The Comanche trade empire stretched from Spanish New Mexico to the Arkansas River in what is now Colorado, as far east as Louisiana and deep into northern Mexico. In East Texas several groups of village-based Indians sought to maintain their way of life, growing corn, beans, and squash, supplemented by hunting. The remnants of the Hasinai confederacy, the Hainai, Nadaco, and Neches, continued to live in the Neches and Angelina watershed as they had for a thousand years. The Kadoha-dacho camped near the great bend of the Red River on the border of Texas and Louisiana as they had for hundreds of years. These two groups merged in the 1850s and became known collectively as the Caddo. Cherokee, Shawnee, Delaware, Kickapoo, Alabama, and Coushatta all immigrated into East Texas and began to plant crops and try to make a new home west of the Mississippi, after being forced out of their homelands by the United States government. Before 1821 they were welcomed by the Spanish government, who saw them as an additional buffer against the aggressively expanding United States. Much as they had in the eighteenth century, Spanish officials hoped a cordon of Indian allies would help defend its borders against other imperial powers.[4]

Even by 1830, when the Anglo and Spanish population had reached 10,000, much of Texas was still largely held and controlled by its Indian occupants. Anglo settlers had concentrated on the lower Colorado and Brazos valleys where the land suited their needs. Settlements as far north as Austin, however, were still very much at risk from Indian attacks. Indians frequently harassed or killed surveying parties in the area. This remained true as the settlement frontier expanded up the Colorado and Brazos rivers in the 1840s. When talk of revolution began in earnest in 1835, both Texan and Mexican officials saw native alliance or neutrality as crucial to their own chances of victory. The brevity of the actual revolution had as much to do with Indians remaining out of the conflict as any diplomatic maneuvering by either side. Nevertheless, both Mexico and the Texians were cognizant of the importance of the Indians in the territory, and diplomatic efforts were made to enlist the Indians or to insure their neutrality.[5]

However, for native peoples in Texas, the Texas Revolution and the Republic must be seen from a longer trajectory. Indians in Texas had co-existed for over 100 years with the Spanish on the frontier. In spite of Spanish attempts to convert Indians into Spanish citizens through missions, Indians in Texas overwhelmingly rejected assimilation and the mission programs. Nevertheless, the Spanish created alliances with many of the groups in Texas, especially the Hasinai confederacy, and in the late eighteenth century with the Wichita villages. The Spanish formed a lasting peace with the Comanche in 1786 that would hold until the end of the Spanish empire in Texas. For the first half of the eighteenth century, the Lipan Apache were the common enemy of the Spanish and most Indian groups in Texas. By mid-century the Apache were under great pressure from the invading Comanche and sought Spanish help and missions. Several missions were established for the Apache, but all failed and suffered attacks by the Comanche, and a combination of Wichita and other Texas tribes. By the 1770s the Spanish realized that they could not support the Apaches without losing almost all other Indian allies and the Apaches once more became enemies to be subdued.

With the possible exception of those in San Antonio, missions were failures in converting Indians into acculturated Spaniards.

The Comanche, Wichita, Hasinai, and others set the terms of their alliances with the Spanish. Trade and gifts maintained the system of alliances between Indians and Spain. This system began to fail with the decline of the Spanish empire in the early nineteenth century. The chaotic period of the Mexican Revolution disrupted alliances and trade networks as there was no longer a stable partner or source for gifts and goods. Once Mexican independence was achieved in 1821, Texas was ravaged by revolts and counter-revolts, filibusters, and invasion. Then Anglo immigration began. It was a difficult time for Indian peoples to navigate and negotiate with new partners. Trade networks had to be rebuilt and alliances reconfigured. Spanish and Mexican authorities could not keep up their practice of providing the gifts necessary to cement relationships with their Indian allies for many reasons. The Spanish and Mexican system failed to maintain peace and alliances in the nineteenth century. Many of those Indian groups returned to raiding to obtain needed supplies and horses for trade, or looked to the new American presence to the east for trade.

During the brief Mexican period (1821–1836), authorities tried to rebuild the system of trade, gifts, and alliances, but continuing turmoil in Mexico City, drastic shifts in government, and lack of funds and support on the frontier left local officials in Texas and New Mexico to temporize and fend for themselves with the Indians. Mexican officials in Texas attempted to maintain relationships with what little resources they had, by rebuilding personal relationships with their native counterparts, but the task was larger than they could handle alone.

For much of the eighteenth century, the French in Louisiana provided access to markets the Spanish could not in Texas. Beginning in the early eighteenth century, the French in Louisiana provided trade goods, especially guns, that penetrated well into Texas through trading posts at Natchitoches, among the Kadohadacho on the upper

Red River, and from the Arkansas Post near the Mississippi River. These trading hubs, and the individual traders operating out of the posts, provided goods and markets for Indians living in Texas. A lively trade in deerskins, horses, and captives functioned through native networks and alliances. This, of course, complicated the task of the Spanish in Texas trying to influence Indian groups who could obtain the trade items they desired from the French. Spanish officials blamed the French and their trade goods as the reason Indians would not succumb to missions and Spanish authority. Of course, they also recognized that the desire of many Indians to live free of European control was an obstacle for their colonial aims.

The end of the Seven Years' War (1763) and the acquisition of Louisiana by Spain created new issues for the empire. What was once a border was now the interior of a larger frontier. Spanish authorities recognized that Louisiana could not be managed as a traditional borderland frontier. The Captaincy General of Havana administered Louisiana rather than the Viceroy and *Audiencia* in Mexico City. Spain continued the French practice of trade and gifts for the Indian groups of Louisiana. However, they maintained the old mission system in Texas and continued to forbid trade between the adjacent provinces. Locally, officials in Natchitoches and San Antonio tried to coordinate and collaborate on Indian policy. It was through the efforts of the commander of the Natchitoches post, the former French officer Athanase de Mezieres, that a peace treaty was finally negotiated with the Wichita villages and Spanish San Antonio. Licensed traders operated out of Natchitoches and other sites in Spanish Louisiana, but were officially restricted to those tribes formerly served by the French. By the early nineteenth century, Spanish officials recognized that trade was a vital component of Indian relations and licensed a trading post at Nacogdoches for the Texas tribes. Supply problems, lack of coordination with officials in San Antonio, and the Mexican revolution prevented the post from living up to its potential for Indian policy. Trade with Natchitoches, now an American trading post, continued for the native groups in East Texas and west along the Red River, further undermining Mexican policies.

By the 1830s native groups in Texas were confronted by an increasingly Anglo Texas. From a small Spanish-speaking population of about 2,500 people in 1820, the non-Indian population of Texas at the time of the Texas Revolution was approximately 40,000, doubling between 1828 and 1836. The native population, swelled by eastern immigrant Indians, was about 40,000. Anglos were streaming into Texas at the rate of 1,000 per month before the revolution. These immigrants were largely southerners who had pushed for removal of the Indians in the south since the War of 1812 and had succeeded. They saw no place for Indians in the Texas they hoped to build. Instead of seeking a form of accommodation with the natives as the Spanish and Mexicans had, most Anglo immigrants sought to remove or exterminate the Indians and take their land.[6]

Austin and his fellow empresarios largely settled in territory along the coastal plain between the Brazos and the Colorado rivers. This was rich land for farming and ranching, was within reach of existing Mexican settlements, and away from the prime hunting grounds of the Comanche and their Wichita allies. Austin largely sought to minimize conflict with the natives of Texas, with the exception of the Karankawa, and until the boom in immigration and expansion of settlement up the Brazos and Colorado river valleys created conflict with the natives whose territory they were invading, relations between Austin's colonists and the natives avoided major conflict. Individual traders established trading posts closer to Indian territory, but they were not acting on behalf of any government or as part of Indian policy until after the revolution. During the Republic, some of those trading posts were intended to provide Indians with an outlet for trade to keep them away from settled areas, not to

provide gifts and trade as part of a strategy of alliance and peace.
Other than Sam Houston, the emerging Texan leadership did not
see a place for co-existence between Indians and Texans. Mirabeau
Lamar, Houston's successor as president of the Republic in 1840,
sought removal or extermination of the Indians as the official policy
of the Republic and aggressively pursued that strategy.[7]

Texas Indian policy was a sharp break with a century and a half of
Spanish and French policy for the Indians of Texas and the southern
plains. During the revolution and the Republic, many groups continued to try to get Texas leaders to conform to established protocols
and practices for friendship and alliance. Houston was experienced
in this and attempted to carry out such a policy, but the treaties he
negotiated with Indian groups were invariably rejected by the Texas
Senate and overturned by later administrations. The Indians found
this confusing and difficult to deal with.

The period of the Mexican Revolution placed Indians in a difficult
situation, as multiple sides attempted to recruit them as allies. Like
the American Revolution, this conflict appeared to the Indians to be
an inter-family quarrel. Even more complicated was the shifting of
sides by individuals within the revolution as they sought advantage
and tried to forecast the eventual winners. More destructive for
some of the Indian groups were the multiple filibusters and invasions during the revolutionary period. Nacogdoches was largely
abandoned at the end of this period (1821) by the settlers who saw
their gateway community become a staging ground for invasions
and attacks on San Antonio. The Hasinai villages near Nacogdoches
moved further up the Trinity, Neches, and Angelina river valleys to
find some relief from the chaos in Nacogdoches. The coastal tribes,
particularly the Karankawa and Attakpa, had been displaced near
Galveston by Lafitte and his band around 1820 and as Galveston
became an entry point for filibusters and invasions. In San Antonio the Tejano settlers also engaged in revolt and counter-revolt,

confusing the Indians in that region over who to deal with and what the conflict was about. To many natives the Texas Revolution appeared to be a replay of the earlier conflicts, but with new players. [8]

The variety of native groups in Texas is reflected in the variety of ways the Texas Revolution affected their ways of life. Some groups, such as the Texas Cherokees, were active participants, at least diplomatically, in the ebb and flow of the period. The Cherokees tried to use the situation to obtain a long-sought land grant and assurance of their future from both sides, Mexican and Texian. They also used their diplomatic connections to maneuver themselves into a real or perceived leadership role among the immigrant and native groups in East Texas. This diplomatic maneuvering cost them credibility with the Anglo settlers. Texian fears of an Indian uprising, or of an Indian alliance with Mexico, were significant. Rumors and evidence of collusion between the Cherokee and their allies with Mexico were difficult for Cherokee leaders to overcome. In addition, factionalism within the Cherokees created confusion among Texians who did not understand divisions among Indian groups. They expected an Indian "leader" to speak for the whole group and have some control over "his people." [9]

Other groups, such as the Comanche and Wichita bands, tried to avoid the entanglements of the revolution. To some extent, their approach to the growing Anglo presence in Texas was to stay clear of settlement. The Comanche consistently attempted to establish a boundary line between themselves and the frontier of settlement. They were able to negotiate something of a truce with the Texans for a time, bypassing their settlements to raid deep into northern Mexico, sometimes with the support of the Texans. [10]

The changing trade network of the southern plains affected the Wichita villages (Tawakoni, Waco, Wichita, Taovayas, and Kichai). As the Comanche absorbed the immigrant Indian tribes into their trade network after their relocation to Indian territory, and extended their trade directly to the advancing Anglo frontier with the Santa Fe trail, the Wichita were replaced by the Anglos as valuable middlemen in the Comanche trade network. However, the Wichita bands were mostly beyond the settlement frontier of early Anglo Texas. Their historic location on the Red River and in north central Texas kept the Wichita and Taovayas out of the direct line of Anglo settlement until after the revolution. However, the Tawakoni, Kichai, and Wacos moved westward to the Brazos River, near what is now Waco, from the upper Sabine and Cypress Creek areas. This was an area where eastern immigrant groups, such as the Cherokee, Delaware, and Kickapoo first migrated into Texas. This also became contested land between Anglo settlers and various Indian groups. Having been displaced in the Comanche trade network, some of the Wichita bands began raiding the Anglo-Tejano settlements near San Antonio and Austin, drawing the wrath of and reprisals from the new Texas republic.[11]

Some native groups, such as the Lipan Apache and the Tonkawa, sought opportunities by assisting the Anglo settlers, especially by serving as guides, scouts, and auxiliaries as the Texans fought their former Indian enemies. Living near the settlements of San Antonio and Austin, the Lipan had over one hundred years of experience with Spanish settlers in San Antonio. Since the mid-eighteenth century, they had sought Spanish assistance from the Comanches, who had driven the Lipan from the Texas high plains. The Spanish founded missions for the Apache in the 1750s and 1760s, only to be overrun by the Comanche and other Texas tribes. The Lipan perceived the new Anglo settlers as potential allies and protection from their Comanche enemies.[12]

The Tonkawa had lived in south central Texas near the Guadalupe River since Spanish settlement of Texas in the early 1700s. The Tonkawa of the nineteenth century was the result of complicated ethnic mixing in the region throughout the eighteenth century, absorbing many smaller groups decimated by disease, warfare, and loss of territory. Relying on hunting and gathering, but not fully dependent on the buffalo, the Tonkawa were resourceful and adaptive people. They also sought opportunities in working with the Anglo immigrants and new allies in their struggle with the constantly shifting and complex set of trade networks, alliances, and conflicts in Texas during the nineteenth century.

This examination of individual native groups provides the historical and cultural context to assess the effects of the Texas Revolution on native women, particularly those members of the Cherokee, Caddo, and Comanche tribes. Each of these groups faced different challenges with the creation of an Anglo Texas. How women fared within these cultures was significantly influenced not only by their unique history and customs, but also by their existing positions within those cultures, and how their societies adapted to the changing circumstances.

These groups of natives included three major subsistence types: village-based groups who relied primarily on corn, beans, and squash supplemented by hunting; groups who relied primarily on hunting and trading; and the hunter/gatherer groups. Each group relied on trade with other Indians and Euro-Americans for survival. The village-based Indians include the Cherokee, Caddo, and Wichita bands—the Wichita, Taovayas, Tawakoni (Waco), and Kichai. The primarily hunting groups were the Comanche, Apache, and Tonkawa. The Karankawa were mostly hunter/gatherers who relied on the rich coastal estuary for subsistence. Each of these groups had distinct experiences and relationships with the Spanish and Mexican governments before the Texas Revolution. Those experiences and other larger forces influenced their actions towards Anglo Texas and their experience during the revolution and republic.

Trade was as old as the groups themselves. It served many functions beyond its more obvious economic and subsistence role. Trade occurs between friends, not enemies. Trade and alliance, therefore, often went hand in hand. Trade networks provided commodities, specialty items, or ceremonial and status items and often held many relationships together. The breakdown of trade and gifts during the Mexican Revolution (1810–1821) unraveled many carefully built alliances. Inter-tribal trade networks were also changing during this period as American traders crossed the Mississippi and became part of the Comanche horse and mule trading network. This displaced the Wichita groups who had been intermediaries in the Comanche trade with Louisiana since the mid-eighteenth century. [13]

The Hasinai villages had served as a trade crossroads since the Mississippian period (800–1400 AD) and their crossroads' location between French Louisiana and Spanish Texas further enabled them to serve as middlemen in a new network, using trade to cement alliances and relationships with other tribes. The Louisiana Purchase, the rise of American traders, and the turmoil caused by the Mexican Revolution however, disrupted these trade networks. The Spanish established a trading post for the Indians of East Texas at Nacogdoches in 1809, thereby displacing the Hasinai as primary middlemen. The post failed during the period of the Mexican Revolution, but the system of trade networks collapsed as well. By the early nineteenth century, the Hasinai population had declined significantly and other trade networks displaced their role as middlemen. As new networks were rebuilt with new players, new alliances emerged and old ones evolved or were shattered. [14]

The Cherokee were late immigrants into Spanish Texas. Spanish authorities, eager to build an Indian barrier to Anglo advancement following the Louisiana Purchase, granted the Texas Cherokees permission to immigrate into East Texas. Just as Indian groups had been part of Spain's imperial strategy in competition with the British and the French, the Spanish perceived the Cherokee and other eastern refugees as a possible solution to creating a human barrier to American advancement into Spanish territory. Led by the peace chief Duwali, who was also known as Chief Bowl or Bowles, the Cherokee settled in East Texas in late 1821 or early 1822 after attempting to settle on the Trinity River. Pressure from the Taovayas (Wichita) in 1820–1821 over hunting territory pushed the Cherokee east to the area just north of the Hasinai. This conflict with the Wichita villages would continue throughout the Cherokee's tenure in Texas.[15]

The Cherokee who migrated west into Arkansas and then into Texas were a product of the factionalism inherent in Cherokee politics, migrating westward to maintain more traditional ways than the acculturation pursued by many of the natives who remained in the east. Thus, they were more traditional in their village politics and life-ways than some other Cherokee groups. This meant that the traditional matrilineal society was more intact than with the more acculturated Cherokees who, under the influence of whites and mixed bloods, were fashioning a Cherokee Republic based upon more patriarchal ways. The villages also maintained the tradition of peace and war leaders, that is, village leaders who dealt with internal matters (peace) and those who dealt with outsiders (war).[16]

In Texas the Cherokee sought locations to plant their staple corn, beans, squash, and cotton and to have access to hunting grounds to supplement their crops. Farming, gathering, and care of the household—managed by the matrilineal clan—was the work of Cherokee women. Hunting, warfare, and diplomacy remained the province of Cherokee men. These gender-based roles were part of the foundation of Cherokee culture, based on mythic values of balanced, not hierarchal, opposing forces. The differing roles did not imply that one gender's role was more important than the other; instead they complemented each other. Once villages were established and seeds were planted, the crops and land belonged to the women of the household. They provided food, woven cotton cloth, clothes, and traded goods, including corn, beans, and cotton cloth to their Anglo and Tejano neighbors in Nacogdoches. This trade was the major source of manufactured goods for the Cherokee. These cultural and economic contributions helped maintain the strong position of women within Cherokee society.[17]

The pressure from Anglo settlement in East Texas directly affected women, who were the keepers of the crops and land. The male leadership, through Duwali, tried to negotiate a land grant from either the Mexican or Texan parties. This attempt to play both sides during the revolutionary period cost Duwali his life. Much like the Cherokee experience during the American Revolution, choosing sides was risky. In the case of the Texas Revolution, it was not at all clear who would win. Mexico was very solicitous of Cherokee assistance and promised a land grant for their help. The Texans, at least under Sam Houston, promised a land treaty as well, but an empresario grant had also been made that encompassed the land the Cherokee were living on and where they hoped to remain. The numerous divisions among the Texian, or Anglo, population made it difficult for the Cherokee to know whom to deal with and whom to trust. A strategy of playing both sides was a time-tested one for southeastern Indians.[18]

Southern Anglo hostility toward Indians and fears of an Indian alliance with the Mexicans, borne out by later evidence, created a barrier of hostility toward the Cherokee and the other immigrant groups they purported to represent for the Anglos of East Texas. While the men pursued diplomatic strategies, women continued to care for their crops and tend their households. After the revolution, when the Cherokee were participating in further political intrigue with Juan Cordova and Manuel Flores, seeking Mexican assistance for the land grant that Houston was unable to deliver, the Cherokee had to move their villages and flee from the militia. This was most difficult on the women, who had to re-establish new fields, starting over in building a household, and find new sources of wild foods to supplement their crops. Hostilities engendered by the revolution and its aftermath also disrupted trade. As hunters, men were much more mobile and able to adapt to new territory. Conflict with other tribes occurred as they moved into existing natives' hunting grounds.

While women took care of crops and the household, men were important in helping clear fields and providing meat and protection. Conflict with Anglos over land or alliance and conflict with other Indians over hunting territory led to the death of Cherokee hunters and warriors. This left women without the support of the males in their household. An increasing number of Anglo settlers squatting on Cherokee land created problems for Cherokee women. They used threats and attacks to chase Cherokee households from their land, allowing Anglos to take over cultivated and improved land. Loss of land, theft of livestock, and outright raids on Cherokee households directly affected Cherokee women, striking at the heart of their role in society. Yet, ultimately, it would be President Mirabeau Lamar's campaign to remove, or exterminate, all Indians that brought the end of the Texas Cherokees. [19]

Following the failure of the "Cordova rebellion" in 1838, an attempt by Tejanos and Indians to gain freedom from Texan rule, and the capture and death of Manuel Flores in the spring of 1839, newly inaugurated President Lamar had the pretext he needed to force a showdown with the Cherokee. In his first message to Congress, Lamar threw down the gauntlet. He announced that it was time for an Indian policy of "no compromise and have no termination except their total extinction or total expulsion." The Cherokee in particular were targets of his animosity. In July 1839, following unsuccessful treaty talks, Duwali and his people began moving north to leave Texas and were attacked by General Thomas Rusk and his troops. After two days, the Cherokees and their allies the Delawares,

Shawnees, and Kickapoo were overrun and Duwali was shot in the
back and scalped. The Anglo Texan forces escorted the survivors to
the Red River and forced them to cross into Indian territory, ending the saga of the Texas Cherokees. The survivors eventually were
absorbed into the Cherokee nation of northeastern Oklahoma or
splintered and joined various Indian groups fighting the Texans.[20]

In some ways the people known as the Caddo had the most
to lose from the Anglo settlement of Texas. Two major groups of
Caddo survived in nineteenth-century Texas, both remnants of
once large and prosperous "confederacies," or groups of villages
encountered by the French and the Spanish in the late seventeenth
century. The Hasinai villages stretched along the Neches and Angelina River valleys while the Kadohadacho lived in several villages
on the great bend of the Red River. The Spanish knew the Hasinai
as the "Kingdom of the Tejas" and the region of East Texas they
occupied as the "province of Texas." Nacogdoches was the site of
one of ten villages occupied by the Hasinai and one of three missions established among the Hasinai by the Spanish. The remaining villages during the early period of Anglo settlement were the
Hainai, Nacogdoches, and Anadarko. These village-based Indians
had been living in the Neches and Angelina valleys since at least
800 AD, growing corn, beans, and squash and hunting deer, bear,
and other game. The Hasinai were descendents of the Mississippian
mound-building culture that existed in the region from 800–1400
AD. The Spanish had known of them through Indians in west and
central Texas and referred to them as the Kingdom of the Texas,
for they were certainly perceived by other Indians as wealthy and
powerful. Similarly, the Kadohadacho had been residents in the
area of the great bend of the Red River since Mississippian times
and were sometimes seen as the "true Caddo." Both occupied prime
agricultural and hunting territory coveted by Anglo immigrants.
By the early nineteenth century, the Kadohadacho had been forced

south to the area around Caddo Lake in the drainage of the Sabine due to pressure from Osage raids and eastern immigrant tribes.[21]

One hundred and fifty years of European contact and introduced epidemic diseases had reduced the Hasinai from about five thousand people in the late seventeenth century to approximately five hundred by 1821. At least three villages remained in their historic territory, the Hainai, Nabedache, and Nacogdoches. The filibusters and invasions of Texas from Louisiana and the unrest of the Mexican Revolution disrupted these villages by organizing or passing through Hasinai territory. Immigrant Indians, such as the Cherokee, Shawnee, Delaware, and Coushatta, also began moving into East Texas by 1820, creating competition for hunting territory and creating conflict for the resident natives of Texas. During the Texas Revolution, Anglos entering Texas to take part in the revolution overran the natives. The Runaway Scrape, a mass exodus eastward as the Mexican army advanced in 1836, passed right through their territory as well. Just as the Tejano settlers of Nacogdoches were losing their land through chicanery and force, the Hasinai villages were being taken over by squatters, speculators, and other fugitives. Pressure for their land was a very destructive force for the Hasinai. [22]

Women held important roles in Caddo society. Households were both matrilineal and matrilocal and the crops of corn, beans, and squash were planted and cared for by the women. Caddo women were known widely for the high quality of their finished deerskins. The dispersed settlement pattern of the Caddo further emphasized the role of the household. Villages consisted of clusters of farmsteads, each occupied by a family group of multiple houses and their fields. Villages stretched as far as twenty miles from end to end. Women also played a key role in diplomacy by hosting visiting delegations, feeding them, and signaling peaceful intentions in interactions with outsiders. Providing the food and household to host dignitaries brought women a key role in the diplomatic arena.[23]

George Catlin, *Caddo Indians Gathering Wild Grapes*, depicts Caddo women engaged in food gathering activities in the 1830s, as they did for hundreds of years. Courtesy Gilcrease Museum, Tulsa, Oklahoma.

The central role that horticulture played in Caddo society and economics, and matrilineal "ownership" of the household and fields, meant that pressure on Caddo landholdings more severely affected women's roles than the more mobile role of men as hunters and warriors. Of course, the disruption to land holdings also impacted Caddo men, but it had a more direct impact on the women who cultivated the fields and gathered other foodstuffs in the area. Building houses and clearing fields were communal activities that involved all people in the village. Once the village moved and households established their fields, however, it was up to the women of the household to take care of the plantings and distribute food.

Following the Green Corn Festival and the harvesting of corn, women dried the surplus corn and stored it for use throughout the winter to feed the household. They ground the dried corn in a wooden mortar (a hollowed tree trunk) with a wooden pestle and the flour was sifted through reeds. The flour was used in a variety of ways to bake loaves, make a warm mush, or in combination with other vegetables. These stores, along with dried buffalo and venison, deerskins and buffalo hides, were products of women's work.

Women were also the most vulnerable to loss from rapidly moving a village or escaping attacks by Texas Rangers or other militia groups. When villages had to be quickly vacated, as they often were during this tumultuous period, women were not able to recover quickly and provide for their households. The effect was to make it very difficult for Caddo women to successfully fulfill their roles in society during this time.

Descriptions of "destitute" Caddoans were usually based on inhabitants of fragmented villages who had been driven from their previous villages and crops. When villages were established and crops given time to mature, the villagers were generally well supplied with corn, beans, and squash. The success of the men in providing meat from hunting varied by location, and especially by the

degree of competition from other natives and Anglos. Each time
the Caddo were forced to move, they re-established their villages,
more concentrated than before, and women renewed their role as
providers through horticulture.[24]

Following the revolution, and especially after the Cordova "rebellion," Texas targeted the Hasinai and Kadohadacho for retalia-
tions since they were allies of the Cherokee and immigrant groups
who occupied prime land in the region of Nacogdoches. The area
north of Nacogdoches and the San Antonio road were the subject
of heated contests over land grants, new immigrants, and land
speculators. Under pressure, the Hasinai relocated to the Three
Forks area of the Trinity River with their relatives, the Wichita
villagers. Attacked in the winter of 1839–1840 by Ranger groups,
they moved again to the Brazos, near the location of current-day
Waco. There they were able to once again establish productive villages with extensive fields of corn, beans, and squash maintained
by the women.[25]

Each move was certainly disruptive to the economy of the
villages, but each time they moved, the Caddoans re-established
their village way of life, including their gender-based division of
labor, and the social roles that sustained their village way of life.
Women's roles remained fairly constant throughout this process. The major impact of Anglo invasion of Texas and the Texas
Revolution and Republic, then, was to force the relocation of
the Hasinai and Kadohadacho from their historic homelands.
Moving from the piney woods of East Texas to central Texas
and the upper Trinity and Brazos river valleys, resulted in more
compact villages, similar to those of their northern neighbors,
the Wichita peoples with whom they consolidated their villages.
The Caddo women, and the native groups as a whole, suffered
from these forced relocations, but the basic structure of society
remained the same.

George Catlin, *Comanche Village, Women Dressing Robes and Drying Meat*, depicts Comanche women dressing buffalo hides for use or trade and drying the buffalo meat that was a staple of the Comanche diet. These were basic work activities for Comanche women. The extensive trade in buffalo hides drove the demand for multiple wives or helpers within some families. Courtesy Smithsonian American Art Museum, Gift of Mrs. Joseph Harrison, Jr.

In the early nineteenth century the Comanche had created an empire on the southern plains that stretched from the Arkansas River
in present day Colorado, through eastern New Mexico, southwestern Kansas, and western Oklahoma, deep into central Texas. They
were reaching the peak of their expansion into northern Mexico
during the 1830s and 1840s. From this longer perspective, the Texas
Revolution appears to be a blip on the radar screen. However, what
the revolution portended was an escalation of Anglo settlement
into Texas and up the Trinity, Brazos, and Colorado River valleys.
This expansion impinged on historic Comanche hunting territory.
More important, the Anglo Texans and their attitude of expulsion or
extermination, coupled with superior firepower, put serious pressure
on the eastern Comanches, the Penateka.[26]

In the 1820s, as Anglo immigration under Mexican rule began,
the challenge and opportunity for the Comanche was to incorporate
the Texans into their vast trade network, through trading or raiding. Initially, the Texans presented an opportunity for new trade
partners or livestock raiding, but the encroaching settlement lines
created more of a problem for Comanche hunting territory. Equally
important, most Texans did not seem interested in the Indian trade.
Initially settling along the coast or in East Texas, the settlers were
more interested in establishing cotton and other marketable crops.
Trading for hides and horses was not as attractive to them as growing marketable crops. The expanding markets for mules in Missouri
and opportunities opened by the Santa Fe trade were attractive to
the Comanche. More troublesome to the Comanche was the flood
of immigrant Indians from the southeastern United States being
re-settled into the "Indian Territory" of what is now Oklahoma.
These immigrants competed for the prime buffalo hunting on the
southern plains and brought additional conflict for the Comanche.[27]

When revolution did emerge in Mexican Texas, the Comanche,
like other Indian groups, were caught in the middle. The decade

of the Mexican Revolution had disrupted Indian relations on the northern frontier and the confusion of the 1820s and early 1830s did nothing to re-establish relationships on the frontier. Thus, the Comanche and other native groups did not have close ties to Mexican authorities. The main concern for the Texans during the revolt was to neutralize the Indian threat. Due to the brevity of the revolution, this was not a problem with the Comanche. Comanche raiding was concentrated on keeping the Anglo line of settlement from pushing up the Colorado and Brazos rivers. Attacks on surveying parties, in particular, were aimed at keeping the Texans out of Comanche territory. Similarly, the attack on Fort Parker in May 1836 was part of this pattern of pushing back at encroaching settlement. Further stimulus for the attack was the role of the fort in supporting earlier Ranger attacks on the Comanche and other Indians in central Texas.[28]

The attack on Fort Parker, and the much discussed capture of Cynthia Ann Parker, however, needs to be seen as part of a larger pattern of Comanche behavior. For at least a century, Comanche had been taking women and children captive on the northern frontier of Mexico. Mexicans and Indians were sold for ransom in New Mexico, traded to other groups, or absorbed into the band to replace members lost to disease and warfare. The expansion of the Comanche empire also created demand for additional labor for herding the large horse herds kept by the bands and to process buffalo hides for trade. As an eleven-year-old girl, Cynthia Ann Parker was the ideal age for a captive girl. Young enough to be acculturated quickly into Comanche ways, she grew up, married, had children and was assimilated into Comanche society. The transition began immediately upon capture. Young girls were put under the supervision of a woman who guided their transition, often a rough one. Yet the captives quickly learned to adapt by acquiring the necessary skills to aid the camp and band, making them useful members of the band. While the attack on Fort Parker may have been in retaliation for earlier conflicts, or to push back the frontier of settlement, captives such as Parker were always sought to supplement the labor pool of the band. Captives became increasingly important in the face of periodic epidemics, such as the 1837 smallpox epidemic that killed a significant number of Comanches.[29]

Cynthia Ann Parker's experience also helps illuminate some of the pressures within Comanche society in this period of expansion. She married and bore three children, two sons and a daughter, helping replenish the population. As a wife, she also would have helped look after horses, processed buffalo hides, and prepared meals for her household. But scholars know very little about her life, such as whether she was an only wife or one of several. The trend throughout the nineteenth century was for successful Comanche men to have increasing numbers of wives. This trend reflected their wealth and status, but also provided the men with the labor needed to take care of their horse herd and to process buffalo hides for trade. We do not have a clear sense of what this meant for the women who were one of multiple wives. This very lack of knowledge about everyday lives of Comanche women makes the historical focus on a captive woman, Cynthia Ann Parker, ironic. Historians have spent far more time writing about this elusive captive, than about the thousands of other Comanche women of the time.[30]

Certainly the tribal experience differed among women. Some scholars argue that the role of "first" wife increased in prestige, directing the work of the later wives. That left the later wives, especially if captives, in a lower position with less influence and more work. Unfortunately, good ethnographic information to understand the complex dynamics that must have been involved is unavailable for this period. We do know that wives were highly esteemed by many Comanche men. As a consequence, Comanche women were often taken as hostages by the Spanish as part of their diplomatic strategy to compel chiefs to discuss peace initiatives, or to recover Spanish captives. The exchange of women between the Spanish and Comanche symbolized and structured peace initiatives. The desire to reunite Comanche families was a strong inducement for peace when trading hostages, indicating a deep attachment between husbands and wives. The presence of women in Comanche parties, therefore, was a signal of their peaceful intentions when visiting Spanish, and later Anglo, settlements.[31]

However, the reciprocal dynamic between the Spanish/Mexicans and the Comanche, and other Indian groups, broke down with the Anglo Texans. The Anglos were not interested in adapting to native protocols of diplomacy and reciprocal relationships. Their attitude towards Indians reflected Lamar's injunction of expulsion or extermination. As historian Gary Clayton Anderson has pointed out, militia and Ranger raids on Indian villages also had the added benefit of rewarding the raiders with captured goods—horses and hides—worth more than a year's salary to most of the men. Anglo Texan raids on Indian villages were focused on expulsion and on destroying the economic basis of survival. In these situations women and children were not hostages or captives to be used in diplomacy, but were typically gunned down or killed during the raid. Killing women and children was considered dishonorable to Comanche and other Indian warriors. Women and children were sometimes allowed to escape to warn others to stay away, but just as often were simply killed to drive out the natives.[32]

Thus, for Comanche women, the Texas Revolution and the population explosion during the Texas Republic years led to deprivation from the loss of hunting territories, pressure on the buffalo, and death from militia and Ranger raids. Mostly this impacted the Penateka bands of central and west Texas. Given the large size and area controlled by the Comanche, those bands north of the Red River experienced little direct impact from the

Texans. As the Penateka, Wichita bands, Caddo, and others were forced beyond the reach of Anglo settlement, it did put increased pressure on the hunting territory of the southern plains north of the Red River.

Overall, the Texas Revolution did not create a social or cultural revolution for native women in Texas. Within their native societies, women continued in much the same roles as before the revolution. Those roles were based upon fundamental assumptions about appropriate divisions of labor, ritual, and position within society by gender. Unlike the fur trade or missionary activity, the Texas Revolution had more in common with the process of removal than with fundamental changes to economies or society. Removal was disruptive of society as subsistence systems were destroyed, villages were displaced, and hunting pressure and competition undermined all groups' ability to support themselves. Women in village-based societies struggled to re-establish new households and fields to support their families. Increased hunting pressures and raids on hunting camps made subsistence for hunting groups less successful. For all native women, militia and Ranger attacks now made them victims of warfare on a larger scale than native women had been in the past. Captivity had always been a risk of warfare with other Indians and the Spanish, but increasingly, Anglo attacks led to death for women and children.

Native women adapted to the changed circumstances as they had in the past. The relatively brief period of the Texas Revolution and Republic did not significantly alter the fundamental roles native women played within their own societies. However, the resulting warfare and forced removal did finally lead to life on federal reservations and a complete reorientation of their lifestyles in the latter half of the nineteenth century. Those changes were part of the larger federal Indian agenda, not necessarily the result of the Texas Revolution.

The larger issue in trying to understand the impact of the Texas Revolution on native women is the lack of basic information on the history of native women in nineteenth-century Texas. Just as Spanish, French, and English writers in the seventeenth and eighteenth centuries focused on their male counterparts when describing native peoples, even fewer American observers of natives in the nineteenth century focused on women. That is not to say that recovering native women's voices is not possible, but it will take a renewed effort at rereading primary documents to uncover those voices and activities. Much basic work needs to be done for the history of Indian women in Texas. Political histories have now been written for most of the Texas groups. What is needed is more basic work on the cultural histories of the native peoples of Texas. Only then can we better understand the histories of the native women and the impact of the Texas Revolution.

Selected Bibliography

Anderson, Gary Clayton. *The Conquest of Texas: Ethnic Cleansing in the Promised Land, 1820–1875*. Norman: University of Oklahoma Press, 2005.

Barr, Juliana. *Peace Came in the Form of a Woman: Indians and Spaniards in the Texas Borderlands*. Chapel Hill: University of North Carolina Press, 2007.

Everett, Diana. *The Texas Cherokees: A People Between Two Fires, 1819–1840*. Norman: University of Oklahoma Press, 1990.

Campbell, Randolph B. *Gone to Texas: A History of the Lone Star State*. New York: Oxford University Press, 2003.

Hämäläinen, Pekka. *The Comanche Empire*. New Haven: Yale University Press, 2008.

Himmel, Kelly. *The Conquest of the Karankawas and the Tonkawas, 1821–1859*. College Station: Texas A&M University Press, 1999.

Perdue, Theda. *Cherokee Women: Gender and Culture Change, 1700–1835*. Lincoln: University of Nebraska Press, 1998.

Shoemaker, Nancy, ed. *Clearing a Path: Theorizing the Past in Native American Studies*. New York: Routledge, 2002.

Smith, F. Todd. *From Dominance to Disappearance: The Indians of Texas and the Near Southwest, 1786–1859*. Lincoln: University of Nebraska Press, 2005.

Smith, F. Todd. *The Caddo Indians: Tribes at the Convergence of Empires,*
    1542–1854. College Station: Texas A&M University Press, 1996.
Weber, David J. *The Mexican Frontier, 1821–1846: The American Southwest under*
    Mexico. Albuquerque: University of New Mexico Press, 1982.

Endnotes

1   David La Vere, *The Texas Indians* (College Station: Texas A&M University
    Press, 2004); F. Todd Smith, *From Dominance to Disappearance: The
    Indians of Texas and the Near Southwest, 1786–1859* (Lincoln: Univer-
    sity of Nebraska Press, 2005); F. Todd Smith, *The Caddo Indians: Tribes
    at the Convergence of Empires, 1542–1854* (College Station: Texas A&M
    University Press, 1996); F. Todd Smith, *The Wichita Indians: Traders of
    Texas and the Southern Plains, 1540–1845* (College Station: Texas A&M
    University Press, 2000); Gary Clayton Anderson, *The Conquest of Texas:
    Ethnic Cleansing in the Promised Land, 1820–1875* (Norman: University of
    Oklahoma Press, 2005); Kelly F. Himmel, *The Conquest of the Karankawas
    and the Tonkawas, 1821–1859* (College Station: Texas A&M University
    Press, 1999); Diana Everett, *The Texas Cherokees: A People Between Two
    Fires, 1819–1840* (Norman: University of Oklahoma Press, 1990).
2   Nancy Shoemaker, *Negotiators of Change: Historical Perspectives on Native
    American Women* (New York: Routledge, 1995); Nancy Shoemaker, ed.,
    Clearing a Path: Theorizing the Past in Native American Studies (New
    York: Routledge, 2002); Patricia Albers and Beatrice Medicine, eds., *The
    Hidden Half: Studies of Plains Indian Women* (Lanham, MD: University
    Press of America, 1983); Theda Perdue, *Cherokee Women: Gender and
    Culture Change, 1700–1835* (Lincoln: University of Nebraska Press, 1998).
    Nancy Shoemaker, "Categories," in *Clearing a Path*, 51–74.
3   Juliana Barr, *Peace Came in the Form of a Woman: Indians and Spaniards
    in the Texas Borderlands* (Chapel Hill: University of North Carolina Press
    in association with The William P. Clements Center for Southwest Stud-
    ies, Southern Methodist University, 2007); Smith, *From Dominance to
    Disappearance*; Anderson, *The Conquest of Texas.* Also for a description
    of how Indians incorporated Europeans into their world in lieu of seeing
    Indians as the colonized, see Kathleen Du Val, *The Native Ground: Indians
    and Colonists in the Heart of the Continent* (Philadelphia: University of
    Pennsylvania Press, 2006); Carlos E. Castaneda, *Our Catholic Heritage
    in Texas, 1519–1936* (New York: Arno Press, 1976), 5: 400; David J. Weber,
    The Mexican Frontier, 1821–1846: The American Southwest under Mexico

(Albuquerque: University of New Mexico Press, 1982), 177. "Journal of Stephen F. Austin on His First Trip to Texas, 1821," *Quarterly of the Texas State Historical Association 7*, no. 4 (April 1904): 289.

4 Pekka Hämäläinen, *The Comanche Empire* (New Haven: Yale University Press, in association with The William P. Clements Center for Southwest Studies, Southern Methodist University, 2008); Gary Clayton Anderson, *The Indian Southwest, 1580–1830: Ethnogenesis and Reinvention* (Norman: University of Oklahoma Press, 1999); Smith, *From Dominance to Disappearance*; Smith, *The Caddo Indians*; David La Vere, *The Caddo Chiefdoms: Caddo Economics and Politics, 700–1835* (Lincoln: University of Nebraska Press, 1998). David J. Weber, *The Spanish Frontier in North America* (New Haven: Yale University Press, 1992), 296; La Vere, *The Texas Indians*, 154.

5 Randolph B. Campbell, *Gone to Texas: A History of the Lone Star State* (New York: Oxford University Press, 2003), 147; Anderson, *The Conquest of Texas*, 103–104.

6 Weber, *The Mexican Frontier*, 177; Smith, *From Dominance to Disappearance*, 161; William R. Hogan, ed., "State Census of 1847," *Southwestern Historical Quarterly 50*, no. 1 (July 1946): 116–118; Anderson, *The Conquest of Texas*, 40–41; Campbell, *Gone to Texas*, 170–171.

7 For the trading posts see George R. Nielsen, "Torrey's Frontier Post No. 2: A Business History," *The Business History Review 37*, no. 3 (Autumn, 1963) and Audy J. Middlebrooks and Glenna Middlebrooks, "Holland Coffee of Red River," *Southwestern Historical Quarterly 69*, no. 2 (Oct. 1965). Houston on co-existence see, Anderson, *Conquest of Texas*, 156; *The Papers of Mirabeau Buonaparte Lamar*, ed. Charles A. Gulick, Katherine Elliott, and Harriet Smither (Austin: Von Boeckman-Jones, 1921–1927), 2: 346–369.

8 Smith, *From Dominance to Disappearance*, 160; George Browning to Sam Houston, September 16, 1836, *The Papers of the Texas Revolution, 1835–1846*, ed. John H. Jenkins (Austin: Presidial Press, 1973), 8:484; Himmel, *The Conquest of the Karankawa*, 18; La Vere, *The Texas Indians*, 178–180.

9 Smith, *From Dominance to Disappearance*, 154; Everett, *The Texas Cherokees*, 68–73; Campbell, *Gone to Texas*, 114.

10 Noah Smithwick, *The Evolution of a State or Recollections of Old Texas Days* (Austin: University of Texas Press, 1983), 123–38; Smith, *From Dominance to Disappearance*, 164.

11 *Ibid.*, 164.

12 Campbell, *Gone to Texas*, 145; Himmel, *The Conquest of the Karankawa and the Tonkawa*, 82–83; Smith, *From Dominance to Disappearance*, 154;

Treaty between Texas and the Tonkawa Indians, November 22, 1837, Dorman H. Winfrey, ed., *The Texas Indian Papers (TIP)* (Austin: Texas State Library, 1959–1961), 1: 28–29; Treaty between Texas and the Lipan Indians, January 8, 1838, *Texas Indian Papers*, 1: 30–32.

13   La Vere, *Caddo Chiefdoms*, 24–25; Hämäläinen, *The Comanche Empire*, 194.

14   *Ibid.*, 23–24; Smith, *The Caddo Indians*, 23–26. J. Villasana Haggard, "The House of Barr and Davenport," *Southwestern Historical Quarterly* 49, no. 1 (July 1945): 66–88.

15   Everett, *The Texas Cherokee*, 23.

16   *Ibid.*, 9, 26.

17   Theda Perdue, *Cherokee Women: Gender and Culture Change, 1700–1835* (Lincoln: University of Nebraska Press, 1998), 40, 43.

18   Everett, *The Texas Cherokees*, 99, 71–73; Campbell, *Gone to Texas*, 147, Houston to Chief Bowles, November 22, 1835, in Sam Houston, *The Writings of Sam Houston,* ed. Amelia W. Williams and Eugene C. Barker (Austin: University of Texas Press, 1938–1943), 3:7; Smith, *From Dominance to Disappearance*, 166.

19   Everett, *The Texas Cherokees*, 88.

20   Campbell, *Gone to Texas*, 169–170. Everett, *The Texas Cherokees*, 109–111.

21   Excellent histories of the Caddo are F. Todd Smith, *The Caddo Indians: Tribes at the Convergence of Empire, 1542–1854* and David La Vere, *The Caddo Chiefdoms: Caddo Economics and Politics, 700–1835*. Herbert Bolton did much of the historical groundwork in a series of articles in the *Quarterly of the Texas State Historical Association* in the first decade of the twentieth century. Bolton's posthumous publication, *The Hasinais: Southern Caddoans as Seen by the Earliest Europeans*, ed. Russell M. Magnaghi (Norman: University of Oklahoma Press, 1987), is an excellent summary of their culture. William J. Griffith, a Ph.D. student of Bolton, published his version in 1954 as *The Hasinai Indians as Seen by Europeans, 1686–1772*, Middle American Research Institute, Philological and Documentary Studies 2, no. 3 (New Orleans: Tulane University Press, 1954).

22   The Nadacos lived on the headwaters of the Sabine and would later join the Hainai and Nacogdoches. Smith, *The Caddo Indians*, 126; John Sibely, *A Report from Natchitoches in 1807*, ed. Annie Heloise Abel (New York: Heye Foundation, Museum of the American Indian, 1922), 95.

23   La Vere, *Caddo Chiefdoms*, 20–21; Bolton, *The Hasinais*, 92–100; Barr, *Peace Came in the Form of a Woman*, 27–33.

24   Smith, *The Caddo Indians*, 149; Statement of Luis Sanchez as taken by Walter Winn, May 1844, *Texas Indian Papers*, 2:64–65.

25 Smith, *Dominance to Disappearance*, 177–180.

26 Hämäläinen, *The Comanche Empire* lays out the argument for a vast economic empire of the Comanche on the southern plains into northern Mexico. Anderson, *The Conquest of Texas* describes the numerous conflicts with the Euro-Americans (Texan) in the mid-nineteenth century.

27 Anderson, *The Indian Southwest*, 251–253.

28 Weber, *The Mexican Frontier*, 102–105; Anderson, *The Conquest of Texas*, 129, 133.

29 Hämäläinen, *The Comanche Empire*, 254–255; Anderson, *The Conquest of Texas*, 135–137.

30 Hämäläinen, *The Comanche Empire*, 248–250; Anderson, *The Conquest of Texas*, 134–135.

31 Barr, *Peace Came in the Form of a Woman*, 252–255.

32 Anderson, *The Conquest of Texas*, 167.

CHAPTER 2

Tejanas

Hispanic Women on the Losing Side of the Texas Revolution

Jean A. Stuntz

In 1821, when Mexico received its independence from Spain, the Hispanic population in Texas had been decimated by the fighting. The three population centers, San Fernando de Béxar (San Antonio), La Bahía (Goliad), and Nacogdoches, had only a few thousand people total. Indian groups dominated the rest of Texas. By 1824, when Stephen F. Austin began bringing in Anglo colonists legally, life for Tejanos and Tejanas, the Hispanic men and women of Texas, had not improved. If anything, life was more unsettled because of the rapidly changing politics in Mexico City.[1]

During the 1820s and early 1830s, most Tejanas raised children, took care of their husbands, and participated in the social and religious rituals of Spanish Texas. They lived in *villas* (small towns) which had grown up around the missions and *presidios* (forts) created over a century earlier. The missions had by then all been secularized and either served as parish churches or had, like the *presidios*, been converted to non-religious uses. This traditional urban lifestyle preserved much of the Spanish heritage including social mores, festivals, and their legal system.[2]

Every day Tejanas got up before the rest of the family to make tortillas for breakfast. This involved kneeling on the ground while grinding dried corn between two stones to make the flour, then forming and cooking the tortillas. After feeding her family, she would get on with the day's chores. This might involve doing laundry by the river, making or mending clothes, tending to sick children or neighbors, or any of the thousands of things pre-industrial women all over the world do. It also might involve activities unique to Spanish-heritage women, such as supervising irrigation of their fields from the *acequias* (irrigation ditches), working in the shops they or their family owned, or taking their spinning to the *plaza* (town square) where they could talk with other women as they worked.

Historians are fortunate that literate people traveled through Texas during this time and left accounts of their travels. In 1828 General Manuel Mier y Terán traveled through Texas on an inspection tour for the Mexican government. His draftsman, José María Sánchez, described the ruins of missions in San Antonio as being populated by poor farmers almost totally at the mercy of hostile Indians. The botanist for the expedition, Jean-Louis Berlandier, also described the town in unflattering terms. The streets were narrow and twisted, the houses were mostly thatched-roof huts (*jacales*), the people indolent and carefree. He wrote that the women dressed more like women of Louisiana than of Mexico City and that the population in general had adopted too many customs of its French and Anglo neighbors.[3]

Once Terán's expedition made it to the next largest town, Nacogdoches, the scene had changed considerably. For one thing, this town situated next to French and later American territory was quite cosmopolitan. The Spanish influence had dissipated, along with the inhabitants, according to Terán. The place was lawless because law-breakers could simply cross the border into another country, and this went in both directions. Terán thought that the Americans were much more industrious in both farming and business than were the Mexicans, and he deplored this, though he stated that Americans also worked much harder at their vices.[4]

Terán visited the tiny town of La Bahía del Espiritú Santo last. The town was poor in every sense of the word. Only about 300 people lived there and they had little food and no luxuries. Only the missionaries kept the town going, for the presidio was run by inept and corrupt officers.[5]

An American visiting San Antonio at about the same time as the Terán expedition, J. C. Clopper, found many contradictions. He praised the lush fields and huge cottonwood trees, but despaired of the architecture and the ruins of previous *presidios*, such as the Alamo. He described the houses as wigwams, with walls woven of small mesquite trees daubed with mud, and with most families having very few possessions. However, he found the young ladies very attractive.[6]

The young ladies found him attractive, too, as his father had opened a successful business in town. One mother even invited him to court her daughter. He accompanied the senoritas to the *fandangos*, or street celebrations involving dancing. These dances were strictly chaperoned to protect the young women's virtues. His detailed descriptions of the women of San Antonio betray his own upbringing as well as theirs. He spoke of their sparkling eyes and bright skin, their long black hair and rich festival clothing. He seemed somewhat chagrined that their ordinary clothing was less than glamorous.[7]

Clopper also described the making of tortillas by the women, from soaking the kernels in lye to the grinding process, done between two stones while kneeling, to the cooking on hot sheets of iron laid over the fire. He said that the women usually sang merry tunes as they worked. He marveled that the tortillas were used in lieu of utensils for eating the rest of the meal, but this was necessary as so few people owned forks. Meals and other household activities took place while sitting on skins on the ground, as chairs were rare.[8]

A young American blacksmith, Noah Smithwick, traveled through Mexican Texas from 1827 through 1836 and recounted his journeys in his memoirs. His description of a woman making tortillas matches Clopper's. Smithwick heard the sounds of singing and what he thought was dancing, but which turned out to be a woman making tortillas. He explained the process as being almost mechanical, as the woman ground the corn into a paste in the *metate* (the flat grinding stones), rolled it into a ball then flattened it with a series of pats, finally tossing it onto the hot sheet of iron to cook, all the while singing as she did so.[9]

When he stayed in San Antonio, Smithwick saw women spinning and weaving in a manner he thought most old-fashioned and inefficient. The women of San Antonio did not use spinning wheels as Americans did. Instead, they tied the end of a long roll of wool to a wooden peg, then set the peg to spinning in a bowl, using the gravity and twirling motion to turn the wool into thread. Smithwick thought this manner of spinning took much longer than did the American way. He also criticized their manner of weaving as being inefficient. Instead of using thread for both the warp and the woof, they used it only to string the loom, then wove rolls of wool under and over the threads with their fingers. He did admit that the blankets thus produced were both beautiful and warm.[10]

It seems that neither Mexican nor American visitors to Texas in the late 1820s were impressed with the inhabitants. However, each had to concede that the women worked all day, even if they then partied well into the night. Tejanas spent many hours each day preparing tortillas and other food and in making the clothing and other textiles for their families. Visitors would not have seen

Tejana type, from *Views of Mexico: Album pintoresco de la Republica Mexicana.* Courtesy DeGolyer Library, Southern Methodist University, Dallas, Texas, Ag2000.1297.

the other duties of the women, such as raising children, cleaning the house, or taking care of their gardens, as all of this was done in private. The life of the Tejana before the Texas Revolution revolved around her family. This would not change much either during or after the conflict.

A few Anglo men did make the acquaintance of Tejanas and some married into the Hispanic community. Jim Bowie may be the most famous/infamous Anglo to do this. He married Ursula de Veramendi, member of a rich and prominent family, in 1831, after officially becoming a Mexican citizen the year before. Bowie often found himself in trouble with the law and his land speculations infuriated President and General Antonio López de Santa Anna. When that general arrived in San Antonio on February 23, 1836, he deliberately took up residence in Bowie's home.[11]

When the tensions began, most Hispanics wanted to stay out of it, seeing the Anglos as the troublemakers. However, when in 1835 Santa Anna overthrew the Constitution of 1824, many in the Tejano communities declared themselves against the tyrant and for liberty (though not for independence, yet). As Tejano men left their homes to join the Consultations, Conventions, and battles, women were left to fend for themselves. They had to do all the work they usually did, plus what the men would have done. No matter how much they supported the principles of liberty, some must have grumbled at all the extra work.[12]

General Martín Perfecto de Cos came to San Antonio with 500 soldiers to secure the area after the first rumblings of resistance. He announced that he would punish the troublemakers at Anahuac and threatened to run all Anglos out of Texas. Those Anglos who had been pushing for war saw this as the last straw. Texan rebels seized Goliad and refused to allow Mexican soldiers to remove the cannon at Gonzales. It was in this struggle that the first shots of the revolution were fired. The banner painted with the words "Come and

Take It" over a cannon became the first symbol of armed resistance to the Mexican authorities even though no shots were actually fired. The Mexican troops retreated to San Antonio empty-handed. The rebel forces proclaimed victory and moved to San Antonio to take it, as well.[13]

The Texan mob arrived at the outskirts of San Antonio in October 1835. The battle of Concepción, fought near the mission Nuestra Señora de la Purísima Concepción de Acuña Mission, was a great victory for the Texans led by Jim Bowie. The Texans then set up a siege of San Antonio, which resulted in the Grass Fight, so called because when the Texans spotted a mule train with large sacks approaching the city they attacked, thinking it was a payroll caravan. Instead, all they found was grass, which the San Antonio natives had gathered to feed their livestock. Infuriated, the Texans burned the grass, only belatedly realizing that they should have used it to feed their own horses.[14]

Finally, on December 5, 1835, as many of the men were cold and hungry and ready to return home for the winter, some of the Texas volunteers decided to attack the city. Ben Milam led about 300 men into San Antonio where they fought house-to-house and hand-to-hand, forcing the Mexican soldiers to retreat from the city into the Alamo on the outskirts of town. There General Cos surrendered and promised to move his troops south of the Rio Grande, never to return to Texas. The Texans moved into the city, either paying for or commandeering quarters and supplies. They also set about fortifying the Alamo to withstand the attack they were sure would come. Santa Anna had already threatened to kill every person who had resisted his authority and had issued arrest warrants specifically for Jim Bowie for his part on the Monclova Speculations. The threat of Santa Anna's army and his reputation for violence drove large portions of the Texas population into hiding in the countryside and sent Anglos rushing east toward the Sabine River and US protection.[15]

The fighting itself, which lasted less than a year, affected Tejanas directly and indirectly. Most of the battles took place in or near the Hispanic towns, so Tejanas had to share their food, their belongings, and sometimes even their houses with soldiers. Once the anti-Santa Anna forces took control of San Antonio in December 1835, Tejanas in town sold food and other goods to the Texian army under the control of Colonel James C. Neill. The army also employed the men living in San Antonio. After Lieutenant Colonel William Barret Travis took command of the forces inside the Alamo, he also issued scrip for cattle purchased from Felipe Xaimes. The Texas government eventually paid these debts.[16]

In February 1836 the people living in San Antonio and those barricading themselves inside the Alamo heard that General Santa Anna and his army were approaching. Many of the Hispanic women and children fled into the countryside to escape his wrath though some stayed in town to convince him of their loyalty. Others joined the forces inside the Alamo.[17]

In the town of Goliad, which had grown up by the mission La Bahía, Tejanas also experienced the fighting first-hand. Captain Manuel Sabriego commanded the *presidio* there and had married a local Hispanic woman. He loyally supported Santa Anna and even raised a company of local men, mostly *vaqueros* (cowboys), to fight off the rebels. On October 10, 1835, Texian commander George M. Collingsworth captured Sabriego and took command of the *presidio*. Philip Dimmitt took charge because he was married to a local Tejana, but he was not especially suited to command. He forced the local townspeople to perform heavy labor without pay, causing many of the families to flee to the countryside and join the forces loyal to Santa Anna. General José Urrea took advantage of these loyalties to defeat Colonel James W. Fannin, Jr. and his garrison at Goliad, which ended in another massacre of surrendered Texian troops on March 27, 1836. "Remember Goliad!" was as much a rallying cry as

"Remember the Alamo!" The fighting ended on April 21, 1836, with the battle of San Jacinto.[18]

After the fighting was over, Hispanics in Texas faced tremendous problems. As more and more Anglos came into the Republic, Hispanics lost status, power, and land. Some lost their lives to Anglo race-based violence. Most of the whites moving in came from the U.S. South and brought their prejudices against people of color with them. Those from Georgia especially had just forced an Indian removal and saw that as a good thing. These new whites saw all Hispanics as lesser because of their skin color and as traitors because they were of Mexican heritage. Even those who had fought with the Texians found themselves branded as disloyal and therefore subject to prejudice and violence.[19]

An example of this prejudice was Juan Seguin. Born in San Antonio to a prominent family, he became *Alcalde* (mayor) in 1833. He supported the movement against Santa Anna and was among the defenders of the Alamo. He survived because he had been sent with a message to the government before the battle. He fought with a troop of Tejanos at the battle of San Jacinto, as much a hero as any man there. He became a senator in the Republic of Texas legislature where he tried in vain to get pensions for the widows and orphans of the Tejanos killed at the Alamo. He also tried unsuccessfully to get the Texas laws translated into Spanish so the Tejanos could defend themselves in court against the Anglos. Eventually, Seguin got tired of fighting the prejudice and joined the Mexican army, though he eventually returned to Texas.[20]

Many of the wealthier Hispanic families dealt with the Anglo invasion by marrying their daughters to promising Anglos, many of whom then became city and state officials because of their wife's money. Both sides benefitted. The Tejanas could protect their families with their Anglo prestige and the men got easy access to land and power. This arrangement only lasted a few years, though, until the influx of so many Anglos and the loss of so much Hispanic land made such marriages less desirable.[21]

Religion was another cause for prejudice against Hispanics. Protestant Anglos held deep-seated hatred of Catholics and all the Tejanos were Catholic. Catholic rituals and festivals continued to take place in the Spanish towns like San Antonio and Tejanas continued to take part in the parades and celebrations. The procession of Our Lady of Guadalupe included the image adorned with flowers, women carrying crosses and banners, and girls dressed in white carrying candles in the parade. Men played music and fired their guns while everyone sang hymns. Protestants saw these parades as idolatry and proof of the ignorance and superstition of the Hispanics.[22]

For most Tejanas daily life did not change much as a direct result of the Texas Revolution, although in the long-term their lives and prospects changed for the worse. They still ground corn to make tortillas, spun thread and wove cloth, took care of their family, and participated in community events. The difference was that they now did all this in occupied territory. After the revolution, immigration from the southern part of the United States increased. These people brought with them the racial attitude that allowed people of color to be treated as less than human and any land they held to be taken from them. So even though most Tejanas did not have much direct experience during the fighting, and their lives did not change immediately, the long-term results of the Texas Revolution on the lives of Tejanas were immense. [23]

The mostly Anglo Republic of Texas legislature moved quickly to change the legal system from the Spanish to the English common law system they were more familiar with. This change took away a lot of rights from Tejanas, as the Spanish system held women to be almost equal to men. Under English common law, married women had no rights at all. Their very existence merged into that of their

Tejana in Baile costume, from *Views of Mexico: Album pintoresco de la Republica Mexicana.* Courtesy DeGolyer Library, Southern Methodist University, Dallas, Texas, vault-folio-2 F1213.L45.

husbands. Under English law, a married woman could not make
a contract, could not own property, could not write a will, could
not sue or be sued, could not even fight for the custody of her own
children because she did not have a legal identity separate from
that of her husband.[24]

This was very different from the Spanish system where married
women could do all of these things. Hispanic women in Texas were
used to being able to transact business, sue someone for transgres-
sions, and own and manage their own property. Legal cases preserved in the Bexár Archives give ample evidence that women in
Spanish Texas knew their rights and exercised them as needed. For
example in 1745, Tomasa de la Garza, a married woman, petitioned
the *cabildo* (local government) for a piece of land for her family to
live on. She and her husband had eight children who lived with
them; one of her daughters was a widow. The government officials
granted title to her, not her husband.[25]

Under Spanish law, women could sue and be sued in their own
names, even if they were married, though usually the husband would
represent the wife. In 1770, don Francisco Caravajal brought suit on
behalf of his wife, doña María, to gain title to land that had belonged
to her grandfather. A city official had illegally given part of this
land to brothers Andrés and Francisco Hernández and Andrés had
sold part of his share to his niece, dona Josepha Hernández, while
Francisco sold part of his share to the son of the original owner,
Joseph Caravajal, dona María's father who should have inherited it
to begin with. Dona Josepha Hernández, the defendant, claimed
that the land was indeed hers, but the authorities ruled in favor of
Dona María. Even though the husband had brought the suit, the
land belonged to the wife.[26]

Spanish married women could also write wills disposing of their
own property. Unlike English common law, married women under Spanish law retained their legal identity and ownership of any

property brought into the marriage. María Melián wrote a will on December 3, 1740, which is a good example of Spanish inheritance laws. María had gained property in each of her two marriages and by settling in Texas. (The Spanish government lured settlers to Texas by giving them land and other property.) She devised each type of property according to the Spanish law. Property brought into a marriage or received as a gift or inheritance after the marriage was separate property, while anything earned during the marriage was community property. María had one cow that she brought into her second marriage, so this cow was her separate property. It had given birth to four calves, which were then community property. Husbands and wives each owned half of this community property. María gave two of these cows—her half of the community property—to her children. She had also received five cows for settling in San Antonio. These were her separate property and she gave all of them to her children. She divided the rest of her own property equally between her sons and daughter.[27]

These cases showed that Tejanas held considerable rights before the Texas Revolution. They could own property in their own name, which is often considered the foundation of citizenship. They could sue if they felt their rights had been infringed upon. They could write wills to dispose of their property as they wished. These rights all disappeared when English common law became the law of Texas. Fortunately, Texas legislators brought back some aspects of the Spanish system when they wrote the statehood constitution in 1845. Though the motivation to re-enact community property laws was to keep Texas lands out of the hands of creditors in the United States, women could still benefit. That was, if they had lawyers. Most people knew nothing about the Spanish community property law and it was only in cases of divorce, intestate succession, and other property battles that these laws were ever used. By that time, though, most Tejanas had been deprived of all land by violence or fraud, and did not have enough money to hire lawyers.[28]

As more and more Anglos came into the Republic and occupied more and more of the territory, Hispanics lost more and more. They lost their land to greedy, unscrupulous H, and violent Anglos. They lost the ability to control their own lives and to guide their children's future. Even in places like San Antonio, which had been mostly Hispanic, Anglos took over and made the town their own. In the process, Tejanas lost their land, lost their rights, and had to struggle just to hold on to the remnants of their culture. In short, the Texas Revolution had a devastating effect on the Hispanic women of Texas.

Selected Bibliography

Acosta, Teresa Palomo, and Ruthe Winegarten. *Las Tejanas: 300 Years of History.* Austin: University of Texas Press, 2003.

Cantrell, Gregg. *Stephen F. Austin: Empresario of Texas.* New Haven: Yale University Press, 1999.

Campbell, Randolph B. *Gone to Texas: A History of the Lone Star State.* New York: Oxford University Press, 2003.

Chipman, Donald E., and Harriet Denise Joseph, *Spanish Texas, 1519–1821.* Rev. ed. Austin: University of Texas Press, 2010.

De la Teja, Jesús F., ed. *Tejano Leadership in Mexican and Revolutionary Texas.* College Station: Texas A&M University Press, 2010.

Dysart, Jane. "Mexican Women in San Antonio, 1830–1860: The Assimilation Process," *Western Historical Quarterly* 7, no. 4 (Oct. 1976): 365–375.

Jackson, Jack, ed. *Texas by Terán: The Diary Kept by Manuel de Mier y Terán on His 1828 Inspection of Texas.* Translated by John Wheat. Austin: University of Texas Press, 2000.

McKnight, Joseph W. "Spanish Law for the Protection of the Surviving Spouse," *Anuario de Historia del Derecho Espanol,* tomo 57 (1987): 373–395.

Montejano, David. *Anglos and Mexicans in the Making of Texas, 1836–1986.* Austin: University of Texas Press, 1987.

Poyo, Gerald E., ed. *Tejano Journey, 1770–1850.* Austin: University of Texas Press, 1996.

Salmon, Marylynn. *Women and the Law of Property in Early America.* Chapel Hill: University of North Carolina Press, 1986.

Smithwick, Noah. *The Evolution of a State or Recollections of Old Texas Days.* Compiled by Nanna Smithwick Donaldson, Barker Texas History Center Series #5, 4th printing. Austin: University of Texas Press, 1994.

Stuntz, Jean A. *Hers, His, and Theirs: Community Property Law in Spain and Early Texas.* Lubbock: Texas Tech University Press, 2005.

Endnotes

1 For more information on the Spanish era of Texas, read Donald E. Chipman and Harriet Denise Joseph, *Spanish Texas, 1519–1821,* rev. ed. (Austin: University of Texas Press, 2010). For more information on the extent of Indian control of Texas, read Pekka Hämäläinen, *The Comanche Empire* (New Haven: Yale University Press, 2009). For an understanding of Mexican politics during the late 1820s and early 1830s, read Gregg Cantrell, *Stephen F. Austin: Empresario of Texas* (New Haven: Yale University Press, 1999), 104–131, 202–296. To get an understanding of the experiences of Spanish and Hispanic women throughout Texas history, see *Las Tejanas: 300 years of History* (Austin: University of Texas Press, 2003) by Teresa Palomo Acosta and Ruthe Winegarten.

2 Randolph B. Campbell, *Gone to Texas: A History of the Lone Star State* (New York: Oxford University Press, 2003), 97.

3 Jack Jackson, ed., *Texas by Terán: The Diary kept by Manuel de Mier y Terán on His 1828 Inspection of Texas,* trans. John Wheat (Austin: University of Texas Press, 2000), 15–17.

4 Ibid., 79–81.

5 Ibid., 151–53.

6 Ibid., 21–23, 26.

7 Ibid., 23.

8 Ibid., 25–26.

9 Noah Smithwick, *The Evolution of a State or Recollections of Old Texas Days,* comp. Nanna Smithwick Donaldson, Barker Texas History Center Series #5, 4th printing (Austin: University of Texas Press, 1994), 9–10.

10 Ibid., 34.

11 William R. Williamson, "Bowie, James," *Handbook of Texas Online* (http://www.tshaonline.org/handbook/online/articles/fbo45), accessed April 18, 2011. Published by the Texas State Historical Association.

12 Campbell, *Gone to Texas,* 116–131; Cantrell, *Stephen F. Austin,* 247–328.

13 Campbell, *Gone to Texas,* 116–122, 128–131.

14 Ibid., 128–136; Alwyn Barr, "Grass Fight," *Handbook of Texas Online* (http://www.tshaonline.org/handbook/online/articles/qfg01), accessed April 17, 2011. Published by the Texas State Historical Association.

15 Campbell, *Gone to Texas*, 138–141. See the chapter in this book on the Runaway Scrape for more on this topic.

16 Stephen L. Hardin, "Efficient in the Cause," in *Tejano Journey, 1770–1850*, ed. Gerald E. Poyo (Austin: University of Texas Press, 1996), 56.

17 Ibid., "Efficient," 63. The stories of the women in the Alamo are told in another chapter of this book.

18 Ibid., "Efficient," 62–64.

19 For more information on the Tejano experience, see Timothy M. Matovina, "Between Two Worlds" in *Tejano Journey*, 73–87 and David Montejano, *Anglos and Mexicans in the Making of Texas, 1836–1986* (Austin: University of Texas Press, 1987), 13–99. For more on Tejanos in leadership roles before, during, and after the Revolution, see *Tejano Leadership in Mexican and Revolutionary Texas,* ed. Jesús F. de la Teja (College Station: Texas A&M University Press, 2010). To focus more on Tejanas, see Jane Dysart, "Mexican Women in San Antonio, 1830–1860: The Assimilation Process," *Western Historical Quarterly* 7 no. 4 (Oct. 1976): 365–375.

20 Matovina, "Between Two Worlds," 75–76; Jesús F. de la Teja, "Seguin, Juan Nepomuceno," *Handbook of Texas Online* (http://www.tshaonline.org/handbook/online/articles/fse08), accessed April 17, 2011. Published by the Texas State Historical Association.

21 Montejano, *Anglos and Mexicans*, 34–35.

22 Matovino, "Between Two Worlds," 81–85.

23 For more on the increase of slavery and racial attitudes in Texas, see Randolph B. Campbell, *An Empire for Slavery: The Peculiar Institution in Texas, 1821–1865* (Baton Rouge: Louisiana State University Press, 1989).

24 The Declaration with Plan and Powers of the Provisional Government of Texas (1836), Article VI, VII. For English common law regarding the status of women, see St. George Tucker, *Blackstone's Commentaries with Reference to the Constitution and Laws of the Federal Government of the United States and the Commonwealth of Virginia* (Philadelphia: William Birch Young and Abraham Small, 1803; repr. New Jersey: Rothman Reprints, 1969), 1:418–445; Marylynn Salmon, *Women and the Law of Property in Early America* (Chapel Hill: University of North Carolina Press, 1986); Jean Stuntz, *Hers, His, and Theirs: Community Property Law in Spain and Early Texas* (Lubbock: Texas Tech University Press, 2005), 99–107.

25 Bexar Archives Translations (BAT) microfilm Reel 3, vol. 17, 1–6.

26 Ibid., reel 7, vol. 48, 16–23, 27, 32, 38–39, 65.

27 Ibid., reel 2, vol. 10, 51–55. For more explanation on Spanish laws of inheritance, see Joseph W. McKnight, "Spanish Law for the Protection of the Surviving Spouse," *Anuario de Historia del Derecho Espanol,* tomo 57 (1987): 373–395.

28 *Debates of the Texas Constitution* (Houston, 1836), 10–11, 53–55, 417–426, 453–462, 505–508, 598–601; Constitution of the State of Texas of 1845, Title 7, Sections 19 and 20. For more on how these Spanish laws were used in the Republic and state of Texas, see Stuntz, *Hers, His, and Theirs,* 133–169.

CHAPTER 3

"Joys and Sorrows of Those Dear Old Times"

Anglo-American Women during the Era of the Texas Revolution

Mary L. Scheer

On April 28, 1833, Dilue Rose from St. Louis, Missouri, celebrated her eighth birthday onboard a schooner traveling from New Orleans to Matagorda Bay, Texas. The small vessel, carrying her parents, brother Granville, sister Ella, and other adventurers, encountered high winds and ran aground on a sand bar off Galveston Island and again at Clopper's Point. Disabled, the ship remained on shore as the frightened passengers spent hours in darkness huddled in the small hold before it turned on its side. The sailors rescued the women and children, as well as Dilue's father who had been ill throughout the two-week journey. After a day without food or dry clothes, the passengers boarded a keel boat for Harrisburg where they were received "with open arms by the good people" of the town. Despite the primitive conditions and rumors of "some talk of trouble with Mexico," the Rose family decided to settle in the region, rented a farm near Stafford Point, fifteen miles from Harrisburg on the Brazos River, and commenced the planting of cotton.[1]

Dilue Rose Harris. Courtesy Nesbitt Memorial Library Archives, Columbus, Texas.

For the next ten years Dilue, a young Anglo-American woman on the Texas frontier, and her family experienced the "joys and sorrows" of revolutionary times. From being shipwrecked on the Texas coast and "threatened by wolves and water" to being "besieged by the runaway negro" and frightened by Mexican troops, she survived those tumultuous years that brought about the unraveling of Mexican Texas, the beginning of the Texas Revolution, and the establishment of the Republic of Texas. In her recollections, recorded in a journal kept by her husband Dr. Pleasant W. Rose, she recalled not only her personal experiences in early Texas, including the year 1836 "with all its horrors," but also the political and social disruptions of the time, proving that women were at the center of the Texas Revolution.[2]

Anglo-American women such as Dilue Rose and others who arrived in Texas in the early decades of the nineteenth century were mostly immigrants from distant American states and territories such as Louisiana, Alabama, Arkansas, Tennessee, and Missouri. "Pushed" from their homes due to financial collapse, suffocating debts, or a desire to start anew, they were "pulled" to the Mexican state of *Coahuila y Tejas* by its liberal land policies and promise of economic opportunity. For the most part Anglo-American women moved to Texas as members of families whose westward treks were initiated by men. With a spirit of adventure and "a fair share of curiosity," these pioneering women loaded their household belongings onto wagons or schooners and followed the established trails and sea lanes to the western frontier. A few, however, came without spouses, such as those single women listed in Austin's Register of Families who received Mexican land grants in 1824. Although native and Spanish women predated their arrival in Texas, Anglo women journeyed westward to "the new El Dorado" as part of a westward-moving Anglo-American quest for fertile soil, commercial expansion, and a better life later promoted as Manifest Destiny.[3]

Most Anglo women in early Texas were southerners in birth and outlook. They had absorbed the values and assumptions of that culture prior to their arrival in Texas. In the antebellum South, according to historian Anne Firor Scott, southerners "put their faith in the family as the central institution of society." Within this milieu southern white women of all social classes, from poor whites to plantation mistresses, sustained themselves through kinship and family ties as wives, mothers, and daughters. Southern men, on the other hand, were designated as heads of families and as such tended to view their wives as subordinate helpmates. Often referred to as the doctrine of separate spheres for the sexes, this viewpoint assigned men and women to their proper places in society—men to the public spaces and women to the private realm. Such prescribed behavior was universally understood at the time, but not always practiced. As historian Ann Patton Malone observed: "Most women, especially in the South, submitted to the code and some [even] enjoyed the view from the pedestal, but an undercurrent of discontent did exist."[4]

Conditions on the Texas frontier often mitigated the model of separate spheres as a metaphor for understanding women's lives. Men naturally outnumbered women in border regions and, according to some scholars, women's value and status increased in frontier settings. Wives typically were called upon to perform male duties such as clearing land and planting crops to make successes of their farms. At the same time the ideals of true womanhood, with its admonitions to purity, piety, submissiveness, and domesticity, accompanied them westward. While Anglo women often struggled to recreate those ideals of southern womanhood on the Texas frontier, the harsh conditions, dangers, and uncertainties of daily pioneer life made many of these precepts obsolete or unattainable.[5]

A few women openly resisted the proscribed feminine roles and gender norms, such as Pamelia Mann, who immigrated to Texas in 1834 and became proficient in the use of firearms and a bowie knife. At the same time she pursued endeavors commonly associated with the male-dominated world, accumulating considerable land and property, such as wagons, livestock, and guns. Another Anglo woman who exhibited a self-reliant, resolute spirit was innkeeper Angelina Peyton Eberly, who fired a six-pound cannon in 1842 to prevent the removal of the state archives from Austin to Houston. Thus, while Anglo women's lives had changed as a result of the frontier experience, their public image did not always match their reality, and according to historian Sandra L. Myres, "remained relatively static."[6]

Prior to Anglo-American colonization of Texas, one of the earliest white women to arrive in the region was Jane Wilkinson Long, wife of Dr. James Long, soldier, adventurer, and filibusterer. Following the birth of her first child in 1819, she set out from Louisiana for Texas, along with her servant girl Kian, to join her husband in Nacogdoches and then at Bolivar Point on Galveston Bay. Dr. Long, along with other opportunists, coveted the lands west of the Sabine River for southern agriculture and expansion. Refusing to recognize the Adams-Onís Treaty (1819) that upheld Spanish claims to Texas, he launched two expeditions into Spanish territory to declare Texas independent, leaving his wife and children behind to wait, scavenge for food, and defend themselves against the Karankawa Indians living along the Texas coast.[7]

The failure of Long's filibustering campaign, his capture, and subsequent death in Mexico City in 1822 left Jane as the sole support of her small family. Abruptly thrown into a world with which she had little previous direct contact, she was lonely, near starvation, and in debt. These adversities, coupled with a self-reliant spirit, however, emboldened her to travel to San Antonio on horseback to demand a government pension from Governor José Félix Trespalacious for her husband's military service during the recent Mexican Revolution (1810–1821). Unsuccessful in this attempt, she returned to Louisiana for a short visit and then journeyed back to Texas. Ignoring warnings that travel to Texas was "too adventurous for a female," Jane set out on her journey to claim title to a league of land in the Austin colony. "When she landed in San Fellipe [*sic*] she was not in possession of 100$ [*sic*] of property" and "had labored under every privation." Although she did not immediately prosper and remained dependent on the good will of friends and suitors, thirty-year-old Jane Long, a woman "with the energies of masculine vigor" and a "tongue not too pliant for a female" demonstrated remarkable courage and fortitude. According to settler J. C. Clopper, she was an active member of the community and was one of "3 or four widows, young and old" who comprised the social life of the capital. Noah Smithwick, a gun-and blacksmith, observed that "the leadership of the 'ton' [*sic*] was accredited to Mrs. Jane Long."[8]

One acceptable avenue open to Jane Long and other Anglo women to live independent lives was to operate a boarding house or inn. The heavy demand for food and housing in early Texas, especially by travelers, provided a secure source of income for many women. At the same time these establishments utilized female domestic skills such as "providing sleeping quarters, food, and drink." But it also required business entrepreneurship and financial acumen. As the sole breadwinner for her children, Jane therefore purchased an inn in 1832 from W. T. Austin and began to make a comfortable living, taking in lodgers traveling between San Felipe and Brazoria.[9]

Other Anglo-American women followed Jane Long into Texas during the 1820s. A surprising number arrived with Stephen F. Austin, the first Anglo *empresario*, as members of the original Old Three Hundred families. Most were married women, but in 1830 at least twenty were widows responsible for the welfare of their children. While married women benefited from immigration through the awarding of land grants to their husbands, widows were eligible for such grants in their own right. Rebekah Cumings was a widow who received title to a league and two *labors* of land in present day Brazoria and Waller Counties. Elizabeth Tumlinson, who was widowed when her husband was killed by Waco Indians, received a league and *labor* of land in 1824 on "the south bank of the Colorado River," near the present-day town of Columbus. And Amy Comstock White, a widow from Louisiana with seven children, who immigrated to Texas to escape the ravages of the Panic of 1819, received a *sitio* of land that included "selected grants along the San Jacinto River."[10]

One Anglo woman who left a detailed record of her experiences in early Texas was Mary Crownover Rabb. In 1823 she traveled from Jonesboro, Arkansas, to Texas with her husband and kinfolk. Her account conveyed the sense of fear and uncertainty she felt in a frontier environment. After traveling for two and one-half months, she crossed the Colorado River, only to find that "thar was no haus thar then nore nothing but a wilderness [*sic*]," Her husband John eventually built a primitive dwelling with an "earthing" floor while Mary busied herself with household chores and spinning in order to "drowded [*sic*]" out the sound of the Indians.[11]

Women shouldered much of the burden of daily life in pre-and post-revolutionary Texas. Depending on their economic status, their lives and survival depended on hard work, resourcefulness, and stamina. Those Anglo women residing on small farms such as Mary Crownover Rabb prepared the food, spun thread into cloth, mended and washed clothes, tended gardens, and took care of the children. Many also worked alongside their husbands, clearing land, planting crops, and tending livestock. Plantation mistresses such as Emily Austin Perry of Peach Point Plantation, although expected to maintain a level of refinement, also performed numerous day-to-day domestic tasks, from feeding, clothing, and nursing children and slaves to making candles, preserving fruits, and tending gardens. Many farm and plantation wives were also engaged in family financial affairs, often making independent decisions in the absence of their planter husbands. In short, "There was nothing which was not her work."[12]

Along with routine chores and child-rearing, Anglo-American women encountered perilous times on the Texas frontier. Tragedy, deprivation, disease, and Indians were frequent visitors to their door. Mary Crownover Rabb remembered camping on an island in the Brazos River where she endured the discomforts of mosquitoes and flies and feared that "alegators [sic] would come up out of the river and get my babe." The river could also take "a sudden rise" and drown her children while they slept in their beds. Mary Ann Maverick, an 1838 immigrant to Texas, recorded "the joys and sorrows of those dear old times" in her Memoirs. She recalled the constant threat from epidemics. "Violent influenza with sore throat and measles and scarlentina," she wrote, as well as cholera and smallpox, felled many residents of San Antonio and the surrounding area. Several of the Maverick children, who were frequently sick, perished from "bilious fever" and other diseases. In addition, Indian raids into Anglo settlements were frequent. Rebecca Burnett Lee, who lived with her family on Cypress Creek, witnessed a Comanche encounter in 1836. In an interview years later she reminisced that the Indians were "all riding barebacked and were almost naked." They entered their yard brandishing "scalping knives" and threatened to break into their home. Only the arrival of friendly Indians frightened them away.[13]

Despite the difficulties and hardships, few Anglo women who arrived in Mexican Texas during the 1820s and early 1830s envisioned a future when the colony would be in full revolt. Many had arrived in Mexico's northernmost province with the expectation of becoming law-abiding citizens under the Mexican Constitution of 1824. In fact Stephen F. Austin had gone to great lengths to remind the colonists "of their obligations to him, to the colony, and to Mexico." Despite the new republican Mexican government's failure to provide important guarantees, such as trial by jury and religious toleration, and fulfill its promises of schools and tax exemptions, most Anglo-American settlers were willing to change their religion, language, and customs, if in name only, in order to comply with Mexican requirements for immigration, land ownership, and settlement. Furthermore, many assumed that Mexicans, who were in the minority in the remote province, would leave them to themselves, thereby permitting the colonists to blend Mexican institutions into Anglo-American patterns. And for a while this accommodation provided peaceful, even harmonious, relations between Anglo colonists and the central government in Mexico City. As late as 1833 Dilue Rose, who had just arrived in Texas, observed that "the people did not appear to anticipate danger." Nevertheless, Anglo colonists' patience was wearing thin over fundamental differences about open immigration, Texas statehood, a responsive judiciary, and the future of slavery. Soon this remote province would stand on the verge of revolt and the ensuing revolution, with its "joys and sorrows," would become for women one of the most difficult and defining moments of their lives.[14]

Anglo-American women in revolutionary Texas could hardly remain aloof from the turbulent events of the 1830s. Despite the absence of a recognizable female public role, they became caught up in the turmoil that enveloped the entire populace. They experienced and wrote about the historic transformation taking place in Texas—from a fledging colony to an independent Republic. Stirrings of political awareness appeared in their letters and diary entries as the public discourse and the impending crisis bore down on their lives, their families, and their homes. While most men and women of the time shared the common assumption that political discussion, like political participation, fell outside the feminine sphere, Anglo women in Texas nonetheless discussed the coming crisis, recorded the disruptions to their normal patterns of life, and even participated in the pre-war resistance and the war itself. Because middle to upper class, educated white females left more records than poor, illiterate, and minority women, scholars know more about their lives, responses, and effects of the revolution than about any other group of Texas women.

One Anglo-American woman who was knowledgeable about the troubled political relations between Mexico and the United States was Jane Long. As the niece of U.S. Army General James Wilkinson, she was well aware of the earlier plots and schemes by her uncle and others to seize a portion of Texas from Spain. As a helpmate and supporter of her husband's unsuccessful expeditions to seize Texas, she had aided his exploits, even stitching the fringed red and white flag that flew over the Old Stone Fort in Nacogdoches. Later, as events escalated during the 1830s, Jane hosted participants on both sides of the conflict at her boarding house, which became "a meeting place" for new arrivals, as well as the unofficial headquarters for the interim government. Both Texan and Mexican leaders enjoyed lodging, meals, and entertainment there. Colonel Juan Almonte, a Mexican officer and diplomat in 1834, was a frequent guest and reportedly was unaware of the "arms and gunpowder" hidden on the property to be used by the rebellious colonists against his government. Attorney and Anglo newcomer William Barret Travis often dined and lodged at her inn and advised her on business and financial matters. Sam Houston was a guest in 1836 while attending the meeting of the Texas Congress in nearby Columbia. And on September 8, 1835, colonists arranged an elaborate dinner and ball at Long's establishment for Stephen F. Austin following his release from a Mexican prison. Afterwards, Austin delivered an impassioned speech to those assembled, supporting the ideals of the emerging war party.[15]

Another astute observer of the political scene was author and diarist Mary Austin Holley, niece of Moses Austin and cousin to

Stephen F. Austin. Widowed in 1827 at the age of forty-three, Holley was "intelligent, talented, and charming," and the sole support of her two children. Living in Kentucky at the time, she made plans for a future in Texas, obtaining a league of land on Dickinson Bayou near present-day Galveston County from her cousin Stephen. Although she never established a permanent residence there, hoping to sell her Texas lands one day to ease her financial straits, her frequent trips, correspondence, and writings concerning Texas helped promote the young colony, garner sympathy for the revolution, and secure the reputation of Stephen F. Austin.[16]

As a writer and member of the Austin family, Holley became "one of the best known women in North America during the first part of the nineteenth century." Since literature was an acceptable activity for women, she wrote several books, including *Texas: Observations, Historical, Geographical, and Descriptive,* a series of letters written in 1831 during her first visit to the Austin colony. The volume, which was dedicated to Col. Stephen F. Austin and his "judicious, disinterested and generous management" of the affairs of his colony, both promoted Texas colonization and answered questions from the London Geographical Society relative to Texas immigration. Envisioning the book as a potential money-making travel monograph, Holley later added an appendix, which included a communication from San Felipe de Austin "relative to late events in Texas, 1832." Therein, she reported on the continued loyalty of the colonists to Mexico, but also their determination to resist "tyrannical acts of the military officers," such as the disturbances at Anahuac, as well as "violations of the constitution and laws" by the Mexican government.[17]

Another member of the Austin clan was Emily Austin Bryan Perry, daughter of Moses Austin and sister to Stephen F. Austin. In 1831, along with her second husband James F. Perry and several children, she had arrived in Texas from Missouri and became the mistress of Peach Point Plantation. "Articulate, hardworking, and [a] very active woman in her own right," according to biographer Light T. Cummins, she was the sole heir of Moses and Stephen F. Austin. After 1836 she inherited thousands of acres of Texas land, of which she retained personal ownership. Although "one of the largest individual landholders in Texas and indisputably its richest woman," Emily Austin, like most married women, was constrained by the doctrine of *feme covert,* a legal stricture that subsumed a married woman's legal identity into that of her husband. This meant that Emily could not enter into contracts in her own name or sue without her husband's consent. Consequently, James "served as her legal agent and as the named party in managing her landed wealth." Nevertheless, Emily remained fully engaged in the affairs of Peach Point Plantation and utilized her unique status to influence "all matters touching on her considerable amount of property."[18]

Despite the legal stricture preventing her independent control of her estate, Emily Austin used her wealth and privileged position to influence public affairs. During the era of the Texas Revolution, she reported to husband James on the political rumors of "another revolution broken out in Mexico," and her hope that "they will let us alone." Throughout 1834 she became increasingly alarmed about political conditions when her brother Stephen was arrested for advocating the separation of Texas and Coahuila and imprisoned in Mexico City, where he languished for months. James necessarily took over his brother-in-law's personal affairs during his absence, and both Emily and her husband "worked very hard in an effort to secure his release." Through regular correspondence they kept in touch with Austin, while openly seeking all avenues, both legal and diplomatic, to secure his release.[19]

Both Austin women, Mary and Emily, fulfilled the traditional roles expected of women of their class and background while also developing an autonomous perspective and independent identity for themselves. They were devoted wives, caring mothers, and attentive daughters. Mary Austin Holley wed in 1805 at the age of twenty and bore two children while overseeing an efficient household for her family. Similarly, Emily Austin Bryan Perry "relished being a wife and caring mother, while maintaining a firm command over the domestic sphere at Peach Point Plantation." Both were educated, married, and then widowed. While she was a *feme covert,* Mary traveled widely, writing poetry and publishing a book about her husband, which was unusual for a woman at that time. To disguise its female authorship, Holley signed her poems with only her initials. Her book later appeared as *Caldwell's Discourses,* utilizing the name of a college professor in Lexington. Twice-married Emily, although "fundamentally defined by her commitment to her family," also worked hard in the Bryan family store in Missouri. During James's long absences, she often managed its business operations. And when their finances declined due to the Panic of 1819, Emily boldly suggested moving to Texas as a solution to their economic woes. However, with widowhood, both women were left to fend for themselves, becoming the sole support of their children. They drew on an inner reserve in the face of grim prospects to make bold and independent decisions for themselves and their children. Mary Austin Holley secured a position as a tutor and traveled to Texas on five separate occasions, while Emily, who was reduced to poverty following James Perry's death, took in boarders and opened a small dame school. "By our industry and economy," Emily wrote Stephen F. Austin, "we have endeavored to live tolerably comfortable...."[20]

As the crises of 1835 escalated into armed revolt, Anglo-American women experienced the revolution in very personal ways. Viewing the Texas Revolution solely from the vantage point of military and political objectives marginalizes the roles of women and families. But a consideration of those events from the domestic front, through personal correspondence and diary entries of the women, allows a many-sided approach to understanding the revolution. Within this context, women's participation on the home front, whether directly or indirectly, demonstrated a level of patriotism that permitted men to fight more effectively on the war front, thereby securing the success of the revolt.

Unlike the American Revolution, in which a number of women took up arms in defense of their homes and property, albeit temporarily, the Texas Revolution was fought mainly by men. Nevertheless, Anglo-American women served the cause in a variety of ways. With the absence of male heads of household during wartime, the balance of work and the exercise of some power necessarily shifted from males to females. As a result Texas women showed their patriotic zeal by supporting their politically active husbands and sons who left them alone for varying lengths of time to attend meetings, make arrangements for their safety, or enlist in the army. Dilue Rose Harris later recalled that nearly every man with a gun and a horse had joined the Texan army in the siege of Bejar, leaving the women and children "behind in the fields to pick the cotton."[21]

With the surrender and retreat of General Martin Perfecto de Cos the men retuned to their farms only to rally again when an enlarged Mexican army under General Antonio López de Santa Anna returned and threatened San Antonio and the Alamo defenses. As a young bride Elizabeth Bertrand Austin, wife of Col. William T. Austin, remembered the anxiety experienced by all those whose husbands and sons had rejoined the Texan army. "From day to day," she stated in 1879, "all those left at home greeted anyone who might bear them tidings, however slight, of the loved ones who were risking their lives for their infant country." These "temporary widows" shouldered not only their domestic duties, but family and business affairs that had previously fallen solely within their husband's control. For months at a time women necessarily became proficient in protecting their homes, maintaining their farms, and independently making financial decisions.[22]

At the same time many Anglo women also took an active and direct role in the Texas Revolution. The October 17, 1835, issue of the *Telegraph and Texas Register* reported that "even the ladies, bless their souls, volunteer their services. . . and if necessary, would enter the ranks, and fight manfully for the rights of the country." Dilue Rose Harris recalled the disturbances of 1835–1836 and the preparations for the fighting. Her mother made "two striped hickory shirts and bags" for her uncle to carry provisions to war while eleven-year-old Dilue spent the day "melting lead in a pot, and dipping it with a spoon, and molding bullets." Mary Austin Holley met with the ladies of Lexington, Kentucky, where she was living at the time, to sew needed garments and gather supplies for the Texas volunteers. Joanna Troutman of Georgia designed and made a battalion flag inscribed with "Liberty or Death" for Georgia recruits to aid the Texan cause. In response to the emergency some women also lent their livestock to the cause, such as innkeepers Angelina Peyton and Pamelia Mann, who placed their oxen in service to the army. A few women of means, such as Jane McManus Storms, a landowner and promoter of Texas annexation, offered to borrow or lend money for the Texas cause using her land as security to support the war effort. She wrote in 1835: "I will with joy contribute my mite to purchase arms for her brave defenders." And others like Susanna Dickinson, who survived the battle of the Alamo, served as a cook and nurse to those Texans within the compound, only to be enlisted as a messenger by Santa Anna to warn Houston against further resistance.[23]

In March 1836 as the battle of the Alamo was taking place, delegates to a constitutional convention met at Washington-on-the-Brazos under difficult circumstances and with little time for deliberation. After formally declaring independence on March 2, these male lawmakers patterned a constitution for the Republic of Texas on the U. S. Constitution. The completed document, adopted on March 17, replaced a federal form of government under Mexico with one independent state, established three branches of government, secured basic rights, settled land issues, and protected slavery.[24]

The government of the newly created Republic of Texas (1836–1845) also merged Spanish law, which gave women extensive legal rights, with English common law, which utilized marital status as the basis for women's legal status. Due to the instability of the fragile Republic, a cohesive legal system developed only gradually. Not until January 20, 1840, did the Texas legislature formally enact the common law of England as the rule in civil actions. This act upheld basic civil liberties for a *feme sole,* or single woman, such as making contracts, owning and controlling property, and if widowed, retaining custody of her children. In practice, however, fathers or male members of families generally handled the affairs of single women. A *feme covert,* or married woman, however, retained only limited rights. She could own separate property that she brought to the marriage and share equally in any wealth amassed from the union, but her legal existence was "covered" or controlled by her husband. Since few women remained single on the frontier, this change in law under the Republic left Texas women worse off legally than women under the Spanish system, but better off than their Anglo sisters coming from the U.S.[25]

One woman who understood her legal rights was Lydia Ann McHenry, a single woman who traveled to Texas from Kentucky in 1833. Having no family of her own, she lived with her sister and brother-in-law "for most of her adult life." In 1835, having "learned enough of the Laws of Mexico" concerning separate property, she defended her sister's property from debt collectors after her brother-in-law's death. "This land was purchased with horses Pa gave myself & sister," she said, "& I do not choose to be turned out of house and home…." Furthermore as a *feme sole,* she stated in unequivocal terms her desire not to be treated "as an idiot who requires a guardian, but what little I have, let it be my own & not par[t]nership property." In short, she demanded: "I ought to be independent."[26]

While certain features of the Texas Constitution of 1836 were revolutionary, the new government did not alter the social or gender roles in place at the time. The delegates' understanding of natural rights and citizenship conformed to the standards of the day, which vested political power in the hands of free white men, while maintaining a patriarchal system in social relations. In their rush to complete their deliberations and flee before the Mexican troops arrived, however, they utilized language in the constitution that was often ambiguous and contradictory. Written at a time when women had few rights—and no direct political rights—the Texas Constitution of 1836 most likely inadvertently permitted women to vote. Article VI, section 11, allowed: "Every citizen of the republic who has attained the age of twenty-one years, and shall have resided six months within the district or county where the election is held, shall be entitled to vote for members of the general congress." In the General Provisions, section 10, the lawmakers then defined citizens without reference to sex as "All persons (Africans, the descendants of Africans, and Indians excepted,) who were residing in Texas on the day of the declaration in independence...." Did this mean that qualified white women in Texas could vote after 1836? No evidence exists that women claimed or exercised that right. Either through oversight, emergency constraints, or imprecise language, lawmakers never intended it, society never expected it, and women never asked for it. Rather, women's roles after independence would remain within the domestic realm, and any involvement in politics would revolve around the informal use of influence rather than direct participation.[27]

After the fall of the Alamo on March 6, 1836, and the defeat and capture of the Texans at Goliad on March 27, a mass exodus of settlers ahead of the Mexican army, known as the Runaway Scrape, ensued. With few defenders to halt Santa Anna's troops and rumors of his plans to rape "the *Fair daughters* of chaste *white women*," thousands of refugees, largely women, children, and slaves, fled eastward toward Louisiana. Many women, who were alone after their husbands had enlisted in the army, braved floods, cold weather, and impassable roads to load their oxcarts and wagons in a desperate rush to save themselves and their families. Widow Angelina Peyton recalled the "great commotion—destruction of property—much left on the river banks—no wagons scarcely—few horses—many on foot mud up to their knees—women and children." Mary Crownover Rabb escaped "with ouer [*sic*] little ones to suffer with cold and hungry." Spring rains caused swollen streams and rivers where ferries became jammed with waiting refugees. Dilue Rose Harris recalled that there were 5,000 people at Lynch's Ferry when her family arrived. Later, Thomas Jefferson Rusk, a signer of the Texas Declaration of Independence whose own family fled the enemy forces, observed: "The women with their little children around them, without means of defense or power to resist, faced danger and death with unflinching courage."[28]

As the Mexican army advanced eastward, Anglo residents abandoned and destroyed cities and towns. Earlier on March 14, General Sam Houston had ordered "his 374 ragged and poorly trained regulars and militia" to leave Gonzales and burn the town. Mexican General Ramirez y Sesma and his troops arrived in time to watch the flames, noting that entire families—men, women, and children— had retreated and "set on fire and abandoned what they could not take with them." Looting and pillaging followed. Days later, when news reached the residents of San Felipe de Austin of the impending arrival of Mexican troops, they evacuated and burned the town to the ground. Many women and families lost almost everything. Afterwards, José Enrique de la Peña, a lieutenant colonel in the

Mexican army, visited the ruins and estimated the destruction at fifty houses, numerous wagons and plows, and "great heaps of broken china." He concluded that "the fruits of many years of hard work had been destroyed in one moment of madness." Angelina Peyton remembered returning to her home in San Felipe after the war: "I went in a day or two—hard rain made road batter brush making streets [sic]—place bare of every thing but ruins all my things burnt up...."[29]

Generally, Anglo women's experiences during the revolution varied according to class and the region in which they lived. Lower to middle class women such as Dilue Rose had limited resources with which to protect their farms and families. They often lacked the means of retiring safely to less exposed areas once the fighting started. A few even decided to remain behind and not flee. Afterwards, those who escaped returned to devastated homes and lands. Upper class women such as Emily Austin Perry had access to wagons, livestock, and slaves to help with securing their farms, packing their belongings, and fleeing eastward. Although panicked women and families from central Texas to as far east as San Augustine, twenty-five miles from the Texas-Louisiana border, felt the effects of the invading army, generally those in the closest proximity to the front suffered the most. As Santa Anna's army brought the conflict nearer to their homes, especially in the Colorado-Brazos rivers region, homes were abandoned, towns were burned, and crops were destroyed. Lydia Ann McHenry, who evacuated to the Trinity River, returned to the Austin colony only to find her bed destroyed and "all [her] clothes stolen by plunderers."[30]

The abrupt end of the military phase of the revolution following the battle of San Jacinto did not necessarily ensure the safety and comfort of Texas families. Rumors circulated about a re-invasion by Mexican troops and a possible alliance between Mexico and the Comanche Indians. In a series of letters to her brother, Lydia Ann

McHenry expressed her concerns about "another invasion" or a "blockade of our ports" from Mexico. She openly sided with those members of the interim government who favored severe punishment for Santa Anna and two of his generals who were held captive. Like many others she feared that if the president were returned to Mexico then his army, which was "driven out almost to the Rio Grande," would soon return. She further wrote on August 25, 1836, that if the Texan army disbanded, "the first thing we should know of the enemy he would be at the Colorado."[31]

In March 1842 their fears were realized when Santa Anna once again sent an army across the Rio Grande River into Texas. The Mexican forces occupied San Antonio, Goliad, and Refugio, but retired after a few days. Despite the short-lived occupation, panic ensued in central Texas, resulting in a second Runaway Scrape. Anglo families, such as the "tribe of Maverick"—Mary, Sam, and their three children—made hasty preparations and fled San Antonio on horseback to points beyond the area threatened by the invaders. Mary recalled that "families ran away from their homes. . . and great losses followed." The Maverick house was "robbed of everything" and "all kinds of damage had been done to anything belonging to Americans." Fearful of returning to San Antonio, only 150 miles inland from the Mexican border, they relocated to land across the Colorado River near La Grange. But Mexican troops returned again later that year, capturing Sam Maverick, who was in San Antonio on business, and imprisoning him in Mexico.[32]

Another danger to the new Republic was from persistent attacks and kidnappings by the Indians on the Texas frontier. The new Constitution of 1836 had been silent on Indian land rights and the new government was both weak and inconsistent in enforcing its policies or treaties. President Sam Houston's conciliatory Indian policy alternated with President Mirabeau Lamar's policy of expulsion and extermination. Amid the chaos, disorder, and uncertainty, Apache,

Mary A. Maverick surrounded by her children, circa 1852. From *Memoirs of Mary A. Maverick*, 1921.

Comanche, Kiowa, and Wichita raiders therefore availed themselves of the opportunity to raid and plunder Anglo settlements.[33]

Women and children were often favorite targets of the Indians. The native peoples frequently seized young Anglo girls and women as additions to their tribe. If the women survived the initial attack and captivity, they became tribal slaves, wives, and concubines, while their children were often held for ransom, sold to traders, or adopted into their captors' tribes. Even the creation of Ranger units by the Congress of the Republic could not eliminate the raids that led to the captivity of the most famous Anglo female captive— eleven-year-old Cynthia Ann Parker, originally born in Illinois. Her family moved to East Texas, living near Fort Parker in current day Limestone County. On May 19, 1836, a party of Comanche warriors attacked the fort and seized Cynthia Ann, her brother John, and three others. Although the other captives were later ransomed, Cynthia Ann subsequently assimilated into Indian society, married a Comanche chief, and gave birth to three children. On December 19, 1860, she was "recaptured" near the Pease River by the Texas Rangers and returned to the Anglo world. But she never reconciled to living in white society, yearning to return to her tribal ways and mourning the loss of her Comanche family.[34]

The inability of the new Republic to protect the frontier allowed other Anglo women to become kidnap victims. Rachel Parker Plummer was a pregnant seventeen-year-old girl abducted by the Comanche who had attacked Fort Parker on May 19, 1836. Beaten and deprived of her children, she was held captive for thirteen months until ransomed by Mexican traders. Thirteen-year-old Matilda Lockhart and four other children also became Comanche captives in 1838. Two years later on March 19, 1840, sixty-five Comanche warriors entered San Antonio to arrange for Lockhart's ransom. The Indians demanded gunpowder, blankets, and paint in exchange for the young Anglo woman who had been severely tortured, burned, and mutilated. Mary Ann Maverick described the scene in her *Memoirs* as a "Day of Horrors," which erupted into a battle known as the Council House Fight. Lockhart escaped to safety, but her "utterly degraded" condition left the young girl "very sad and brokenhearted" the rest of her life.[35]

After the revolution some Anglo women who had been negatively affected by the war expected compensation for their losses and sacrifice. Widow McElroy, who had lost cattle and a wagon during the war, appealed to Interim President David G. Burnet for the loss of her property. Pamelia Mann, who had lent Houston a yoke of oxen while he traveled toward Nacogdoches, displayed her spunk and independent spirit by demanding their return—at the point of a pistol—after Houston turned toward Harrisburg. And Rebecca Burnett Lee requested repayment from the Texas legislature for the loss of her father's "cattle, hogs, chickens, turkeys, potatoes and corn" that the Texan army confiscated. The new government considered her petition, but concluded that it was "too old and payment was denied by the committee on claims."[36]

One benefit for Anglo-American women after the revolution was a renewed emphasis on female education. Prior to 1835 the failure of the Mexican government to provide an adequate school system for Texas children was a source of continuing concern to the colonists. As a result, Anglo families living in Mexican Texas turned to private schools with instruction in English or, in the case of girls, they founded boarding schools for "young ladies and misses." The first of these schools was located at Coles Settlement in 1834, founded by Frances Trask Thompson.[37]

One grievance listed in the Texas Declaration of Independence was that Mexico "failed to establish any public system of education." With independence and increased population growth, the prevailing sentiment was that the future of the Republic depended on an "educated and enlightened" citizenry, including women. In

his message to the Texas Congress in December 1838, President
Mirabeau B. Lamar, therefore urged those assembled to set aside
"lands to the purpose of general education" and thereby "lay the
foundation of a great moral and intellectual edifice." But Lamar's
vision failed to materialize immediately and private schools, such as
female academies, separate departments, or home schooling were
the only choices for many Anglo families. Curriculums for girls were
"both solid and ornamental," ranging from literature to needlework,
and aimed at training girls for "refined and cultured womanhood."
But by 1850 the Republic still lagged behind in educational opportunities and no "female Seminary of high order" existed for young
women to acquire "a complete and thorough course of education."
Nevertheless, Anglo women benefited from and contributed to
the overall expansion of education in Texas. They gained access to
learning, established schools, served as teachers, and helped increase
literacy rates of white Texans, which by 1860 was about 96 percent
for men and 94 percent for women.[38]

Overall, the era of the Texas Revolution brought both "joys and
sorrows" to Anglo women. With a spirit of adventure, curiosity, and
hope, many willingly followed their husbands westward in search
of a new and better life. Most were young women of childbearing
age who endured multiple pregnancies and bore numerous children without complaint. Some successfully managed businesses and
farms, while others played an important role in building schools,
churches, and communities. For many women, however, their suffering was great: harsh living conditions, Indian raids, loneliness,
and loss of children. As the Texas Revolution intruded into their
lives, they patriotically sent their husbands and sons to war, supported the Texan cause, and maintained the home front. When
danger threatened, many women were directly responsible for saving the lives and possessions of their families. Following the war
some Anglo women, especially those near the war front, lost almost

everything, including family members and most of their belongings. The experience of Mrs. George Sutherland was especially tragic: She lost a son at the Alamo and returned to a home where she "found nothing in the world worth speaking of."[39]

Although the Texas Revolution increased women's visibility and activism, it did not significantly improve their lives or overall status. Historian Paul D. Lack credited the brevity of the conflict for limiting "the degree to which revolution had wrenched apart the political order and social fabric." Success on the battlefield, then, did not necessarily result in shifts in power or property. Women continued to tend to the day-to-day welfare of their families and reside within the confines of the domestic realm. While scarce frontier conditions and educational opportunities improved somewhat, there was no apparent change in gender relations between the sexes. At the same time, with independence and a new Republic, English common law supplanted the Spanish legal system, which represented a loss of women's rights. For Anglo women this meant that the doctrine of coverture continued unimpeded, women remained excluded from political life, and society in general continued to view them as mental and physical unequals. Although separate property rights were preserved, Anglo women under the Republic and statehood could not vote, hold office, nor if married, control their property, write a will, or expect custody of their children. By the mid-nineteenth century only a few eastern women, such as Elizabeth Cady Stanton, Lucretia Mott, and Susan B. Anthony, had begun to question their subordination. For Texas women on the western frontier, with fewer places to gather, learn from each other, or act in concert, such challenges would have to wait another twenty years until the Constitutional Convention of 1868–1869. Even then the woman's question died for lack of support. In the meantime, the first generation of Anglo-Texas women, who helped free themselves and their families from an autocratic regime, realized little positive political, legal, or social benefit from the Texas Revolution.[40]

Selected Bibliography

Austin's Old Three Hundred: The First Anglo Colony in Texas. Austin: Eakin Press, 1999.

Bryan, J. P., ed. *Mary Austin Holley, The Texas Diary, 1835–1838.* Austin: University of Texas Press, 1965.

Crawford, Ann Fears, and Crystal Sasse Ragsdale. *Women in Texas: Their Lives, Their Experiences, Their Accomplishments.* Austin: State House Press, 1992.

Cummins, Light Townsend. *Emily Austin of Texas, 1795–1851.* Fort Worth: TCU Press, 2009.

Downs, Fane. "'Tryels and Trubbles': Women in Early Nineteenth-Century Texas." *Southwestern Historical Quarterly* 90 (July 1986): 35–56.

Green, Rena Maverick, ed. *Memoirs of Mary A. Maverick: A Journal of Early Texas.* San Antonio: Maverick Publishing Co., 2005.

Harris, Mrs. Dilue. "The Reminiscences of Mrs. Dilue Harris." *Quarterly of the Texas State Historical Association* 4 (July 1900–April 1901).

Holley, Mary Austin. *Texas: Observations, Historical, Geographical and Descriptive.* Baltimore: Armstrong & Plaskitt, 1833.

Hogan, William Ransom. "Pamelia Mann: Texas Frontierswoman." *Southwest Review* 20 (Summer 1935): 360–370.

Marks, Paula Mitchell. *Turn Your Eyes Toward Texas: Pioneers Sam and Mary Maverick.* College Station: Texas A&M University Press, 1989.

Rabb, Mary Crownover. *Travels and Adventures in Texas in the 1820s.* Waco, TX: W. M. Morrison, 1962.

Smithwick, Noah. *The Evolution of a State, or Recollections of Old Texas Days.* Austin: University of Texas Press, 1983.

Endnotes

1 Title quotation from Rena Maverick Green and Maverick Fairchild Fisher, eds., Preface, *Memoirs of Mary A. Maverick: A Journal of Early Texas* (San Antonio, TX: Maverick Publishing Co., 2005); Dilue Rose Harris died on April 2, 1914, at the age of 89 in Eagle Lake, Texas. See Dilue Rose Harris, "The Reminiscences of Mrs. Dilue Harris," *The Quarterly of the Texas State Historical Association* 4 (July 1900–Apr. 1901): 85–127, (Jan. 1901): 155–189 and Jeanette Hastedt Flachmeier, *A Rose of Texas* (n.p.: n.p., 1986).

2 Ann Fears Crawford and Crystal Sasse Ragsdale, *Women in Texas: Their Lives, Their Experiences, Their Accomplishments* (Austin: State House

Press, 1992), 25–35; Harris, "The Reminiscences of Mrs. Dilue Harris," 120.

3   Although the term "Manifest Destiny" was not used until the 1840s, westward expansion into frontier regions was already a reality. Linda Hudson in *Mistress of Manifest Destiny* argues that Jane Mcmanus Storm Cazneau, a land speculator and advocate of Texas annexation, coined the term in 1845. See Elizabeth Tumlinson, Rebekah Cumings, and Amy Comstock White in *Austin's Old Three Hundred: The First Anglo Colony in Texas* (Austin: Eakin Press, 1999). Lester G. Bugbee, "The Old Three Hundred," *Texas Historical Association Quarterly* 1, no. 2 (October 1897): 108–117.

4   Anne Firor Scott, *The Southern Lady: From Pedestal to Politics, 1830–1930* (Chicago: University of Chicago Press, 1970), 4–21, 213; Elizabeth Fox-Genovese, "Family and Female Identity in the Antebellum South: Sarah Gayle and Her Family," in *In Joy and in Sorrow: Women, Family, and Marriage in the Victorian South*, ed. Carol Bleser (New York: Oxford University Press, 1991), 19; Ann Patton Malone, *Women on the Texas Frontier: A Cross-cultural Perspective* (El Paso: Texas Western Press, 1983), 14–19.

5   Since most Mexican and Republic censuses enumerated only heads of household, the total number of women in Texas before 1850 is difficult to determine. A partial census in 1847 showed 43 males to 34 females of the Anglo population; however, some report the figures to be 2 to 1. Viktor Bracht, *Texas in 1848* (San Antonio: Naylor Pub., 1931), 63–64, 106; Angela Boswell, *Her Act and Deed: Women's Lives in a Rural Southern County, 1837–1873* (College Station: Texas A&M University Press, 2001), 13–14, 16; Barbara Welter, "The Cult of True Womanhood: 1820–1860," *American Quarterly* 18 (Summer 1966): 151–174.

6   William Ransom Hogan, "Pamelia Mann: Texas Frontierswoman," *Southwest Review* 20 (Summer 1935): 360–370; Sandra L. Myres, *Westering Women and the Frontier Experience, 1800–1915* (Albuquerque: University of New Mexico Press, 1982), 269; C. Richard King, *The Lady Cannoneer: A Biography of Angelina Belle Peyton Eberly, Heroine of the Texas Archives War* (Burnet, TX: Eakin Press, 1981), 120–125.

7   Although Jane claimed she was the first English-speaking woman to bear a child in Texas, censuses between 1807 and 1826 reveal a number of children born to Anglo-American women prior to 1821. Martha Anne Turner, *The Life and Times of Jane Long* (Waco: Texian Press, 1969), 1–84; Ron Tyler, et al., eds., "Jane Herbert Wilkinson Long," *The New Handbook of Texas* (Austin: Texas State Historical Association, 1996), 4: 274–276.

8 Turner, *The Life and Times of Jane Long*, 95–96; "Jane Herbert Wilkinson Long," *The New Handbook of Texas*, 4: 274; J. C. Clopper, "J. C. Clopper's Journal and Book of Memoranda for 1828," *The Quarterly of the Texas State Historical Association* 13 (July 1909): 59–60; Noah Smithwick, *The Evolution of a State or Recollections of Old Texas Days*, comp. Nanna Smithwich Donaldson, Barker Texas History Center Series #5, 4th printing (Austin: University of Texas Press, 1994), 48.

9 Jane Long ran two boarding houses, one in Brazoria (1832–1834) and another in Richmond (1837–1838). Pamelia Mann was also a proprietor of an inn at Washington-on the-Brazos during the meeting of the constitutional convention in 1836 and later in Houston. Angelina Eberly ran boarding houses in San Felipe and Austin. Ellen Garwood, "Early Texas Inns: A Study in Social Relationships," *Southwestern Historical Quarterly* 60, no. 2 (October 1956): 219–244; "Reminiscences of Jno. Duff Brown," *Southwestern Historical Quarterly* 12, no. 4 (April 1909): 302; William R. Hogan, *The Texas Republic* (Norman: University of Oklahoma Press, 1946), 106–107; Turner, *The Life and Times of Jane Long*, 105–108; King, *The Lady Cannoneer*, 68, 91–92.

10 A *labor* was about 177 acres and a *sitio*, or league of land, was about 4,428 acres. *Austin's Old Three Hundred*, 24, 87, 89; Lester G. Bugbee, "The Old Three Hundred: A List of Settlers in Austin's First Colony," *Texas Historical Association Quarterly* 1, no. 2 (October 1897): 108–117.

11 See Mary Crownover Rabb, *Travels and Adventures in Texas in the 1820s* (Waco, Texas: W. M. Morrison, 1962) and Crawford and Ragsdale, "'Trials and Troubles' in Texas," in *Women in Texas*, 13–21.

12 See Rabb, *Travels and Adventures in Texas in the 1820s*. Light T. Cummins, *Emily Austin of Texas, 1795–1851* (Fort Worth: TCU Press, 2009), 157–178; Scott, *The Southern Lady*, 29; Malone, *Women on the Texas Frontier*, 20.

13 Rabb, *Travels and Adventures in Texas in the 1820s*, 5–8; Green and Fisher, *Memoirs of Mary A. Maverick*, 76–84; *Houston Daily Post*, April 15, 1900.

14 For a discussion of whether the Texas Revolution was a genuine revolution, see Paul D. Lack, *The Texas Revolutionary Experience: A Political and Social History, 1835–1836* (College Station: Texas A&M University Press, 1992), xix–xxv. Also see Crane Brinton, *The Anatomy of Revolution* (N.J.: Prentice-Hall, 1952); Harris, "The Reminiscences of Mrs. Dilue Harris," 4: 89; Gregg Cantrell, *Stephen F. Austin: Empresario of Texas* (New Haven: Yale University Press, 1999), 151.

15 Turner, *The Life and Times of Jane Long*, 114–116; Nan Hillary Harrison, "Jane Long, The Mother of Texas" manuscript (Austin: University of Texas Archives), 50; Garwood, "Early Texas Inns," 227; Robert E. Davis,

ed., *The Diary of William Barret Travis* (Waco: Texian Press, 1966), 74, 130.

16 Holley made a total of five trips to Texas between 1831 and 1843. J. P. Bryan, ed., *Mary Austin Holley, The Texas Diary, 1835–1838* (Austin: University of Texas Press, 1965), 7–10.

17 *Texas* was the first known history of Texas written in English. Mary Austin Holley, *Texas: Observations, Historical, Geographical and Descriptive* (Baltimore: Armstrong & Plaskitt, 1833), 141–167; Bryan, *Mary Austin Holley,* 7.

18 Cummins, *Emily Austin of Texas,* 4–5.

19 Stephen F. Austin was released from prison on December 25, 1834, although he was required to remain in Mexico City. He ultimately returned to Texas in July 1835. Cummins, *Emily Austin of Texas,* 104, 112–117; Stephen F. Austin to James F. Perry, November 6, 1834, Moses and Stephen F. Austin Papers, 1676, 1765–1889, Center for American History, University of Texas, Austin, Texas, 3:17–22.

20 Ragsdale, *Women in Texas,* 40; Cummins, *Emily Austin of Texas,* 3, 55–57, 65–70; Bryan, *Mary Austin Holley,* 7; Cantrell, *Stephen F. Austin,* 165.

21 Anglo women only occasionally took up arms, mainly to defend their property. A few Mexican women, referred to as camp followers or *soldaderas,* did accompany the Mexican armies. Harris, "The Reminiscences of Mrs. Dilue Harris," 4: 157.

22 *Galveston Daily News,* April 20, 1879.

23 See Linda Hudson, *Mistress of Manifest Destiny: A Biography of Jane McManus Storm Cazneau, 1807–1878* (Austin: Texas State Historical Association, 2001). *Telegraph and Texas Register* (San Felipe), October 17, 1835; Harris, "The Reminiscences of Mrs. Dilue Harris," 4: 160; Hogan, "Pamelia Mann: Texas Frontierswoman," 360–361; Fane Downs, " 'Tryels and Trubbles': Women in Early Nineteenth-Century Texas," *Southwestern Historical Quarterly* (July 1986): 47–48; Paul D. Lack, *The Texas Revolutionary Experience,* 211, 227; Mr. William L. Cazneau, *Eagle Pass or Life on the Border,* ed. Robert Cotner (Austin: Pemberton Press, 1966), 2.

24 The Texas Declaration of Independence, March 2, 1836, *Laws of the Republic of Texas* (Houston 1838), 1: 3–7; The Constitution of the Republic of Texas, *Laws of the Republic of Texas,* 1: 9–26.

25 H. P. N. Gammel, comp., *The Laws of Texas, 1822–1897* (Austin: Gammel Book Co., 1898), 1: 1074, 2: 1777; Jean Stuntz, *Hers, His, and Theirs: Community Property Law in Spain and Early Texas* (Lubbock: Texas Tech University Press, 2005), 101–103, 133–145; Tyler, et al., eds., *The New Handbook of Texas,* 6: 1046–1047.

26 George R. Nielsen, ed., "Lydia Ann McHenry and Revolutionary Texas," *Southwestern Historical Quarterly,* no. 3 (January 1971): 393, 402.

27 The Constitution of the Republic of Texas, Art. VI, sec, 11 and General Provisions, sec. 10.

28 Harris, "The Reminiscences of Mrs. Dilue Harris," 4:162–167; Lack, *The Texas Revolutionary Experience,* 224.

29 Houston's army burned Gonzales and San Felipe de Austin while Fannin set fire to Refugio and La Bahia. David M. Vigness, *The Revolutionary Decades* (Austin: Steck-Vaughn Co., 1965), 192; King, *The Lady Cannoneer,* 80–85; José Enrique de la Peña, *With Santa Anna in Texas: A Personal Narrative of the Revolution* (College Station: Texas A&M University Press, 1975), 65–66, 106.

30 Green and Fisher, *Memoirs,* 46; Nielsen, "Lydia Ann McHenry and Revolutionary Texas," 404; Lack, *Texas Revolutionary Experience,* 224–237.

31 Nielsen, "Lydia Ann McHenry and Revolutionary Texas," 393–408.

32 Sam Maverick was released on March 30, 1843, after more than six months' imprisonment. Green and Fisher, *Memoirs,* 50–59.

33 Linda Hudson, "Women in Texas, a Pioneering Spirit," in *The Texas Heritage,* ed. Ben Procter and Archie P. McDonald, 4th ed. (Wheeling, Illinois: Harlan Davidson, Inc., 2003), 255.

34 See Margaret Hacker, *Cynthia Ann Parker: The Life and the Legend,* Southwestern Studies, no. 92 (El Paso: Texas Western Press, 1990) and Paul H. Carlson and Tom Crum, *Myth, Memory, and Massacre: The Pease River Capture of Cynthia Ann Parker* (Lubbock.: Texas Tech University Press, 2010). Tyler, et al., *The New Handbook of Texas,* 57–58.

35 Maverick, *Memoirs,* 23–27, 32–33; S. C. Gwynne, *Empire of the Summer Moon* (New York: Scribner, 2010), 36–52, 84; Tyler, et al., *The New Handbook of Texas,* 243.

36 Frank X. Tolbert, *The Day of San Jacinto* (New York: McGraw-Hill, 1959), 93–94; *Houston Daily Post,* April 15, 1900.

37 Tyler, et al., *The New Handbook of Texas,* 1041–1042.

38 Efforts to establish a public school system in Texas did not succeed until after the Civil War. William Ransom Hogan, *The Texas Republic: A Social and Economic History* (Norman: University of Oklahoma Press, 1946), 136–159; Journal of the House of Representatives of the Republic of Texas, 3d Congress, 168–170; Melinda Rankin, *Texas in 1850* (Waco: Texian Press, 1966), 116–117; Wreathy Aiken, *Education of Women in Texas* (San Antonio, TX: Naylor Publishing Co., 1957), 27, 30, 33; Tyler, et al, *The New Handbook of Texas,* 6: 1041–1043. See also the Texas Declaration of Independence, March 2, 1836.

39 George Sutherland to sister, June 5, 1836, in John H. Jenkins, ed., *The Papers of the Texas Revolution, 1835–1836* (Austin: Presidial Press, 1973), 7: 24–26; Lack, *The Texas Revolutionary Experience*, 236.

40 Tirus H. Mundine of Burleson County unsuccessfully proposed an equal suffrage motion at the 1868–1869 convention. The committee on state affairs approved Mundine's proposal, but the delegates later rejected it by a vote of 52 to 13. Lack, *The Texas Revolutionary Experience*, 259; *Journal of the Reconstruction Convention, which met at Austin, Texas* (Austin: Tracy, Siemering & Co., 1870), 1: 245–246, 580, 2: 414; Elizabeth Taylor, "The Woman Suffrage Movement in Texas," in *Citizens at Last: The Woman Suffrage Movement in Texas*, ed. Ruthe Winegarten and Judith N. McArthur (Austin: Ellen C. Temple, Pub., 1987), 13–14, 56–61; Tyler, et al., *The New Handbook of Texas*, 6: 1039.

CHAPTER 4

Traveling the Wrong Way Down Freedom's Trail

Black Women and the Texas Revolution

Angela Boswell

Spanish Texas was not a great place to be a woman of African descent. Black women in Texas suffered from social and legal constraints upon their freedom. Spanish society left a legacy of racism that relegated blacks to the lowest caste and allowed many to be held as property until the Mexican Revolution concluded in 1821. However, Spanish laws and then the Mexican Revolution held some opportunities for black women to gain their freedom and even rise in social and economic stature. However, the Texas Revolution, supposedly fought for freedom from tyranny, erased centuries of the promise of freedom for black women in Texas and fastened the legal and social distinction of slavery upon them much more firmly.

Africans and their descendants accompanied the Spanish from the earliest years of conquest of America both as free and as slave, and they continued to occupy an important place in the development of the Spanish colonies. In areas where labor demands were high, such as in Peru, the Spanish brought in hundreds of African slaves. However, the predominant labor force in most of Spanish

America continued to be Native Americans who were not enslaved but treated as peasants who owed tribute to the conquering Europeans. Spanish authorities might have preferred three distinct classes—free Spaniards, Indian peasants, and African slaves—but what actually evolved was much more complicated. The paucity of Spanish women enticed many Spanish men to have liaisons with women of the other classes, and whether or not the liaisons were legally sanctioned through marriage, the children of such unions often were recognized. Additionally, Native Americans and Africans living and working in proximity often formed liaisons of their own, so that there emerged a complex caste system with full-blooded Spanish at the top, full-blooded Africans at the bottom, and gradations in between including full-blooded Indians, and mixed-blooded people of every group.[1]

These sexual liaisons and intermarriage created children of African descent who were often free. Yet, this was not the only avenue to freedom for blacks in Spanish America. Masters manumitted their slaves for a variety of reasons, including exemplary service, religious convictions, and the raising of the purchase price by the slaves. These manumissions were recognized and even encouraged by the spirit of the Spanish law. The thirteenth-century "statement of legal and moral principles," *Las Siete Partidas,* loosely guided the laws of Spanish America. Interpretations in America erred significantly on the side of oppression and creating and keeping a ready labor force, but *Las Siete Partidas* declared that slavery was a necessary evil and should be considered only temporary. The true condition of human beings was freedom. Thus Spanish legislation for America increasingly favored individual achievements of freedom. By the end of the eighteenth century, fueled by a booming economy (making self-purchase more feasible), with an abundance of labor (easing the pressures to legally create an unfree laboring population), and guided by the ideals of personal freedom, a colony like Mexico had created a large free black population. By 1810, of approximately 624,000 *afromestizos*, only 10,000 were slaves.[2]

The social classifications of people in Spanish America were thus confused by racial intermixing and significant percentages of free blacks and mulattoes before the Spanish ever began their first settlements in Texas. In Texas, as in other communities on the periphery, the social caste system became even more fluid. The terms related to race—Spanish, black, Indian, mestizo, and mulatto—were still used to indicate social position in society. However, one's economic and social position in society affected one's racial designation as much as biology. Especially in frontier areas such as Texas, based upon marriage, social respect, and economic factors, people passed from darker-skinned designations to lighter-skinned ones. Race became a matter of social status that could change, rather than a biological determinant of social status. A census compiler in 1777 labeled the Texas colonists as "una quadrilla de trapientos de todos colores"—"a ragged crew of all colors."[3]

The very small population of blacks who lived in Texas in the late eighteenth and early nineteenth centuries, therefore, either enjoyed their freedom or could look forward to the possibility of freedom. In 1790, only 37 of the 2,417 people were slaves. But a 1792 census of Texas recorded nearly 450 *negroes* or *mullatoes*. Of those, 167 mulattoes were female and 19 negroes were female. The possibility of a female slave gaining freedom was probably not less than that of a male slave. In a study of other parts of early Spanish America, specifically Peru, manumission operated primarily for the benefit of women and small children. María Rosa de la Rosa y Valle and María Gertrudis de la Peña are but two examples of Texas women who were freed, in these two cases by other women.[4]

Even women who remained enslaved in Spanish Texas could call upon the protection of the legal system. According to historian Dedra S. McDonald, Maria Simona de Jesus Moraza of San Antonio left her home and petitioned the governor for redress in 1791. Maria claimed that the daughter and daughter-in-law of her masters had whipped her without cause, beat her with small sticks, kicked her, and continued to threaten her. The alcalde found in her favor and granted Maria and her husband Santiago Phelipe el Pierro the right to seek another work situation. It took two years to locate a potential buyer, during which time Maria's owners were able to appeal and have the decision overturned (after all, it had been the daughter, not the owner, who had abused the slave). Despite the negative outcome, these slaves were aware that they could appeal to outside authorities to mitigate the worst abuses of slavery.[5]

Free mulattas and black women could also avail themselves of the court system. Antonia Lusgardia Hernández filed a petition in San Antonio to legally retrieve her son from the household of her former employers. Although it noted that the head of the household, don Miguel Nuñez, was the father of the child, the court returned the child to his mother "on the condition that she provide a proper home for him."[6]

Clearly equality of condition did not exist between those on the bottom of the social ladder and those at the top. Socially, those who could claim pure birth were the most respected and powerful in the community, and legally punishments were more severe for persons of mixed race. Nonetheless, black women in Spanish Texas could look forward to the possibility of emancipation, the possibility of even moving up the social ladder, and the protection of laws even if they were enslaved.[7]

The fluidity of society in Spanish Texas attracted both free black immigrants and runaway slaves from the United States. It is impossible to document clearly how many slaves ran to freedom in Texas, but there are numerous reports. For instance in 1807, the explorer Zebulon Pike met some blacks in Texas at the Trinity River whom he believed to be runaway slaves. And although statistically most runaway slaves in the United States were male, the nearness of unsettled Texas attracted families as well as single men. Free blacks immigrating to Spanish Texas included women. In the early 1800s Mary Ortero moved to Texas from Louisiana with her husband, Felipe Elua, and their children after Elua purchased his own freedom and that of his family. They educated their children in both Spanish and French, and accumulated property including land and houses. According to the traveler (and abolitionist) Benjamin Lundy, Elua also had a sister who married a Frenchman and lived in San Antonio.[8]

By 1810, when an independence movement began in Mexico that would finally culminate in separation from Spain eleven years later, slavery in Mexico had already become insignificant economically, socially, and legally. According to historian Dennis Valdés, "alternative sources of laborers, the increasing difficulty of obtaining slaves from Africa and the introduction of wage labor, which made the supply of workers more elastic," as well as the ability of slaves to escape to towns and cities where thousands of free blacks and mulattoes lived, made the system moribund. Revolutionary sentiment had voiced strong opposition to slavery and announced its abolition on several occasions during the fight for independence. With the recognition of Mexico's independence, the system of slavery was legally near its end.[9]

Yet the year of Mexican independence, 1821, also marked the beginning of the first Anglo settlements in Texas and the re-introduction of slavery. Under an impresario contract, Stephen F. Austin led a group of American settlers—and their slaves—into Texas. Upon the news of Mexican independence, Austin traveled to Mexico City to confirm his contract and to lobby the officials to allow slavery in the settlements. Most of the bills debated clearly indicated that the legislators assumed slavery, if any were allowed, would be temporary; however, due to political developments unrelated to the

new Americans, none were passed in those first few years of settlement. According to historian Randolph Campbell, "developments
in 1822–24 were typical of Texas' experience with slavery during the
entire period of Mexican rule. Mexican leaders showed disapproval
of slavery but did nothing effective to abolish it." When the Mexican
government forbade the slave trade, they still continued to allow
Anglo Americans who were migrating to bring their slaves with
them. When slavery was abolished in Mexico, Texas was granted an
exemption. And when Texans wanted more slaves, Mexico allowed
them to bring in people from outside the United States bound to
labor by "voluntary" contracts, often for ninety-nine years. When
Mexico set a limit of ten years for labor contracts, the Anglo Texans
ignored it.[10]

At the local level, Austin pronounced laws necessary to protect
the institution of slavery within his colony, including prescribing
punishments of whites for enticing a slave to run away or buying
goods from a slave. Other laws prescribed whipping slaves for steal-
ing or being away from home without a pass. In other words, Austin's
colony reenacted the basic slave codes of the southern United States.
These laws and the profitability of the fertile cotton fields of Texas
encouraged slaveholders to emigrate and bring slaves. By 1825 nearly
25 percent of the population of Austin's colony were slaves. Even after
Texans followed the letter of the law, but not the spirit, by bringing
in slaves under ninety-nine-year contracts, the actual practice was
to continue buying, selling, and using slaves as collateral, just as in
the southern United States. For instance, William Hunter wrote to
James Perry in January 1832 describing the purchase of two slaves:
"I have bought two Negroes one of Col. Best a mulatto man about
21 years old, stout and of excellent character raised by Best. Price
600.$ the other about 13, a very smart boy I got of R. M. Williamson
price 400.$" James F. Perry recorded numerous bills of sale for slave
property including the purchase of a 15-year-old girl for $450 in 1834

and a mulatto girl for $440 in 1835 who was warranted as a "slave for life." An estate inventory in 1834 listed three men, three women, five girls, and five boys as property.[11]

Although the Austin colony and other Anglo settlements often operated as if slavery were legal in much the same way as in the southern states, the frontier conditions and the attitude of Mexican authorities toward slavery affected the character of the institution in Mexican Texas. According to Campbell, the uncertainty over slavery's status "retarded the development of slavery in Texas" leading to a lower percentage of slaves in Texas than would be expected. Prospective immigrants often expressed concerns about bringing slaves to Texas when the future of such investment was so insecure. James A. E. Phelps wrote to Stephen F. Austin that "nothing appears at present to prevent a portion of our wealthy planters from emigrating immediately to the province of Texas but the uncertainty now prevailing with regard to the subject of slavery."[12]

The Anglo American slaveholders already in Texas also expressed frequent and sometimes significant concerns about Mexico's intentions toward slave property. Noah Smithwick remembered that "Jesse Thompson, living on the San Bernard though possessed of a number of slaves, devoted his attention mostly to stock. There was much dissatisfaction over the uncertainty of legislation on the slavery question and Thompson, among others, was at one time on the point of returning to the United States with his slaves, and it was probably due to this uncertainty that he had neglected farming interests." Dilue Rose Harris described a family who left Texas in 1834 with their slaves and who would not return because they "did not intend to bring any more slaves to Mexico."[13]

Although some settlers such as Jared Groce from South Carolina brought over a hundred slaves to plant cotton and corn, most plantations in Texas were considerably smaller and most slaveholders claimed only a few slaves. Dilue Rose Harris remembered two families who traveled on the same ship with her family to Texas, one of whom had two slaves (man and woman), another who had one slave woman.[14]

The smaller concentration of slaves in a frontier area such as this would have affected black women. Plantations and farms could be quite distant from each other leading to relative isolation, making it more difficult for women to find husbands, to create families, and to establish communities of support. Despite the distances, there was one aspect in favor of women finding mates: the gender ratio among slaves in Texas seemed to be even. Because slave women could not make a choice to move or not move, they found themselves brought to Texas in an even ratio.[15]

The even gender ratio among slaves was in stark contrast to the gender ratio among free whites in Texas. The opportunities of the frontier enticed a much greater proportion of white men than white women. Single men, married men who found moving west easier than divorce, and even happily married men who often left wives behind temporarily until setting up a home for their families were more likely to find Texas an exciting choice. In the 1825 census of one county, only 36 percent of the white population was female. As William B. Aldridge wrote to his brother: "We are truly a herd of bachelors here five out of six belonging to our establishment are bachelors past 30 years one youth only and not a married man among us."[16]

The shortage of white women and the availability of black women created favorable circumstances for interracial liaisons and concubinage. Abolitionist Benjamin Lundy noted in his travels that "I reached the farm and house of two brothers, named Alley, where I stopped for the day. . . . The two Alleys are industrious immigrants from the State of Missouri. They have never married. They purchased, however, a handsome black girl, who has several fine-looking partly coloured children—specimens of the custom of some countries." The implication that the two men shared sexual access to one slave woman indicates a relationship other than love and affection. Testimony in court years later contended that William Alley never acknowledged the children as his and treated the woman and her children as property for decades. In no southern state in the U.S. was the rape of a slave considered a crime against the woman, and in Texas, the pattern continued as masters had sexual rights to their slaves. The frequency of these voluntary or involuntary sexual liaisons can never be accurately measured, but they clearly occurred. Early settlers John McFarland, William Primm, and Monroe Edwards were all recorded as living with black women.[17]

Historian Ann Patton Malone believed that "black female concubinage, often an arrangement based on affection as well as convenience, was common on the early Texas frontier." And there were examples of interracial marriages in Texas before the revolution that were based upon affection. After moving to Nacogdoches from Georgia, David Town freed his slave "who was in fact his wife" and her children. John F. Webber became "entangled in a low amour" and subsequently purchased from her master the woman of his affection and their child and acknowledged them as his family. According to his friend Noah Smithwick, who immigrated to Texas from Tennessee in 1827, Webber built a home in an unsettled area where they "were constrained to keep to themselves" because they could mingle neither with whites nor slaves. However, due to the kindness and generosity of Puss Webber, they "merited and enjoyed the good will, and, to a certain extent the respect, of the early settlers."[18]

The Webbers fared better in Texas than they probably would have in the settled portions of the southern United States. The shortage of people in frontier areas generally led to greater willingness to bend social rules. And under Mexican rule there were no laws forbidding interracial marriages. Although the Anglo settlements in Texas operated as if Anglo laws regarding slavery were in effect, the actual Mexican laws did occasionally shape African American realities. Slaves may not have gained their freedom by the acts of Mexican laws, but slaves in Texas did have certain rights under Mexican law, such as the right of petition, a right that slave owners did not relish their slaves exercising. Anglo Texans must have exercised some restraint against their slaves in order to avoid any greater Mexican interference and a widespread dissemination of Mexico's antislavery sentiments amongst their slaves. Noah Smithwick described how when the slaves "became aware of the legal status of slavery in Mexican territory, ... it was probably owing to their ignorance of the language and country that more of them did not leave." It was probably because of the fear of Mexico's influence over their slaves that Mary Austin Holley, the cousin of *empresario* Stephen F. Austin who published a travel narrative and promotional tract of Texas, came to believe that slaves were "invested with more liberty and less liable to abuse" in Texas. The reminiscences of a white frontiersman described how one slave who ran away to freedom returned voluntarily "preferring slavery under [his master] Thompson's lenient rule to freedom in Mexico."[19]

Black women might have found a bit more social fluidity and a bit more timidity on the part of owners to greatly abuse slaves in Texas. But the work in frontier Texas, as in any frontier region, was very hard on women as well as men. African American women brought valuable "female" skills with them that, due to the shortage of white women in Texas, were in short supply: cooking, sewing, weaving, canning, washing, and cleaning. And women could be put to tasks that white women would never be allowed to do, such as clearing fields, hoeing, planting, picking, and even plowing if necessary. Some gendered division of work was still honored: men were carpenters, builders, and blacksmiths. But nearly all other tasks, including caring for cattle, were also performed by black women on the Texas frontier. When James Perry offered to let his place for free to someone who would take care of his cattle, Isaac Mansfield applied and explained his anticipated division of labor: "I have a negro boy and Negro woman to help me—the boy to make a crop and the woman to cook and take care of your cows."[20]

Even traditional tasks were made more difficult by scarcity. The family of even a "well-bred man" such as Thomas B. Bell lived "in a little pole-cabin in the midst of a small clearing upon which was a crop of corn." Noah Smithwick described how Bell, his wife, and his children showed "in their every manner the effects of gentle training," but "the whole family were dressed in buckskin, and when supper was announced, we sat on stools around a clapboard table, upon which were arranged wooden platters. Beside each platter lay a fork made of a joint of cane. The knives were of various patterns, ranging from butcher knives to pocketknives. And for cups, we had little wild cymlings, scraped and scoured until they looked as white and clean as earthenware..."[21]

Many a traveler and settler noted the hardships that such rugged scarcity caused for white women. But few recognized the tremendous toll on black women. For instance, the white woman Jane Hallowell Hill remembered some of the difficulties and sacrifices her mother made: "Our first year spent in the new home, before we had had time to raise corn, we often were deprived of having bread; at one time for three weeks." When the family finally obtained a very small quantity of corn-meal, Hill's mother "at once had the cook to make some bread, and with tears in her eyes she divided it among the children, both white and black, not tasting it herself." Hill's mother, of course, made a tremendous sacrifice, but the unnamed slave woman, "the cook" was the one who turned the cornmeal into bread and was never even given choices on how the bread should be distributed.[22]

As difficult as life could be for black women in Texas, under Mexican rule there remained hope of continued fluidity in laws and social mores concerning race. White southerners generally believed in slavery as a permanent condition for a race of people they believed to be inferior. But Mexicans had a tradition of seeing slavery as transitory and encouraging manumission even before the Mexican Revolution in which the ideology of freedom for all played a major role. For Mexican legislators who understood the Anglo Americans' need for laborers in frontier Texas, slavery was a temporary expedient. Abolitionists such as Benjamin Lundy entertained hopes of settling a colony of free and freed blacks in Texas and was encouraged by Mexican officials in those hopes. In 1834 Mexican authorities sent Colonel Juan Almonte on a mission to report on the state of Texas, and his reports urged the Mexican government to change its course on slavery: "From the population which is shown, we must subtract about a thousand souls of imported slaves. This abuse is quite notable now, and if we do not stop the flow quickly, it will be difficult to correct it later without causing a revolution of far-reaching consequences." Even some slaveholding Anglos seemed, at least to the abolitionist Benjamin Lundy, to be willing to end the practice: William "Stafford thinks slavery a bad thing, but he says it is no harm for him to hold slaves and treat them well until all will agree to abolish the institution...."[23]

Anglo Texans feared Mexico's intentions regarding slavery, and as conflicts between the Texans and the new government under General Antonio López de Santa Anna heated, many slaveholders did not know whether war or peace provided the best protection of their property. As John Linn remembered: "During the months of August and September 1835, there was much uneasiness felt in regard to the threatened loss of the slave property; and the owners of slaves were disposed to favor the peace policy, although there was for them little more to hope from that horn of the dilemma than from war, if indeed as much."[24]

The question of peace or war was soon answered, and the Texas Revolution caused immediate and long-term changes for black women in Texas. After taking no prisoners at the Battle of the Alamo, Santa Anna's army marched through Texas causing panic. With many men away fighting in the revolution, women, children, and slaves were left to gather what they could and run to the east ahead of Santa Anna's advance. Many families tried to save what they could before leaving, asking slaves to help bury the white families' prized possessions. Former slave Jeff Parsons remembered that "we buried the wash tubs, pots, kettles, cooking utensils, and old master's secretary."[25]

After hiding what they could, families packed for travel. Some had to leave so quickly that they literally left their dinner on the table. Jane Hallowell Hill's "mother was so distressed when she heard of the fall of the Alamo that she only took one trunk, some bedding and provisions, leaving a good supply of everything at home." Others, however, like Dilue Rose Harris' family, had prepared weeks earlier in case they had to leave. On February 20 her "mother had packed what bedding, clothes, and provisions she thought we should need, ready to leave at a moment's warning."[26]

Black women in the path of Santa Anna's army were also caught in the scramble, but as most were slaves, they had the fewest choices in what treasures would be saved by hiding or taking. Ann Raney Thomas Coleman's "negroes were told they could only take one change of cloaths with them, myself the same, the enemy were only seven miles from us, and it would not do to take aney thing that would retard our progress…. The negroes were all in tears at the prospect of looseing their all, which was felt by them as much as we felt our loss…." While Coleman limited the slaves to one change of clothing, she tried to slip some of her more cherished and less necessary belongings into the cart: "I packed up my china set, and put them in the wagon, and thought my husband would think they were my little boys cloaths and mine, a foolish thought." Although she had to forgo the china, she was able to take "some letters and papers belonging to my father, and mother all the rememberance I had of them and some other small mementoes which did not take up much room."[27]

Preparing for an extended trip was hard work and the slave women spent all day at the Coleman farm "cooking some provision … about five hundred head of chickens, a good maney which were killed and cooked for our travel."[28] And then the travel itself was dangerous and grueling. Reminiscences by white women such as Dilue Rose Harris, Ann Raney Thomas Coleman, Elizabeth Craw, and Jane Hallowell Hill leave no doubt as to the dangers and the fear of the "runaway scrape." However, black women shared these same dangers and fears, and most likely did not get the chances to ride in the carts or on horseback for at least part of the journey described by the white women.

Jane Hallowell Hill's party had at least one adult female slave and slave children. "We had a terrible time travelling through mud and water, as it rained most of the time. Some of the rivers were more than three miles wide, which we had to cross in small ferry-boats all through the bottoms, or valleys. We kept on until within twenty-five miles of the Sabine river, stopping at San Augustine." Dilue Rose Harris' group of travelers faced equally treacherous conditions and included twenty or thirty slaves from a neighboring plantation so that "there were more negroes than whites among us and many of them were wild Africans." After a particularly difficult river crossing, the men had to drive the horses and oxen to the prairies but "the women, sick children, and negroes were left in the bottom" without anything to eat. The white women and children stayed in a wagon with a canvas cover, but the black women and their children stayed in carts "and the water [came] up in the carts."[29]

Harris remembered "no insubordination among" the slaves in her party; "they were loyal to their owners." However, other slaves saw the war and the dislocations as their opportunity to gain their freedom. Anglo Texans repeated far and wide that "the proclamation of Santa Anna announced his purpose to emancipate the slaves." As a result, reports of runaway slaves abounded. William Fairfax Gray recorded in his journal on April 22, 1836, that he startled "three runaway Negroes, who fled and plunged through a bayou at our approach." As Noah Smithwick and his friends tried to avoid capture by the Mexican army, they "discovered two men in the road ahead, who, on being hailed, dropped their bundles and ran. We examined the contents of the packs and were satisfied the owners were only runaway negroes who would keep out of the Mexicans' clutches, and so give no information."[30]

Most slaves who chose to run away in the midst of the war were probably male. Six of the Coleman slaves "ran away to the Mexican armey been promised their freedom, on doeing so." The only two who remained were women. However, at least some black women also made their escape. In Juan Almonte's journal on April 2, 1836, he recorded that "Two blacks (slaves), a man and a woman, presented themselves. They had discovered where there was corn and salt." Historian Paul Lack also found evidence of entire families seeking freedom with the Mexican army.[31]

Some African American women found their freedom as a result of the Texas Revolution, but most did not. They returned to homes that had been destroyed by Mexican troops and American plunderers. Armies had burned fence rails, "swept the country of poultry, sheep, hogs, and horses," and torn up houses and floors looking for food and valuables. And surviving in the aftermath of the war would be most difficult for female slaves who had to make food out of nonexistent supplies. "On our return we found nothing but the wild animals on the prairies, and hard times met us at home. We had to live there months on game and without the taste of bread. We built scaffolds for drying the meat. We ate it dried, fried,

DOCTOR PARROTT

AGAIN offers his professional services to the citizens of Texas. He can always be found at his residence, except when absent on professional business.   Tranquility, August 16, 1836.—4t.

FOR SALE.

A NEGRO WOMAN aged 22 years. A first rate cook, washer and ironer, and general house servant, also a good hand in the field and to manage cows. She has been 10 or 12 years in this country, and is sober and honest. She would not be parted with, but the owner is going to the United States for his health, apply at Mrs. Fearis's in Columbia.
August 15th, 1836.   3 times—August 16

FIVE DOLLARS REWARD

WILL be given to any one who will deliver to the subscriber a DIRK, lost by him, on the evening of the 10th instant, at Bell's Landing. The Dirk has a horn handle, decorated with silver. Has a cork screw and tweesers attached, and has a crown at the hilt.
Aug. 16   S. L. HAVENS.

"For Sale" advertisement from *Telegraph and Texas Register*, August 16, 1836. Courtesy The Dolph Briscoe Center for American History, University of Texas at Austin.

boiled, broiled, stewed, baked and roasted, but we had to live on it so long we became tired of it, anyway we could cook it." But the black women did not merely have to worry about preparing nourishment, they also had to immediately work in the fields to prepare the next food and/or cotton crop. Jane Hallowell Hill remembered that "the negroes had to work in the day-time preparing for the support of the family, for we had been robbed of nearly everything we had left when we fled from the Mexicans."[32]

But the physical difficulties in the aftermath of the Texas Revolution would not compare to the long-term consequences for slave women of the Texans' victory. Proponents of the revolution almost immediately began speculating on the hopes of changes in the laws regarding slavery. Before the war was won, William Fairfax Gray recorded that "it is the opinion of all the *Texanos* with whom I have conversed on the subject that the new government of Texas must sanction the holding of slaves as property." Some with whom he conversed were convinced also that "new government will authorize the introduction of slaves into Texas."[33]

By March their hopes were confirmed. The Constitution of the new Republic of Texas recognized slavery for life and guaranteed the rights of immigrants to bring with them slaves. Thus, property rights in slaves that had been unstable before the Revolution became ensconced in the constitution and further upheld by judicial findings and legislative enactments. Legally affixing that status of property, the Republic made it increasingly difficult for slaves to become free. A slave could only be emancipated by the owner and only if the owner made provisions to remove the slave from Texas.[34]

Not only was slavery more firmly fastened upon the slaves and future slaves of Texas, but the new government took steps to restrict the presence of free blacks as well: "No free person of African descent, either in whole or in part, shall be permitted to reside permanently in the republic, without the consent of congress." In the years following the adoption of the constitution, several free black women petitioned to remain in Texas. Patsey's petition was supported by five citizens of Rutersville in 1840; over fifty people signed washerwoman Zelia (Zylpha) Husk's two petitions in 1841; while Betsy's much later petition had twenty-nine whites vouch for her in 1856. Citizens of Galveston found forty-two-year old nurse Mary Madison to be "a very valuable citizen" and petitioned for her right to stay. According to historian Ruthe Winegarten, the "Texas Congress usually ignored or rejected petitions for the right to remain in Texas."[35]

Many free black women not granted the right to stay in Texas remained anyway, but in a quasi-legal limbo that could have been threatened at any time. Margaret Gess's freedom was threatened in 1848 when the heirs of the recently deceased Adam Smith claimed that she and her child were still slaves. Smith and Gess had lived together and had a child before the revolution. Smith had signed a document recognizing that Gess was "free and at liberty to go and do the best she can to make an honest livelihood in the world." Although in this case Gess won her freedom, she did so only after a costly appeal to the Supreme Court and another trial at the district level, demonstrating the precarious nature of even maintaining property rights in her own person.[36]

In 1840 Congress moved to expel all free blacks by threatening that all who did not leave by 1842 (later extended to 1845) would be sold into slavery. In 1858 the Texas legislature took yet another step at eliminating all free blacks from Texas by enacting a law allowing a free black person to voluntarily enslave him or herself. After being jailed and forced to leave or choose a new master, Rachel Grumbles chose Aaron Burleson as her new master because, as her son remembered years later, Burleson "thought mo' ob his slaves dan most anyone I ever saw."[37]

The clear purposes of the new government formed as a result of the Texas Revolution was to erase all possible racial fluidity and to erase any ideas that blacks were to have any other status than slaves. After Texas gained statehood in 1845, the Texas Supreme Court proved to be one of the most progressive of the southern courts in recognizing the humanity of the slave property and certain rights of free blacks, who were never great in numbers. Nevertheless, in 1859 Justice Oran M. Roberts succinctly articulated the goal of legislation and the assumption of white Texans that "Negroes are, in this country, *prima facie* slaves."[38]

Not only did legal proscriptions make it nearly impossible for black women to live freely or aspire to freedom in Texas, but social attitudes hardened. As more immigrants came to Texas bringing slaves, the Mexican influences regarding racial and class fluidity abated. The interracial couple John and Puss Webber had been tolerated and even respected by their neighbors in Texas before the revolution. After the revolution and the Indian threat lessened a "new lot of people came" to Webber's prairie "and they at once set to work to drive Webber out." When Webber hired a private teacher for his children, the neighbors "raised a hue and cry about the effect it would have on the slave negroes, and even went so far as to threaten to mob the tutor." The free black woman Puss Webber and her husband found that they could not withstand "the bitter prejudice" which became ever more threatening. The Webbers sold out and moved to Mexico "where there was no distinction of color."[39]

As opportunities for free black women to even exist in the state declined, the legal protections of slavery encouraged more slave-holders to bring more and more women as slaves for life to Texas. Although it is impossible to establish exact numbers, it is clear that immediately following the revolution the slave population increased significantly and the rate of increase continued to grow. Campbell estimated that between 1836 and 1847, the percentage of the population of slaves in Texas rose from 13 to 27 percent. And that number of slaves continued to grow, increasing 50 percent between 1847 and 1850.[40]

Many of these slaves came with the families who claimed them as property. However, even when migrating with masters, black women were often torn from family members in the previous location who were owned by different masters. In frontier states such as Missouri and Arkansas from where many of the settlers in Austin's colony came, the rate of abroad marriage (marrying someone from a different farm or plantation) was very high. Slave owners also bought black men and women at slave markets and brought them to Texas, thus separating them from families and any familiar community whatsoever.[41]

In addition to losing permanent touch with loved ones, the actual journey to Texas was often grueling. Interviewed by a WPA worker in the 1930s, Silvia King recounted a much later journey overland to Fayette County: "He buys some more slaves and dey chains us together and marches us up near La Grange, in Texas. Marse Jones done gone ahead and de overseer marches us. Dat was a awful time, 'cause us am all chained up and whatever one does us all has to do. If one drinks out of de stream we all drinks, and when one gits tired or sick, de rest has to drag and carry him."[42]

The large increase in the population of Texas as a whole, as well as the slave population in particular, following the revolution probably did have one small advantage for black women. The larger population became more concentrated, making life less isolated. It became easier for black women to form networks within the slave community to help them cope with the system of slavery. And it increased the likelihood of forming families.

Overall, however, the Texas Revolution was not a positive development for black women. Americans had brought with them to Texas attitudes about slavery and the permanent inferiority and proper place of black women as laborers. However, as long as Texas remained under Mexican rule, there were opportunities and hope that the system of slavery would be abolished or mitigated. Efforts to colonize free blacks, the right of slaves to petition, and even the small level of acceptance of interracial liaisons could serve to retard the progress of an institution which gave all black women only one role: slave. Indeed, life improved after the Texas Revolution in some ways as scarce frontier conditions improved and the possibility of forming families increased. However, these improvements could not counterbalance the legal and social strictures that immediately emerged as a result of the revolution. Black women, under the new "free" Texas government, were the least able to look forward to freedom.

Selected Bibliography

Bowser, Frederick P. "Colonial Spanish America." In *Neither Slave Nor Free: The Freedman of African Descent in the Slave Societies of the New World*, edited by David W. Cohen and Jack P. Greene. Baltimore: Johns Hopkins University Press, 1972.

Campbell, Randolph B. *An Empire for Slavery: The Peculiar Institution in Texas, 1821–1865*. Baton Rouge: Louisiana State University Press, 1989.

Campbell, Randolph B., ed. *The Laws of Slavery in Texas: Historical Documents and Essays*. Austin: University of Texas Press, 2010.

Glasrud, Bruce A., and Merline Pitre, eds. *Black Women in Texas History*. College Station: Texas A&M University Press, 2008.

Lundy, Benjamin. *The Life, Travels, and Opinions of Benjamin Lundy, including his Journeys to Texas and Mexico...* Philadelphia: William D. Parrish, 1847.

Malone, Ann Patton. *Women on the Texas Frontier: A Cross-Cultural Perspective. Southwestern Studies* Monograph No. 70. El Paso: Texas Western Press, 1983.

McDonald, Dedra S. "To Be Black and Female in the Spanish Southwest: Toward a History of African Women on New Spain's Far Northern Frontier." In *African American Women Confront the West, 1600-2000*, edited by Quintard Taylor and Shirley Ann Wilson Moore. Norman: University of Oklahoma Press, 2003.

Lack, Paul D. "Slavery and the Texas Revolution." *Southwestern Historical Quarterly* 89 (July 1985): 181–201.

Shoen, Harold. "The Free Negro in the Republic of Texas." *Southwestern His-torical Quarterly* Part I: 39 (April 1936): 292–308; Part II: 40, no. 1 (July 1936): 26–34 ; Part III: 40, no. 2 (Oct. 1936): 85–113; Part IV: 40, no. 3 (Jan. 1937): 169–199; Part V: 40, no. 4 (Apr. 1937): 267–289; Part VI: 141, no. 1 (July 1937): 83–108.

Smithwick, Noah. *The Evolution of a State; Or Recollections of Old Texas Days.* Austin, 1900.

Winegarten, Ruthe. *Black Texas Women: 150 Years of Trial and Triumph.* Austin: University of Texas Press, 1995.

Wortham, Sue Clark. "The Role of the Negro on the Texas Frontier, 1821–1836." M.A. Southwest Texas State University, 1970.

Endnotes

1 Frederick P. Bowser, "Colonial Spanish America," in *Neither Slave Nor Free: The Freedman of African Descent in the Slave Societies of the New World,* ed. David W. Cohen and Jack P. Greene (Baltimore: Johns Hopkins University Press, 1972), 20, 26–27, 37; Donald E. Chipman, *Spanish Texas, 1519–1821* (Austin: University of Texas Press, 1992), 188.

2 Bowser, "Colonial Spanish America," 21–22, 37; Dedra S. McDonald, "To Be Black and Female in the Spanish Southwest: Toward a History of Afri-can Women on New Spain's Far Northern Frontier," in *African American Women Confront the West, 1600–2000,* ed. Quintard Taylor and Shirley Ann Wilson Moore (Norman: University of Oklahoma Press, 2003), 43; Dennis N. Valdés, "The Decline of Slavery in Mexico," *The Americas* 44 (Oct. 1987): 167–194.

3 Quoted in Harold Shoen, "The Free Negro in the Republic of Texas, I," *Southwestern Historical Quarterly* 39 (April 1936): 292; Chipman, *Spanish Texas,* 188–89.

4 Shoen, "The Free Negro, I," 292; Ruthe Winegarten, *Black Texas Women: 150 Years of Trial and Triumph* (Austin: University of Texas Press, 1995), 2 (hereafter cited as *Black Texas Women: 150 Years*); Randolph B. Campbell, *An Empire for Slavery: The Peculiar Institution in Texas, 1821–1865* (Baton Rouge: Louisiana State University Press, 1989), 11; Bowser, "Colonial Spanish America," 31; Valdés, "Decline of Slavery in Mexico," 173–74; Teresa Palomo Acosta and Ruthe Winegarten, *Las Tejanas: 300 Years of History* (Austin: University of Texas Press, 2003), 35.

5 McDonald, "To Be Black and Female," 47.

6 McDonald, "To Be Black and Female," 47–48.

7 Chipman, *Spanish Texas,* 188–89.

8 Sean Kelley, "'Mexico in His Head': Slavery and the Texas-Mexico Border, 1810–1860," *Journal of Social History* 37 (Spring 2004): 709–723; Stephen Harding Hart, Archer Butler Hulbert, Mark L. Gardner, eds., *The Southwestern Journals of Zebulon Pike, 1806–1807* (University of New Mexico Press, 2007), 237; Benjamin Lundy, *The Life, Travels, and Opinions of Benjamin Lundy, including his Journeys to Texas and Mexico...* (Philadelphia: William D. Parrish, 1847), 54–55.

9 Valdés, "Decline of Slavery in Mexico," 193–94; Campbell, *Empire for Slavery*, 14–15.

10 Campbell, *Empire for Slavery*, 16–34; Paul D. Lack, "Slavery and the Texas Revolution," *Southwestern Historical Quarterly* 89 (July 1985): 183–84.

11 Campbell, *Empire for Slavery*, 18–19; Wm. Hunter, San Felipe de Austin, January 8, 1832, to Mr. James F. Perry, and Bill of Sale, May 12, 1834, Estate Inventory, April 4, 1834, Volume III, Typescript Correspondence; Bill of Sale, May 18, 1835, Volume IV, Typescript Correspondence, Box 2R137, James F. and Stephen S. Perry Papers, 1785–1942, Dolph Briscoe Center for American History, The University of Texas at Austin.

12 James A. E. Phelps to Stephen F. Austin, January 16, 1825, *The Austin Papers* I, 1020, quoted in Sue Clark Wortham, "The Role of the Negro on the Texas Frontier, 1821–1836" (M.A. Southwest Texas State University 1970), 21; Campbell, *Empire for Slavery*, 33.

13 Noah Smithwick, *The Evolution of a State; Or Recollections of Old Texas Days* (Austin, 1900), Southwestern Classics Online, <http://www.old-cardboard.com/lsj/olbooks/smithwic/otd.htm>, Chapter 3; Dilue Harris, "The Reminiscences of Mrs. Dilue Harris, I," *The Quarterly of the Texas State Historical Association* 4 (Oct. 1900): 111, 124.

14 Smithwick, *The Evolution of a State,* Chapter 1; Harris, "Reminiscences, I," 87.

15 Angela Boswell, "Black Women during Slavery to 1865," in *Black Women in Texas History,* ed. Bruce A. Glasrud and Merline Pitre (College Station: Texas A&M University Press, 2008), 16–17.

16 Census Report, December 31, 1825, summarized and reprinted in Bill Stein, "Consider the Lily: The Ungilded History of Colorado County, Texas, Part 1," *Nesbitt Memorial Library Journal* 6 (January 1996): 32–33; William B. Aldridge to brother, Alexander Aldridge, April 28, 1837, Marion, Texas, William B. Aldridge Papers, Dolph Briscoe Center for American History, The University of Texas at Austin; Angela Boswell, *Her Act and Deed: Women's Lives in a Rural Southern County, 1837–73* (College Station: Texas A&M University Press, 2001), 13–14.

17 Lundy, *Life, Travels, and Opinions,* 41; the Alley children who had been held as slaves sued for their father's inheritance after the Civil War. Not

surprisingly in Reconstruction Texas, they lost the case. Estate of William Alley, June 12, 1871, through October 10, 1873, Probate Final Record, Book H, pp. 701–15, 720–21, 730–48, Colorado County Clerk's Office, Columbus, Texas; Wortham, "The Role of the Negro," 69–70.

18   Ann Patton Malone, *Women on the Texas Frontier: A Cross-Cultural Perspective, Southwestern Studies* Monograph No. 70 (El Paso: Texas Western Press, 1983), 31, 37; Lundy, *Life, Travels, and Opinions,* quoted in Shoen, "The Free Negro, I," 296; Smithwick, *The Evolution of a State,* Chapter 17.

19   Smithwick, *The Evolution of a State,* Chapter 3; Mary Austin Holley quoted in Lack, "Slavery and the Texas Revolution," 188–89. See Mary Austin Holley, *Texas: Observations, Historical, Geographical, and Descriptive, in a Series of Letters Written during a Visit to Austin's Colony, with a View to a Permanent Settlement in That Country in the Autumn of 1831* (Baltimore, 1833).

20   Isaac Mansfield to James Perry, March 19, 1833, James F. and Stephen S. Perry Papers, Volume III. See also Boswell, "Black Women during Slavery," 17–18.

21   Smithwick, *The Evolution of a State,* Chapter 3.

22   Recollections of Mrs. Jane Hallowell Hill, Austin, Texas, 1898, Thomson Family Papers 1832–1898, Woodson Center Research Center, Rice University, Houston, Texas.

23   Lundy, *Life, Travels, and Opinions,* 38, 63–66; *Almonte's Texas: Juan N. Almonte's 1834 Inspection, Secret Report and Role in the 1836 Campaign,* ed. Jack Jackson, trans. John Wheat (Austin: Texas State Historical Association, 2003), 253.

24   John J. Linn, *Reminiscences of Fifty Years in Texas* (Austin: State House Press, 1986), 114.

25   Uncle Jeff Parsons of Jackson Municipality. *Sons of DeWitt Colony Texas, Texas A&M University,* <http://www.tamu.edu/faculty/ccbn/dewitt/mustergon2.htm#parsons>.

26   Recollections of Mrs. Jane Hallowell Hill; Dilue Harris, "The Reminiscences of Mrs. Dilue Harris, II," *The Quarterly of the Texas State Historical Association* 4 (Jan. 1901): 161.

27   Ann Raney Thomas Coleman Reminiscences, Pt. 1, p. 151. Box 2Q483, Ann Raney Thomas Coleman Papers, 1849–1892, 1958, Dolph Briscoe Center for American History, The University of Texas at Austin.

28   Coleman Reminiscences, 151.

29   Harris, "Reminiscences, II," 163–66.

30   Harris, "Reminiscences, II," 164; Linn, *Reminiscences of Fifty Years,* 114; *The Diary of William Fairfax Gray, from Virginia to Texas, 1835–1837,*

Friday, April 22, 1836, William P. Clements Center for Southwest Studies, Southern Methodist University, Dallas, Texas, 1997 < http://smu. edu/swcenter/FairfaxGray/wg_cont.htm>; Smithwick, *The Evolution of a State*, Chapter 9; Lack, "Slavery and the Texas Revolution," 194–196.

31 Coleman Reminiscences, 151; *Almonte's Texas,* 398; Lack, "Slavery and the Texas Revolution," 194.

32 Recollections of Mrs. Jane Hallowell Hill; Uncle Jeff Parsons; Harris, "Reminiscences, II," 177.

33 *Diary of William Fairfax Gray,* January 5 and January 10, 1836.

34 Randolph B. Campbell, "Human Chattels: the Laws of Slavery in Texas," in *The Laws of Slavery in Texas: Historical Documents and Essays,* ed. Randolph B. Campbell (Austin: University of Texas Press, 2010), 4–5; The Constitution of the Republic of Texas (1836), General Provisions, Sections 9 and 10, Tarlton Law Library, Jamail Center for Legal Research, University of Texas at Austin, http://tarlton.law.utexas.edu/constitutions/ text/ccGP.html; Campbell, *Empire for Slavery* 45–47.

35 The Constitution of the Republic of Texas (1836), General Provisions, Sections 9 and 10, Tarlton Law Library, Jamail Center for Legal Research, University of Texas at Austin, http://tarlton.law.utexas.edu/constitutions/ text/ccGP.html; Winegarten, *Black Texas Women: 150 Years,* 8; Ruthe Winegarten, *Black Texas Women: A Sourcebook, Documents, Biographies, Timeline* (Austin: University of Texas Press, 1996), 5, 11–13 (hereafter cited as *Black Texas Women: A Sourcebook);* Campbell, *Empire for Slavery* 45–47.

36 Harold Shoen, "The Free Negro in the Republic of Texas, VI," *Southwestern Historical Quarterly* 41 (July 1937): 106; Mark Davidson, "One Woman's Fight for Freedom: *Gess v. Lubbock,* 1851," in Campbell, *Laws on Slavery,* 87–93.

37 Winegarten, *Black Texas Women: 150 Years,* 8; Winegarten, *Black Texas Women: A Sourcebook,* 5, 11–13.

38 Quoted in Campbell, *Empire for Slavery,* 112. See also Campbell, "Human Chattels," 4–5; A. E. Keir Nash, "The Texas Supreme Court and Trial Rights of Blacks, 1845–1860," *The Journal of American History* 58 (Dec. 1971): 624.

39 Smithwick, *The Evolution of a State,* Chapter 17.

40 Campbell, *Empire for Slavery,* 55; Lack, "Slavery and the Texas Revolution," 201–2.

41 Boswell, "Black Women during Slavery," 15–18.

42 "Silvia King" in Jo Ella Powell Exley, ed., *Texas Tears, Texas Sunshine: Voices of Frontier Women* (College Station: Texas A&M University Press, 1985), 125.

CHAPTER 5

Two Silver Pesos and a Blanket

The Texas Revolution and the
Non-Combatant Women Who Survived
the Battle of the Alamo

Dora Elizondo Guerra

On February 23, 1836, seven women and seven children took refuge in the Alamo for thirteen days as Mexican General Antonio López de Santa Anna, with a major part of his army, entered San Antonio's main plaza to do battle against insurgent Texans, both Anglos and Tejanos. The women with their children entered the Alamo not as combatants, but as civilians who either chose to remain or waited too long to escape safely. They included six Hispanics and one Anglo woman: Concepción Charlé Gortari Losoya, Andrea Castañon de Villanueva, known also as Madam Candelaria, Juana Navarro Pérez Alsbury, Gertrudis Navarro, Ana Salazar Castro Esparza, Juana Francisca Losoya Melton, and Susanna Wilkerson Dickinson. Each had a husband, son, brother, or brother-in-law fighting on the Texas side of the revolution.[1]

In 1995 historian Timothy M. Matovina published *The Alamo Remembered: Tejano Accounts and Perspectives,* in which he stated that he was "probing the collective legacy of Tejano Alamo accounts" and was bringing them together "in a single volume for the first time." Among those accounts gathered by Matovina were three interviews from survivors and eyewitnesses of the battle that specifically mentioned these women. Namely, they were the accounts of Juana Navarro Pérez Alsbury, Enrique Esparza, and Madam Candelaria.[2]

For many years the narrative of the Alamo story identified Susanna Wilkerson Dickinson and her infant daughter Angelina, referred to as the "babe of the Alamo," as the sole survivors of the battle. This Anglo-centric narrative, told and retold, became an allegory of courage, defiance, and survival. Through conversations with a curious public and interviews with journalists, which were given national newspaper coverage as the first news out of the Alamo by an eyewitness and survivor, Dickinson's account became well known. Susanna and Angelina's experience was repeated, written about, and applauded, while totally excluding the fact that there had actually been at least six other women and six more children present about whom nothing was reported.

In the late 1880s Mary Maverick, a prominent San Antonio citizen and wife of Colonel Sam Maverick, and newspaper editor John S. Ford interviewed Juana Navarro Pérez Alsbury, establishing the fact that she and her unmarried sister Gertrudis Navarro had also been survivors, and that Juana had also held an infant in her arms. The Maverick-Ford interview stated that "Mrs. Alsbury and her sister were in a building not far from where the residence of Colonel Maverick was afterwards erected."[3]

More inclusive interviews confirming the presence of women and children other than Susanna and Angelina Dickinson were left by Enrique Esparza. Enrique was the son of Gregorio Esparza, one of the Alamo defenders killed in the battle. Only eight years old, Enrique, along with his mother and three siblings, joined Gregorio and took refuge inside the Alamo. As an eyewitness to the events that took place during the thirteen-day siege and fall of the Alamo, he witnessed the death of his father and other participants. Esparza's recollections appeared in the *San Antonio Light* on November 10, 1901, when he was seventy-three years old. He recalled: "Within the Alamo courtyard were also other refugees who were saved— Mrs. Alsbury and one child and sister, Gertrudes [*sic*] Navarro; Mrs. Concepción Losoya, her daughter and two sons: Victoriana de Salina and three little girls; Mrs. Susanna Dickinson and baby (hitherto believed to have been the only ones who escaped alive); and an old woman Petra."[4] In several interviews Andrea Castañon de Villanueva, or Madam Candelaria, changed what she said about the Alamo events and her role in them. Her interviews appeared periodically in San Antonio and national newspapers in which she described her heroic exploits during the siege. Although filled with inconsistencies, they did establish that she had been a survivor and an eyewitness. In a March 6, 1892, interview published in the *San Antonio Express*, Villanueva conceded that other women beside herself were present in the Alamo at the time of the battle. She observed: "Santa Anna made the attack … on March 6. The Alamo was filled with Texans, a number of women among them…." However, she did not mention their names or number.[5]

Survivor accounts given years after the event are always filtered through each participant's memory, and for Juana Navarro Pérez Alsbury, Enrique Esparza, and Madam Candelaria, who did not speak English, sifted once again through random and unidentified Spanish to English interpreters; then yet again distilled and written by journalists at the time in the romantic post-Civil War language of hyperbole that was fashionable in the 1880s and 1890s. It was during the late nineteenth century that such lofty phrases as "The Cradle" or "The Shrine of Texas Liberty" were used in reference to the Alamo. It seems unlikely that these three Tejano interviews assigned such gilded epithets to the compound where for thirteen days their lives and their families were at such high risk.[6]

Nevertheless, the accounts by Esparza, Alsbury, and Madam Candelaria describing their personal experiences on that morning at the Alamo remain among the most relied upon sources about these non-combatant women and children. Dissimilar as the accounts are regarding how many women were actually present, what was their location within the compound, what events they witnessed, whether Juana Navarro Pérez Alsbury or Madam Candelaria nursed Jim Bowie, what illness Bowie suffered, typhoid or tuberculosis; or the manner and order in which the leaders on the Texan side were killed, on one point the three accounts do agree: There were other women and children who survived the assault besides Susanna Dickinson and her daughter Angelina.

Between 1994 and 1999 three seminal works were published: *Women and Children of the Alamo* (1994) by Crystal Sasse Ragsdale; *The Alamo Remembered: Tejano Accounts and Perspectives* (1995) by Timothy M. Matovina; and *Echoes from Women of the Alamo* (1999) by Gale Hamilton Shiffrin. Two in particular—the Ragsdale and Shiffrin books—focused exclusively on the women and children who experienced and witnessed the battle. To this day these works remain among the most important, often-quoted, and credible sources of information about the women and children survivors at the Alamo. Collectively, these three publications confirmed the names of Ana Salazar Castro Esparza and her four children—a daughter from her Castro marriage, María de Jesús Castro—and three sons from her Esparza marriage, Enrique, Manuel, and Francisco Esparza; Juana Navarro Pérez Alsbury and her infant son Alejo Pérez; Juana's unmarried sister Gertrudis Navarro; Andrea Castañon de Villanueva or Madam Candelaria; Concepción Charlé Gortari Losoya and her sons, Toribio, a slain Alamo defender, an adolescent son, Juan, and her married daughter Juana Francisca Losoya Melton; and, of course, Susanna Wilkerson Dickinson and her infant Angelina.

Six of those seven women who had taken refuge in the Alamo were *Bexareña* women, some with remarkable lineages and considerable social standing. Of the seven children, six were *Bexareño* boys and girls, including one other infant, another "babe of the Alamo." The story of these Hispanic women and children has been largely ignored or marginalized.[7]

Many of the Hispanic women of San Antonio de Béxar were descendants of the original founding families whose ancestors had come as military, civilian, or mestizo settlers. Their ancestors shaped and developed Bexar's economy, its trade routes, religion, language, customs, and society, as well as its emotional and cultural connectedness to Spain and later Mexico. Women's backgrounds as members of each of those groups determined their social standing in the community, setting up a hierarchy that separated one social group from another. Women from affluent households kept within their own elite circle of friends, socializing with other well-to-do women of their class. Working-class women were either Indian captives brought into local homes or wives and daughters of men who were farm hands, drovers, stone masons, blacksmiths, millers, or day laborers. The women served as house maids, laundresses, nannies, cooks, seamstresses, or healer-midwives. Despite the rigid class system in place, the dangers and adversities they faced from Indian raids to epidemics forced the community to come together in mutual cooperation, making social barriers less of an issue in frontier areas.

Some Hispanic women exercised their legal right to petition and acquire land, as well as conduct business by selling and buying cattle, horses, sheep, goats, and farm produce. Female land owners often rented part of their land to neighbors for farming. Gertrudis Sánchez petitioned and received "a lot of fourteen *varas* by six *varas* near the town plaza in order to construct a house for her eighteen-member family."[8]

By the 1830s the increase of settlers from the United States to Texas and San Antonio was one more change to which the Hispanic resident community had to adapt. In 1834 Juan Almonte, a Mexican official and diplomat, estimated the "civilized population" in the Department of Béjar as 4,000, composed of Mexicans and Anglos. As a central, more developed and larger township, San Antonio tended to attract more affluent, enterprising Anglo settlers, such as Samuel Maverick and his wife Mary, James Bowie, John W. Smith, and others. These Anglo American newcomers came with their own set of mores, customs, and traditions. As Anglo and Hispanic women became neighbors, curiosity about each other brought them together, but their respective social standing determined their close friendships. The Seguins and the Navarros, prominent San Antonio families, for instance, had close social ties with the Mavericks who were considered their social equals. Intermarriage between Anglo men and Hispanic women also helped to close the ethnic and cultural gaps, as did a need for mutual survival. In time, frontier life and women's common needs and interests lessened the language and social barriers. For example, non-slave-holding Anglo households looked to the working-class Hispanic community for staffing their homes with maids, cooks, seamstresses, and nannies, and bilingualism became common, as Anglos necessarily learned Spanish in order to conduct their affairs with the Mexican authorities in charge.[9]

As political conditions between the two groups deteriorated and military preparations began, many families were caught in the middle of the dispute. The approach of the Mexican army toward San Antonio caused many of those families to flee, joining others in a major exodus from the town. Those who were unable to get away, such as the Hispanic women and children at the Alamo, cast their lot with the Texans and sought safety and refuge behind the mission walls. Susanna and Angelina Dickinson, recent settlers from Gonzales, also stayed behind when Susanna's husband, artillery

Captain Almeron Dickinson moved them to San Antonio and at the last minute inside the Alamo compound.

At the conclusion of the battle, the Mexican army assembled the Alamo survivors. The women requested to search for the bodies of their loved ones and give them a Christian burial, but were denied by General Santa Anna. The women and their children were then marched out of the Alamo at gunpoint into a sea of blood and dead bodies. Viewed as traitors to their mother country—Mexico—their Mexican soldier-captors demeaned, jabbed, and prodded them onward from the Alamo to the main plaza and then to the home of Don Ramón Músquiz, a high ranking political official at the time. That same day, following a brief stay at the Músquiz boarding house, the women were taken before General Santa Anna for interrogation, during which he forced them to pledge allegiance to Mexico. The general, who had hours earlier been merciless in his exercise of power at the Alamo, in an ironic and uncharacteristic gesture of compassion, made a show of personally rewarding each woman with "two silver pesos and a blanket." The women were then released to return to their families and resume their lives. After a few days' stay at the Músquiz household, Susanna Dickinson and her infant Angelina, with only two black men to accompany her—one in the service of the Mexican army and the other Travis' slave Joe—traveled east to inform General Sam Houston and the Texas army of the fate of the Alamo defenders.[10]

The fate of the *Bexareña* survivors was precarious. To Anglo Texans they were the enemy; to some of the native *Bexareños*, many of whom had remained loyal to Mexico and were their relatives, they were traitors. Mexican nationals as well held them in contempt, accusing them of treason. These *Bexareña* widows with their fatherless children were now pariahs in a land where their Hispanic dominance was fading.[11]

Susanna Dickinson didn't fare any better. While most of the Hispanic women had some hope of shelter with neighbors, friends, or eventually their own relatives, Susanna, without her husband Almeron as the sole source of her support, left the Músquiz house without a single person to whom she could turn for assistance or solace. She had to rely on the kindness of strangers along the way until she could reach Gonzalez, her former place of residence. There she had hope of finding someone who remembered her and could give her assistance and comfort.[12]

An examination of the lives of these non-combatant women must necessarily include members of their families and the societal norms of both the Hispanic and Anglo cultures of that era. Within those societies, men were the heads of the household and their activities in the public sphere were dominant. Women's lives, for the most part, generally centered on domestic concerns such as the home and family. Whatever good fortune or misfortune befell their male partners, the women automatically inherited the benefits as well as the difficulties. This was true in times of peace and during times of military confrontation when they were in as much risk of opprobrium, prison, or a firing squad as were their husbands. In short, the status of the women and children at the Alamo, Hispanic or Anglo, was subordinate and dependent.

Mexican historian Erika Quiróz of the Universidad Autónoma del Estado de México, Toluca, described the nineteenth-century Mexican family as an institution of moral and Christian instruction held together by a loyal, loving, self-sacrificing, and virtuous woman. She further suggested that the Catholic Church and nineteenth-century society had control over how women thought, acted, and believed. The church and society promoted the idea that the highest virtue in womankind was to give up her self interests in favor of their husband and children. They were to be "respectable and respectful." Their role in life and in God's divine plan was to preserve family values of purity, piety, and domesticity, according to the ideals of the church, society, and their station in life.[13]

To an extent nineteenth-century mores, as they applied to Hispanic and Anglo women, were also true on the Texas frontier, only more elastic. Frontier life demanded a more assertive woman in the face of Indian attacks or other dangers. When their husbands were away, which on the Texas frontier was very often, women frequently crossed gender boundaries to defend their families and household, place food on the table, and keep life and limb intact during alternating periods of crop failures, livestock decimation, and damaging droughts or floods. For example María Josefa Becerra, a daughter of a prominent ranching family from La Bahia, wrote a letter to her husband Erasmo Seguin, a San Antonio businessman and politician away on business in Saltillo. In it she informed him that two neighboring lots had become available, and not wanting to lose the opportunity of extending their existing property, she purchased them. Becerra further explained that not knowing how long he would be away, she saw the urgent need to acquire the land and chose to act in his absence. For both Hispanic and Anglo women, necessity and survival on the Texas frontier required them to perform tasks normally reserved for men.[14]

While the seven female survivors of the Battle of the Alamo conformed to societal strictures of the time, with occasional opportunities to step out of their sphere, they also represented a diverse mix of women, ethnically and socially. Concepción Charlé Gortari Losoya was fifty-seven years old at the time of the battle and came from French and Spanish military stock who had resided in San Antonio since the late 1770s. She was first married at age sixteen to Ignacio Miguel Gortari, who was killed by the Comanches in May of 1802. Concepción re-married as was common on the frontier due to the high mortality rate among both men and women. Her second marriage was to Ventura Losoya. Concepción's status as an elite *Bexareña* came from her ancestors' military service, as well as the family's long-time presence, first in Louisiana, then at Los Adaes in Spanish Texas, and eventually in San Antonio where her father was "granted a two-room stone house, [which had been] an old Indian dwelling that ... was situated on Plaza de Valero near the southwest corner of the mission's compound ...."[15]

A 1979 archaeological survey conducted by Anne Fox and James Ivey of the Department of Archaeology at the University of Texas at San Antonio, described the Losoya property: "In 1786 Fray José Francisco López, Father President of the Missions in the province of Texas granted a house and workshop and their lots of land together with a large garden at the southwest corner of mission [Valero] to Pedro de los Ángeles Charlé...." Concepcion's father had been of service to the mission for thirteen years as "carpenter, barber and sacristan" and received the land and workshop in reward. When the missions were secularized and their lands distributed in 1793, the Losoya brothers—Miguel and Cipriano—acquired grants to the "lands on the north and west sides of the Plaza de Valero...." Having married into the Losoya family, Concepción Charlé, "eventually inherited title to most of the land on either side of Losoya Street ... at the southwest corner of Alamo Plaza ...."[16]

Concepcion's estate and other holdings were additionally augmented when she inherited her mother's properties. "Her parents were important members of the Alamo mission community. María de Estrada [Concepción's mother] owned cattle and acquired land of her own on the flowing Acequia Madre near the Alamo...." In combination her properties gave Concepción the élan and social prominence that *Bexareño* society held as being prestigious.[17]

Yet it was the precise location of her Alamo property that was snatched away without her consent or cooperation and destroyed during the 1835 siege of Bexar when Mexican General Martín Perfecto de Cos and his army simply took over her property. "[General

Andrea Castañon Villanueva (Madam Candelaria). Courtesy Daughters of the Republic of Texas Library, San Antonio, Texas, Gift of Mrs. Carlis Allison, SC12025.

Cos] selected a strategic cannon site on the southwest corner of Alamo Plaza—at Concepción's house…." Following the destruction of her house, "work began on repairs of the shattered Alamo, and the eighteen-pound cannon remained on the Charlí [sic] corner…." However, Concepción did own other town lots. Most likely after the battle Concepción, her daughter Juana Francisca Losoya Melton, and her adolescent son Juan moved to a Losoya family ranch, as many San Antonio families retreated to their ranches when hostilities put them at risk. Local tradition, however, suggests that Concepción took her remaining family to Natchitoches.[18]

In contrast, what is known about thirty-three-year-old Andrea Castañon de Villanueva or Madam Candelaria is unclear. Her story has been embroiled in controversy, contradiction, and hearsay, mostly of her own making, leaving behind many unanswered questions.

On March 6, 1892, in an interview given to the *San Antonio Express,* she stated that she was born in Laredo, on November 30, 1785. However, during a personal interview with Mrs. Vee Gómez (Olga Villanueva Gómez) a great-great-granddaughter of Madam Candelaria, a copy of Andrea's baptismal certificate showed her birth date as December 1, 1803, in Presidio de San Juan Bautista del Río Grande, present day Guerrero, Coahuila. Candelaria then stated, "My father said he was the tailor of Ferdinand VII…." It is unlikely that a presidial soldier in frontier New Spain would have served in King Ferdinand VII's court as a personal tailor. Furthermore, she continued, "I was the daughter of [a] Spanish soldier Antonio Castañon, who had seen service in Cuba before he came to fight against the Indians at the remote [sic] presidio. My mother, Francisca Ramírez was Mexican." In Candelaria's baptismal certificate her mother's name was Francisca Martínez, not Ramírez as she stated in the newspaper interview. In fact many of her statements to the press were contradictory and misleading.[19]

In the same interview with the *San Antonio Express* she strongly claimed that not only was she inside the Alamo compound during the battle, but that she was also brought in specifically to nurse James Bowie, a defender and brother-in-law of the Navarro sisters. Years later (1901), Adina de Zavala, granddaughter of Lorenzo de Zavala, first Vice President of the Republic of Texas, disputed Candelaria's presence at the Alamo in a story given to the *San Antonio Light*. In that article de Zavala, who was not an eyewitness to the battle, did not provide evidence for her claim. Enrique Esparza, interviewed in November 1901 by the same newspaper, said he did not dispute Candelaria's claims about being inside the Alamo nursing Bowie. Newspaperman John S. Ford, in his interview with Juana Navarro Alsbury, added: "She says she does not know who nursed him [Bowie] after he left the quarters she occupied and expresses no disbelief in the statement of Madam Candelaria." Alsbury continued, that "there were people in the Alamo I did not see." Given that several of the eyewitness accounts stated that the women and children were scattered in different areas throughout the Alamo compound, one plausible explanation is that Madam Candelaria might have been there, but was simply not seen by some of the others.[20]

In another interview with the *San Antonio Light* on February 19, 1899, Madam Candelaria contradicted her earlier statement that her father came from Cuba to Texas. In that interview she stated that she didn't love Spain because, "her father's family was forcibly moved to Texas from the Canary Islands about the middle of the last century for the purpose of carrying out a colonization scheme, concerning which her people were never consulted." The Spanish Crown had authorized the colonization of Texas by Canary Islanders in 1729 for the purpose of increasing Spain's presence in its northern province of Texas. Included among the incentives offered candidates was the lesser title of nobility: Hidalgo. No evidence exists that Spain coerced Canary Islanders to move to Texas as Madam Candelaria suggested.[21]

In the course of the interview with Candelaria's great-great-granddaughter, Mrs. Gómez, she mentioned that Madam Candelaria had six siblings, which oddly enough Candelaria never acknowledged in any of her previous interviews with the press. In addition, Mrs. Gómez also stated that Madam Candelaria had four children: Francisca, by her first marriage to Silverio Flores de Abrego, who was killed in the 1813 Battle of Medina, and three others—Amado, Candelario Jr., and Santiago—by Candelario Villanueva, who abandoned his family at some point in their lives, leaving Madam Candelaria to bring up her children alone. The existence of her offspring was also omitted from her accounts to the press, as well as other unsubstantiated stories that Madam Candelaria was an innkeeper and also operated an orphanage.[22]

Despite the contradictory evidence concerning Madam Candelaria and her Alamo role, sufficient evidence existed, specifically the Esparza-Navarro eyewitness interviews, for the Texas legislature to award her a government pension of $120 per year on April 13, 1891, for her nursing services rendered to the sick and wounded during the battle of the Alamo, putting to rest any doubts, at least officially, about her presence there. In fact, she confirmed her nursing role in many interviews, and the March 6, 1892, newspaper article described Madam Candelaria as a charitable woman and a capable nurse.[23]

Two other non-combatant women at the battle of the Alamo were the Navarro sisters. Juana Navarro Pérez Alsbury was twenty-four years old and her unmarried sister Gertrudis Navarro was twenty years old in 1836. They were the daughters of José Ángel Navarro, a politician, businessman, and rancher, as well as nieces of two landed, political activists, José Antonio Navarro and José Francisco Ruiz, both participants on the Texas side of the revolution and signers of the Texas Declaration of Independence at Washington-on-the-Brazos. Furthermore, the Navarro sisters were the adopted daughters of Juan Martín de Veramendi, governor of the Mexican state of *Coahuila y Téjas*, businessman, and Texas patriot. Another significant though lesser connection was their relationship to James Bowie, who had married their cousin and adopted sister Ursula Veramendi. One explanation of the presence of Juana and Gertrudis at the Alamo is that Bowie urged them inside after Juana's second husband, Dr. Horace Alsbury, left on a mission and was unavailable to remove the sisters from harms way.[24]

Gertrudis Navarro, the unmarried younger sister, was automatically under the protection of her older sister Juana, who had been married, widowed, and then re-married as her Pérez and Alsbury names show. Juana's first husband Alejo Pérez was related to the De Leon family of Victoria. The Bexar County records indicate that "Alejo Pérez was a merchant ... He was given a permit in August 12, 1833, to transport listed goods to and from Monclova." He died in 1835 in a cholera epidemic that swept San Antonio. A year later Juana married Horace Alsbury.[25]

The sisters' prominence originated from their ancestral lines, but it was those same affiliations that also kept their lives in turmoil. Before and during the Texas Revolution both benefited and suffered from the political fortunes and misfortunes of their family. Their father remained loyal to Mexico and to General Santa Anna, while their uncles and adopted father and by now also Juana's husband, Horace Alsbury, sided with the Texas patriots. When their father, José Ángel, died in June of 1836, each sister inherited twenty-five head of cattle; but it was Horace's signature that appeared on the acceptance document for his wife Juana's inheritance. After the revolution these gendered spheres remained intact. No matter how large their dowries or how powerful their family, women remained subordinate to their husbands.[26]

Fortunes rose and fell on the frontier and everyone, including the Navarro family, teetered between prosperity and potential financial disaster. However, during the Texas Revolution the Navarro sisters were less affected by the devastation and general poverty it caused. Juana followed her husband "to [a Navarro-owned] Calaveras Ranch on the Goliad Road... [when] after an absence, Dr. Alsbury was with his family, Juana and Alejo." Gertrudis eventually married Miguel Cantu, who was a grandson of Concepción Charlé Gortari Losoya. She lived "the remainder of her long life on the old Cantu Calaveras ranch near present-day Elmendorf."[27]

The life of Ana Salazar Castro Esparza, another Alamo survivor, unfolded through accounts given to local journalists by her son, Enrique Esparza, from 1901 to 1911. Although Esparza mentioned his mother casually, rather than as a central focus in those interviews, she emerged as a person of courage and determination. He related how his mother was willing to die by her husband's side at the Alamo, and in fact, expected such a fate.[28]

Ana Salazar Castro Esparza, the daughter of Gregorio Salazar and María González, was born on January 23, 1812, in San Antonio de Béxar. Her birth occurred at a crucial moment in San Antonio's political history as the insurrection in Mexico against Spanish rule spilled over into Texas. Between 1811 and 1813 San Antonio and its environs suffered anti-Spanish filibustering expeditions that forced San Antonio residents to take sides and flee for their safety. Like most families, when hostilities began, *Bexareños*, including the Salazar family, "left for their ranch homes for safety." This was especially difficult for women and children, who on a moment's notice had to pack or otherwise secure what they valued, and attempt to escape safely, sometimes without the protection of their husbands or other male relatives who stayed behind to defend the city.[29]

In 1836 Ana was twenty-four years old and married to second husband Gregorio Esparza, an Alamo defender and cannoneer with whom she had three sons: Enrique, Francisco, and Manuel. In an interview with University of Texas at San Antonio archaeologist Kay Hinds, Lina Olivares, one of Ana's great-great-grandchildren, related an often-repeated family story of events following the release of Ana and her children by Santa Anna. She told of the thirteen-day siege in which Ana lost her husband, became very sick with pneumonia, and subsequently experienced hard economic times. Enrique's 1902 account also suggested her difficult circumstance. He stated: "After the president had given my mother her two dollars and a blanket, he told her she was free to go where she liked. We gathered what belongings we could together and went to our cousin's place on North Flores Street, where we remained for several months." Ana's great-great-grandson J. R. Peche described the poverty in which the family found themselves. For many years they struggled to keep their family fed and housed. He remembered that his great-great-grandmother worked from time to time as a servant in the more affluent homes and also took in laundry in order to survive.[30]

Ana and her sons continued unsuccessfully to petition the legislature for the land that was due them as Gregorio's heirs. The land was eventually granted many years later. After suffering through years of want, the hard-working and dedicated Esparza brothers became successful farmers and developed a lucrative freighting business that afforded them the ability to live a better, less financially strapped life in Atascosa County. The brothers established their ranches and farms near each other and with time constructed and bequeathed a church and a school to their community. Ana Salazar Castro Esparza died in 1849.[31]

Alamo survivor Juana Francisca Losoya Melton was the daughter of Concepción Charlé Gortari Losoya and Ventura Losoya. She was born on December 20, 1816 in Natchitoches, Louisiana. She married Eliel Melton who later came to Texas in January of 1830 and settled in Robertson's colony, where he obtained several leagues of land. Although he did not initially come to San Antonio, present-day Melton family descendants list Eliel and Juana Losoya as having three children together, Tabitha in 1819, Stroud in 1820, and Jonathan in 1821. This was highly unlikely since Eliel registered as a single man when he arrived in Texas, and in 1819, according to present-day family descendants, Eliel and Juana had their first child Tabitha. If correct, then Juana would have only been three years old. Furthermore, none of the Alamo survivor's accounts mention that Juana brought children with her.[32]

Juana Francisca was at the Alamo with her mother and two brothers, Toribio who died in the battle, and her younger brother Juan. In his 1907 account Enrique Esparza stated that the first thing he remembered upon entering the Alamo was seeing Mrs. Melton, "a Mexican woman married to an American," making circles on the ground with an umbrella. Enrique who was eight years old had not seen many umbrellas, and referred to Melton as a woman, rather than a girl of fifteen.[33]

Juana disappeared from history after 1836. There is no record that she ever claimed the land due to Eliel as a defender at the Alamo. She furthermore failed to receive the land her husband was granted upon his arrival in Robertson's colony to which she had every right. According to the prevailing legal system, Eliel's brother Ethan Melton became the executor of Eliel's estate and Juana's name vanished from census and tax rolls.[34]

Juana's mother Concepción, however, appeared in the 1840 census, which described her as a San Antonio widow and a land owner in Bexar County. In addition, the tax rolls revealed that she paid taxes on three town lots while her son Juan was listed as her agent. Concepción and her family were also behind the Alamo walls during the siege and took refuge afterwards at her brother-in-law Domingo Losoya's ranch. Conversations with members of Los Bexareños Genealogical and Historical Society of San Antonio suggest that

Concepción and her surviving children eventually left Domingo's ranch and went to Natchitoches.[35]

Among all the non-combatant women at the battle of the Alamo, Susanna Wilkerson Dickinson has received the most attention. Journalists conducted interviews about her experiences during the siege and fall of the Alamo; archival files in libraries hold copies of newspaper clippings and photographs of Susanna and Angelina; and in 1978 C. Richard King published a biography, *Susanna Dickinson Messenger of the Alamo*. In Austin, Susanna's last home will soon become a museum to her memory.[36]

Susanna Wilkerson Dickinson was born in Tennessee sometime in 1814. By the time she was twenty-two-years old, she had eloped, married a man twice her age, and traveled from Tennessee to Texas to Green DeWitt's colony. Her husband Almeron was a man of means who had served in the U.S. Army as an artilleryman. He made a good living as a blacksmith and gunsmith. They arrived in Gonzalez in 1831, received 4,428 acres, and immediately settled and improved the land. Almeron and Susanna prospered and Almeron became a leader in their community. Then in 1835, Almeron joined the Texas forces as a volunteer.

On the Texas frontier Susanna's life held a wide range of un-expected challenges. She survived an assault by a gang of newly arrived American volunteer troops, who in a drunken and disorderly spree broke into homes in Gonzalez. When they reached the Dickinson property Almeron was away defending San Antonio during the siege of Bexar. Launcelot Smither, who was to protect the Gonzalez community, described the event, in his unschooled hand, in a letter to Stephen F. Austin: "Such a savage and hostile CONDUCT as was comitd by some of the troops that ... come into the place ... numbers of the men broke open all most Every house in town and Robed all they could lay their hands on—and such Insults wire never offered to American women before ...

Susanna Wilkerson Dickinson. Courtesy Daughters of the Republic of Texas Library, San Antonio, Texas, Gift of Mrs. R. E. Nitschke, SC12294.

thire is no tribe of savages or Mexicans that would be guilty of such conduct...."[37]

With news from Gonzalez about the attack on his family and with the escalation of political and military events related to the Texas Revolution, Almeron traveled to Gonzalez, gathered his family, and moved them to San Antonio. He installed his wife and baby girl in the boarding house of Don Ramón Músquiz, where Susanna served as cook and laundress for the new arrivals. Almeron, promoted to captain in charge of artillery at the Alamo, then left to help with the preparations for the approaching siege. At some point he then moved his small family inside the Alamo compound where they remained during the siege.[38]

Following the Alamo battle, twenty-year-old Susanna and the other surviving women were escorted back to the Músquiz house. While on their way, a stray bullet struck Susanna in the leg. She received treatment and after a few days of recovery Susanna and her baby girl were brought before General Santa Anna for questioning. Years later, in her statements to the press, Susanna told how General Santa Anna had inquired about her wound, asked if she felt better, and offered to adopt her child Angelina and raise her in luxury. She refused his offer.[39]

Susanna soon learned the conditions for her release. The Mexican general wanted to intimidate the Texas forces and their leader with the strength and size of his army. He therefore permitted her freedom in exchange for her passing the information along to General Sam Houston and all Texans. To further impress upon her with his power, he ordered his troops to pass in review with Susanna at his side. Afterwards, Santa Anna released her with instructions written in English warning General Sam Houston that "the treatment accorded rebels at the Alamo will be the treatment to which the remainder of the country will be subjected."

On March 8, 1836, Santa Anna provided Susanna and Angelina with a horse for their journey. They began their long and dangerous trek, along with two black servants, toward Gonzalez. Subsequent interviews and reports do not mention whether she was provided with food or water. Along the way the small party was at the mercy of the cold weather and possible attack from Indians. Ten miles from the town she encountered three of General Houston's scouts, Deaf Smith, Henry Karnes, and Robert Hardy. She immediately informed them of the events at the Alamo and showed them the warning from the Mexican general. Deaf Smith gave Susanna and her little girl safe conduct to Gonzalez. Seeing the urgency of the situation, Smith then pushed on to Houston's camp with General Santa Anna's directive. Safe within the Gonzalez community, Susanna and her child rested and received food and shelter; however, her respite didn't last long. With orders from General Houston to burn the town to the ground, they soon joined the mass exodus eastward in front of the Mexican troops, known as the Runaway Scrape.[40]

Following the Texas Revolution, Susanna's hope for a better life for herself and her daughter turned into a nightmare of loss, want, despair, and suffering. Susanna, with nothing left for her in Gonzalez, remained in Houston for a few years, working in boarding houses, cooking, and taking in laundry. As a widow with little means of support, she re-married several times as a means of securing a male protector for her survival. She moved to Lockhart and eventually to Austin where she spent the rest of her life. Fortunately, on December 9, 1857, Susanna married for the fifth time. Her new husband Joseph William Hannig was a cabinet maker and businessman from Germany who was kind and supportive. They settled in Austin, where the family prospered and became distinguished members of the community.[41]

Susanna's recollections of the battle of the Alamo appeared frequently in national newspapers. On March 6, 1986, the *Lockhart*

Post-Register re-printed her account of the battle that she gave during an 1881 visit to the Alamo. Forty-five years after the events of 1836, she recalled: "There were about a 160 sound persons in the Alamo when the enemy appeared in overwhelming numbers and from environs to the west. There were others who were either sick or wounded, among them being Colonel Bowie, who was in the last stages of consumption." In the same interview she related: "As we passed through the enclosed ground in front of the church, I saw heaps of dead and dying. I recognized Colonel Crockett lying dead and mutilated between the church and the two-story barrack building, his peculiar cap by his side." José Enrique de la Peña, a Mexican army colonel who kept a daily account of the army's Texas campaign, confirmed Susanna's description of Crockett's cruel end.[42]

Susanna's daughter Angelina grew up with a flirtatious and irresponsible disposition and didn't fare much better than her mother. She too went into loveless marriages, divorced, and bore four children by different husbands or liaisons, whom she later abandoned to her mother and other relatives. Angelina continued to live a life of despair, drifting to New Orleans and later to Galveston, following Jim Britton, a railroad man. Upon her death in 1869, the Galveston *Daily Bulletin* on July 14, 1869, reported: "The death last evening of 'Em Britton'... a name being that of a woman connected forever ... at the Alamo ... She embraced the life of a courtesan and so died last evening."[43]

This study has focused only on the seven women and children whose presence and survival at the battle of the Alamo is known with some certainty. But undoubtedly other women were there. The accounts of Enrique Esparza, Madame Candelaria, and Susanna Dickinson confirmed the presence of a number of other local women and described their departure during the three-day armistice. Their names, unfortunately, are lost to history.

All of the female survivors of the battle of the Alamo demonstrated inner strength and courage during the battle and afterwards. But their lives were never the same, as many became
widows, their children became fatherless, and their futures became
uncertain. In particular the Texas Revolution affected the ability of the new Republic to compensate the survivors for the loss
of their husbands and damages to their homes. Financially, the
conflict added a considerable number of claims to the already
existing roster of debts to be paid from a non-existent treasury.
Susanna Dickinson petitioned the new government in October
1836 for $500, but was refused. Land, rather than specie, then
became a more frequent source of compensation, but it took most
of the Alamo women years before any of the land grants due their
husbands for military service were awarded. In 1839 Susanna and
Angelina Dickinson received a donation certificate for 640 acres
and later a bounty warrant for 1,920 acres of land in Clay County.
Of the six Hispanic women survivors, only Ana Esparza's heirs
were awarded a bounty warrant for 1,920 acres and a donation
certificate for 640 acres in 1854.[44]

Following the revolution, the female survivors of the Alamo
found themselves living amidst two societies—Mexican and Anglo. The Hispanic survivors became socially marginalized in a
culture that was increasingly foreign and sometimes even caustic.
While they continued to maintain many of their cultural practices and traditions, they were increasingly outnumbered by an
Anglo-American population that viewed them with animosity
and sought to impose an alien economic and political system.
While some of the Hispanic women survivors had the advantage
of taking refuge on family ranches, others encountered a poverty
they had not expected. For example, Madam Candelaria and Ana
Salazar Castro Esparza experienced prolonged periods of loss and
deprivation following the revolution. On the other hand, Juana

Navarro Pérez Alsbury and her sister Gertrudis Navarro Cantu, as well as Concepción Charlé Gortari Losoya, being women of considerable means prior to the Texas Revolution, fared much better. Each had inherited ranches, cattle, and several homes, which they managed to hold on to in the face of uncertain times. Susanna Dickinson also failed to negotiate successfully her role in Anglo society. With only her fame as an Alamo survivor and claimant for her husband's pension and land rights, she had only those meager means to navigate between her previous life and the new circumstances.

While the Texas Revolution brought long-term political change to Texas by securing independence from Mexico and creating an independent Republic, it failed to significantly benefit the women who survived the battle of the Alamo. For the *Bexareña* women the successful revolution meant a loss in social status, although leaving their Spanish legacy of legal and property rights in place under the Republic. For many it also brought an immediate decline in their economic standing and prospects for their future. While Susanna Dickinson, as the lone Anglo American woman, enjoyed widespread acknowledgement as an Alamo survivor, she personally did not improve her condition after the war. As a widow on the Texas frontier with few resources, only the traditional avenue of marriage allowed her some semblance of respectability and security. At the same time the Texas Revolution, due in part to its brevity, failed to alter the gendered roles or responsibilities of Texas women. Although much affected by the loss of their husbands and fathers, the day-to-day lives of the Hispanic and Anglo widows after 1836 continued much as before, as mothers, daughters, and even wives again. For the foreseeable future the non-combatant women who survived the battle of the Alamo would sustain themselves through their family ties and self-reliance in a male-dominated, Anglo society under an independent Republic and then statehood.

Selected Bibliography

De la Teja, Jesús F. *San Antonio de Béxar: A Community on New Spain's North-ern Frontier.* Albuquerque: The University of New Mexico Press, 1995.

De la Teja, Jesús F., ed. *Tejano Leadership in Mexican and Revolutionary Texas.* College Station: Texas A&M University Press, 2010.

Matovina, Timothy M. *The Alamo Remembered: Tejano Accounts and Perspec-tives.* Austin: University of Texas Press, 1995.

———. *Tejano Religion and Ethnicity: San Antonio, 1821–1860.* Austin: Uni-versity of Texas Press, 1995.

McDonald, David. *José Antonio Navarro: In Search of the American Dream in Nineteenth-Century Texas.* Denton: Texas State Historical Association, 2010.

McDonald, David R., and Timothy M. Matovina, eds. *José Antonio Navarro: Defending Mexican Valor in Texas José Antonio Navarro's Historical Writings, 1853–1857.* Austin: State House Press, 1995.

Ragsdale, Crystal Sasse. *Women and Children of the Alamo.* Abilene, TX: State House Press, 1994.

Shiffrin, Gale Hamilton. *Echoes From Women of the Alamo.* San Antonio: AW Press, 1999.

Tijerina, Andrés. *Tejanos and Texas Under the Mexican Flag, 1821–1836.* College Station: Texas A&M University Press, 1994.

Weber, David J. *The Mexican Frontier, 1821–1846: The American Southwest Under Mexico.* Albuquerque: University of New Mexico Press, 1982.

Endnotes

1 Timothy M. Matovina, *The Alamo Remembered: Tejano Accounts and Perspective* (Austin: University of Texas Press, 1995), xi.

2 *Ibid.*

3 Rena Maverick Green, ed., *Samuel Maverick, Texan, 1803–1870: A Col-lection of Letters, Journals and Memoirs* (San Antonio: privately printed, 1952.), 55; John S. Ford, "The Alamo's Fall: A Synopsis of the Display of Heroism," *San Antonio Express*, March 6, 1889; Matovina, *The Alamo Remembered*, 131.

4 Enrique Esparza, "Another Child of the Alamo," *San Antonio Light*, No-vember 10, 1901; Matovina, *The Alamo Remembered*, 65.

5 Andrea Castañon Villanueva, "Historical Reminiscences of the Aged Madam Candelaria," *San Antonio Express*, March 6, 1892; Matovina, *The Alamo Remembered*, 53.

6 Esparza, *San Antonio Light*, November 10, 1901; Matovina, *The Alamo Remembered*, 63.

7 Timothy M. Matovina, *Tejano Religion and Ethnicity: San Antonio, 1821–1860* (Austin: University of Texas Press, 1995), 28–35.

8 A *vara* is 33 1/3 inches. Jesus F.de la Teja, *San Antonio de Bexar: A Community on New Spain's Northern Frontier* (Albuquerque: University of New Mexico Press, 1995), 8, 18, 41.

9 de la Teja, *San Antonio de Bexar*, 24–29; Gifford White, *1830 Citizens of Texas* (Austin: Eakin Press, 1983), 239.

10 Esparza, *San Antonio Light*, November 10, 1901. In the account Esparza explained how he and his mother and siblings, at the urging of their father Gregorio, entered the Alamo at the very last minute. Enrique explained that his father's body was the only one of the defenders' bodies that was given Christian burial. After finding his Tejano in-laws huddled in a corner of the Alamo compound, Gregorio's brother Francisco, a soldier in the Mexican army, requested and was granted permission by his commander to recover his brother's body and give it a Christian burial.

11 *Ibid*. Esparza stated that the "father" José Antonio Navarro removed the Navarro sisters from the Músquiz household prior to their interview with Santa Anna. This is highly unlikely. In a personal interview with historian David R. McDonald, who has recently published the biography of José Antonio Navarro, he confirmed that José Antonio and Francisco Ruiz left immediately for New Orleans after signing the Texas Declaration of Independence at Washington-on-the-Brazos. They did not return to San Antonio until 1837, thereby avoiding the price General Santa Anna had placed on their heads. José Antonio Navarro was definitely not in San Antonio, as Esparza's account states. Furthermore José Antonio was not their father. The sisters were the daughters of José Ángel Navarro and the adopted daughters of Juan Martín de Veramendi, who had married the Navarro brother's sister, Josefa Navarro. Esparza was in his 70s at the time of the interview and might have confused the brother's names. It is also to be noted that Esparza, in another interview that appeared in the *San Antonio Express* in 1907, stated that the Navarro sisters were the first to be interrogated by Santa Anna, which is completely contrary to his own 1901 statement that they had been removed from the Músquiz home prior to the interrogation. In her own words Juana Navarro Alsbury stated in the Maverick-Ford interview that her former brother-in-law Manuel Pérez, also a soldier in the Mexican army, took her, her sister, and infant son under his wing and was given permission to appoint a black female slave to accompany them to their father José Ángel Navarro's home. Discrepancies and contradictions of this nature within and between

the Navarro, Esparza, and Madam Candelaria's accounts abound and continue to muddle what might have happened on that cold morning of March 6, 1836. It is important to recall that Ana Esparza also had an ex-brother-in-law serving in the Mexican army who was given permission to assist her. The Texas Revolution is comparable to the U.S. Civil War in that relatives with differing political loyalties fought against each other. Matovina, *Tejano Religion and Ethnicity*, 24, 28–34.

12 Bess Carroll, "Survivor Tells of Fall: Santa Anna's Ultimatum Carried to General Sam Houston," *The San Antonio Light,* March 13, 1936; Dickinson, Susanna, Dickinson Biography File, Daughters of the Republic of Texas at the Alamo, San Antonio, Texas..

13 Erika Leticia Bobadilla Quiroz, "Condición de la Mujer Durante el Siglo XIX en México," http://www.monografias.com/trabajos 42/mujer-mexicana/mujer-mexicana.shtml (accessed May 10, 2010). "La familia del siglo XIX representaba toda una institución de enseñanza moral y religiosa … la iglesia se encargaba de controlar la forma de pensar, actuar y sentir de la mujer… [la mujer debería ser] conservadora de la riqueza, la sangre y la religión, abnegada, sumisa, respetable y respetuosa, servir al marido, educar a sus hijos de acuerdo a los ideales de categoría [y de la fe]…."

14 Erasmo Seguin, File 163, Spanish Archives, Bexar County Courthouse, San Antonio, Texas.

15 Steve Gibson, comp. "Charlé, Pedro Carlos de los Ángeles"(www.http.//bexargenealogy.com) (accessed September 30, 2010). Ignacio Miguel Gortari, Microfilm Reel 030.0657-58, May 11, 1802, Béxar Archives, Chihuahua, University of Texas, Austin, Texas.

16 Anne A. Fox and James E. Ivey, "Historical Survey of the Lands within the Alamo Plaza – River Linkage Development Project," Archaeological Survey Report No. 77, 1979, Center for Archaeological Research, University of Texas, San Antonio, Texas.

17 Crystal Sasse Ragsdale, *Women and Children of the Alamo* (Abilene, TX: State House Press, 1994), 70.

18 *Ibid.,* 72.

19 Matovina, *The Alamo Remembered,* 53; Ragsdale, *Women and Children of the Alamo,* 41; "Alamo Massacre as told by the Late Madam Candelaria; Her Vivid Story of the Great Battle, Where 177 Brave Men Met Death as True Heroes—Colonel Bowie Died in Her Arms—Blood was Ankle Deep," *San Antonio Light,* February 19, 1899. Andrea Castañon de Villanueva, Baptismal Certificate 1803 (obtained by her descendants from the *Mormon Church Stake Genealogy Microfilm Library,* San Antonio, Texas.)

20 *San Antonio Express*, March 6, 1892; Matovina, *The Alamo Remembered*,
    46, 53, 59; Gale Hamilton Shiffrin, *Echoes From Women of the Alamo* (San
    Antonio, TX: AW Press, 1999), 90.
21 de la Teja, *San Antonio de Béxar*, 18.
22 Michael Soler, MD. (great-great-great-grandson of Andrea Castañon de
    Villanueva), email correspondence, October 2010, San Antonio, Texas.
23 Madam Candelaria died in February 10, 1889. "Andrea Castanon Vil-
    lanueva," *The New Handbook of Texas,* ed. Ron Tyler, et. al. (Austin: Texas
    State Historical Association, 1996), VI: 752; HR Bill No. 464 (April 13,
    1891) in Cadwell Walton Raines, ed., *The Laws of Texas, 1822–1897* (Austin:
    The Gammel Book Co., 1898).
24 Ruben M. Perez and Bonnie Kuykendall, eds., *Lest We Forget: A Tribute
    to Those Who Forged the Way* (San Antonio, TX: n.p., 2010); Spanish
    Archives, Bexar County Courthouse, San Antonio, Texas, 112; David
    R. McDonald, "Juan Martín de Veramendi," in *Tejano Leadership in
    Mexican and Revolutionary Texas,* ed. Jesus F. de la Teja (College Station:
    Texas A&M University Press, 2010), 29; Alsbury, Horace Arlington, *The
    Handbook of Texas Online,* http://www.tshaonline.org/handbook/online/
    articles/AA;fal48 (accessed May 28, 2010).
25 Pérez and Kuykendall, *Lest We Forget*, 111.
26 José Ángel Navarro, "Jose Angel, Testamento de José Ángel Navarro,
    1830–1840," Spanish Archives.
27 Pérez and Kuykendall, *Lest We Forget*, 122; Ragsdale, *Women and Children
    of the Alamo*, 39.
28 Matovina, *The Alamo Remembered*, 62–66, 67–72, 77–88, 101–103.
29 Steve Gibson, comp. "Descendants of Pedro Carlos de Los Angeles Char-
    lé," www.bexargenealogy.com (accessed April 22, 2010); Kay Thompson
    Hinds, "A Historical Study and Archaeological Notes on the Esparza
    Site: The Esparza Farms, the San Augustine Mission Church and the San
    Augustine School with Relevant Character Histories and Biographical
    Information," Center for Archaeological Research, University of Texas
    at San Antonio, 6.
30 Hinds, "A Historical Study and Archaeological Notes," 6.
31 *Ibid.*
32 A league of land equaled 4,428 acres. Eliel Melton, Biography File, Daugh-
    ters of the Republic of Texas Library at the Alamo; Eliel Melton, "Jonathan
    and Tabitha Melton of Georgia, USA, http://familytreemakergenealogy.
    com/users/l/e/i/Vera-M-Leisure/BOOK-0001/0003-0071.html (accessed
    May 29,2010).
33 Gibson, "Descendants of Pedro Carlos de Los Angeles Charlé. "

34 Eliel Melton, "Jonathan and Tabitha Melton of Georgia, USA, http://
    familytreemakergenealogy.com/users/l/e/i/Vera-M-Leisure/BOOK-
    0001/0003-0071.html (accessed May 29, 2010).

35 Gifford White, ed., *1840 Census of the Republic of Texas* (Austin: Pem-
    berton Press, 1966), v, 3.

36 See C. Richard King, *Susanna Dickinson Messenger of the Alamo* (Austin,
    TX: Shoal Creek Publishers, 1976). Steve Campbell, "Museum to Open
    at Austin Home of Alamo Survivor Susanna Dickinson," *Dallas Morning
    News*, March 2, 2010.

37 Shiffrin, *Echoes from Women of the Alamo*, 5-9.

38 *Ibid.*, 8.

39 Shiffrin, *Echoes from Women of the Alamo*, 8.

40 Carroll, "Survivor Tells of Fall," *San Antonio Light*, March 13, 1936.

41 B. J. Benefiel, "Alamo Remembered: Messenger of Defeat Made Home
    in Lockhart Following Battle," *Lockhart Post-Register*, March 6, 1986;
    Dickinson Biography file, Daughters of the Republic of Texas Library at
    the Alamo.

42 *Lockhart Post-Register*, March 6, 1986.

43 Obituaries, Galveston *Daily Bulletin*, July 14, 1869; Dickinson Biography
    file, Daughters of the Republic of Texas Library at the Alamo.

44 Hinds, "A Historical Study and Archaeological Notes," 6; *The New Hand-
    book of Texas*, 2: 637.

CHAPTER 6

"Up Buck! Up Ball! Do Your Duty!"

Women and the Runaway Scrape

Light Townsend Cummins

The Runaway Scrape during the spring of 1836 constitutes one of the most noteworthy and poignant chapters of the Texas Revolution, in large part because it touched the lives of almost all Anglo-Americans in the province whether soldier or civilian. The "Runaway Scrape" quickly became the term used by those involved to describe the flight of Texans towards Louisiana and the United States at they moved eastward during the spring of 1836. Thousands of people rolled before the movement of the Mexican armies and eventually became involved in this exodus. The military forces commanded by General Sam Houston constituted a significant part of this movement, but the largest number of people proved to be the men, women, and children of the families living in the areas from San Antonio to the Sabine River. The Runaway Scrape accordingly involved a considerable number of women who took to the roads with their families and children. Many of them experienced profound hardships and privations. Some of them lost their lives in the process.

The scrape first began in the areas south of San Antonio when settlers heard news of Santa Anna's arrival in Texas. The number of people heading to the east accelerated steadily during February 1836. With the fall of the Alamo and the Goliad Massacre, the exodus quickly became a full-scale rout of the civilian population. Many of the roads running to Louisiana became choked with masses of people, some with carts and wagons hauling their possessions, all of them bound towards supposed safety. In places where the road crossed streams and rivers, the backups sometimes ran for miles as travelers anxiously waited to cross in order to continue their journey. By the time of the Battle of San Jacinto almost six weeks later, a majority of the English-speaking population of Texas had joined the flight and was on the move.[1]

For many Texas women, participation in the Runaway Scrape thereafter remained one of the most memorable and defining events in their lives. This certainly proved to be the case for Dilue Rose, the daughter of Dr. Pleasant W. Rose, one of the provinces' early physicians. Born at St. Louis in 1825, Dilue Rose moved to Texas with her family in 1833. She participated in the Runaway Scrape as an eleven-year-old girl. Settling in the Houston area after the Texas Revolution, she married former Texas Ranger Ira Harris and they eventually made their home at Columbus. Prior to his death in 1869, Ira and Dilue had nine children. In 1900, during her seventy-fourth year, Mrs. Harris published her reminiscences of the Runaway Scrape in the *Quarterly of the Texas State Historical Association*, edited by University of Texas Professor George P. Garrison. Although presented to the *Quarterly's* readership as Mrs. Harris's reminiscences, Professor Garrison carefully noted that the actual narrative was based on a journal kept by Dr. Pleasant W. Rose, a document that had been lost at some earlier time. His daughter Dilue, however, had earlier access to the journal before it was lost and based her narrative on her notes from it, augmented by her own memories as a child. She wrote her narrative in the late 1890s, in consultation with both George P. Garrison and Adele Looscan, an early twentieth-century historian of Texas. Even to this day, Dilue Rose Harris's recounting of the Runaway Scrape constitutes the best-known and most widely read source for the Runaway Scrape, having been cited and reprinted many times.[2]

The Rose family lived near Stafford Point in the vicinity of the lower Brazos River, the heart of Texas's most viable plantation belt. Prior to the outbreak of the Texas Revolution, Dr. Rose and his family had the opportunity to meet and know most of the important people in Texas, including Sam Houston, William B. Travis, Erastus Smith, and many others. The family had been following the revolution during late 1835 and early 1836 by means of reports brought by travelers. When news of the fall of the Alamo arrived in their locality, they decided to flee east. They made very quick arrangements for their departure, "hauling clothes, bedding, and provisions on the sleigh with one yoke of oxen." The Roses traveled eastward in the company of several other families. The rivers and streams of the region had swollen badly because of the unusually heavy rains that spring. The Roses and thousands of others made their eastward trek along muddy and boggy roads, some little more than wagon tracks. "Our hardships began at the Trinity," Dilue later recounted in her memoir of the scrape. They made their crossing of that river on what proved to be the last trip across by the ferry boat. It swamped badly while they were aboard, leaving the Roses and the rest of the passengers stranded with water rushing dangerously around them. They stayed in this perilous situation for several hours before being rescued.

Once across the Trinity, the Roses continued east for five days, experiencing additional difficulties of travel, until they reached the small settlement of Liberty, where Dilue's little sister died from the rigors of the trip. After several weeks there, Dilue and her family heard what they first thought to be sounds of distant thunder until someone recognized the sounds as cannon fire. The noisy Battle of San Jacinto some thirty-five miles to the southwest was in the process of ending the Texas Revolution. When news of Sam Houston's victory arrived at Liberty, the Roses eventually made their way back home along with the thousands of other Anglo-American settlers who had been part of the Runaway Scrape.[3]

The experiences of Dilue Rose Harris in the Runaway Scrape proved to be typical for many of the women, young and old, who participated in it. The rigors of the trip, its physical hardships, and the stark discomforts experienced by Dilue and her family were representative of the problems faced by most settlers who participated in this exodus. This proved especially to be the case regarding the Rose family's difficulty in crossing the flood-swollen rivers of the region, a dangerous problem for everyone involved. Illnesses such as cholera and other maladies ravaged many of those moving along the wet, muddy roads and also discomfited the Roses, directly contributing to the death of Dilue's younger sister. A number of families lost members to illness, especially in the case of infants, small children, and elderly people. Juan N. Seguin, a Tejano settler and prominent citizen of San Antonio, recalled his family's participation in the Runaway Scrape: "All the members of my family, not excepting a single person, were attacked by fever. Thus, prostrated on their couches, deprived of all resources, they had to struggle in the midst of their sufferings to assist one another."[4]

Often many of the traveling parties did not include the men of a family, either because they were deceased, in military service, or had been called elsewhere by their duties. The majority of those who participated were Anglo-American women and children, but the scrape also involved African American men, women, and children (most of them slaves who left no records of their experiences) along with the families of some Tejanos. Several of Dilue's brothers, indeed, did not travel with the Roses because they had remained behind in order to herd the family's cattle to a safe location. The Runaway Scrape thus represented a rare moment in early nineteenth-century Texas when by chance many women found themselves independently empowered to provide for the safety and security of their families. It is also significant that several of these women, including Dilue Rose Harris, later found historical voices for themselves and provided stirring accounts of their experiences.[5]

The Runaway Scrape began when the Mexican army commanded by General Antonio López de Santa Anna entered Texas. Many settlers believed the Mexican army would engage in the wanton slaughter of women and children accompanied by wholesale destruction of property. Texans had already heard reports, no doubt embellished, about the cruelties Santa Anna had thrust on the interior Mexican province of Zacatecas the previous year when he put down a revolt there. As well, most of the Anglo-American civilian populace had come to Texas from the southern, slave-owning region of the United States, and many of them had an inbred fear of slave rebellion. What better time for a revolt by slaves, many settlers speculated, than an invasion by the Mexican army? As historian Randolph B. Campbell has pointed out: "The Runaway Scrape may have been prompted in part by a concern for the reaction of the bondsmen to the invading Mexican army . . . and many Texans fled eastward with the conviction that Santa Anna meant to create a servile insurrection." Some settlers who worried about such a development also improbably spoke highly at the same time about the loyalty of their own slaves, many of whom participated in the flight eastward with their masters' families. The exodus eastward also owed its motivation to the fact that word quickly spread among the Anglo-American population that General Edmund Pendleton Gaines commanded a United States Army force that was stationed in Louisiana just across the Sabine River. This became a panacea to the fleeing settlers and in their minds the guarantee of a safe refuge to them, especially when Sam Houston's army itself joined the eastward moving throng of men, women, and children.[6]

Beyond fears of the Mexican army and problems with the slave population, the ever-present threat of Indian attack never strayed far from the daily worries of most Anglo-American settlers, who feared that such depredations might come to pass if a Mexican invasion made unstable the usual defenses against the tribes. A number of rumors, most of them untrue, circulated along the roads of Texas during the exodus that Indian depredations had already occurred at various places due to the breaking down of defenses. H. M. Wilson, newly arrived from the United States, appeared at Nacogdoches while the scrape was underway, spreading tales that the Cherokees in Texas were planning to levy organized attacks against the Anglo-American settlements. His stories may have been motivated by the fact that General Gaines across the Sabine in Louisiana was suspicious that such raids would occur. Gaines had been specifically cautioned by authorities in Washington D. C. to guard against anticipated violence from the various tribes of the region spilling over into United States territory.

There were indeed isolated attacks by Indian war parties during the Runaway Scrape that impacted directly on women, most notably one that occurred along the banks of Cummins Creek, an area several miles northeast of where the San Antonio–San Felipe Road crossed the Colorado River. This area had been settled in the 1820s by the Townsend and Cummins families, almost all of whom departed during the scrape. One local family, however, decided to remain: Conrad Juergens, his wife Mary, and their two young sons. They were recent arrivals from Germany and likely decided to remain along the creek because Mary was expecting to give birth at any moment. They believed that the Mexican army would most likely pass a number of miles to the south along the main road, and in that they proved correct. However, they instead found themselves the object of an Indian attack. Shortly after the Mexican forces had moved through the area, which was otherwise depopulated of settlers, a marauding party of braves struck their cabin in the dead of night. In the ensuring gunfire, Conrad Juergens was wounded but managed to save himself and escape into the woods. Mary and her two boys were not as lucky. The Indians captured all three of them and struck out thereafter for the Red River valley with the pregnant mother and her two sons. Three months later, after Mary had been separated from her sons, she appeared at a trading post belonging to Holland Coffee in the Indian Territory. Battered and abused, she had given birth to a daughter during the time of her captivity. Some of her relatives who had been searching for her learned of her presence at a Red River trading post. They arrived to pay a $300 bounty for her release. This ransom, however, did not involve her two sons, whose ultimate fate became lost to history. An additional attack south of San Antonio during the spring of 1836 resulted in the capture of another young woman, Sarah Ann Horn, along with a Mrs. Harris, and Sarah Ann's two sons. Horn, Harris, and the children suffered at the hands of their captors. As was the case with Mary Juergens, Sarah Ann's sons were taken from her and, although she saw them once while in captivity, they never returned from their ordeal. Both Sarah Ann and Mrs. Harris eventually found their way back after two years of captivity.[7]

The Runaway Scrape occurred in several stages. It began as an evacuation, starting south of San Antonio in February before it spread eastward to Gonzalez and Victoria early in the following month, culminating in civilian flight from the Colorado and Brazos valleys in mid- to late March. The arrival of the Mexican army on the banks of the Rio Grande in mid-February set in motion the chain of events that would start these panicked evacuations. Santa Anna had come to Texas for the purpose of putting down a revolt in what he saw as the most recalcitrant of his errant and obstreperous provinces. The Anglo Americans of Texas and their Tejano allies had been waiting for the appearance of the self-exalted Mexican commander who styled himself as the "Napoleon of the West." There had already been watchers along the Rio Grande for several weeks, most notably a man dispatched from San Antonio by Juan N. Seguin for such a purpose. News thus arrived in San Antonio and surrounding areas as soon as the Mexican army began its crossing into Texas. Fears among the civilian population there precipitated evacuations from Bexar even before reports of Santa Anna on the Rio Grande arrived. James C. Neill, then commanding in San Antonio, wrote to the nascent government at Washington-on-the-Brazos: "There can exist little doubt that the enemy is advancing on this post from the number of families leaving town today and those preparing to follow." Seguin's spy along the Rio Grande reported to San Antonio that the main Mexican army had crossed the river by mid-February. It was at this time that the exodus of families began as a presage to the Runaway Scrape, which would occur later in larger numbers. The Seguin family became one of the first to evacuate even as Santa Anna marched northwards to Bexar from the Rio Grande. Seguin later recalled in his memoirs: "When we received intelligence from our spies on the Rio Grande he was preparing to invade Texas, my father with his, my own, and several other families, removed toward the center of the country."[8]

A healthy measure of panic among civilian settlers also occurred to the southeast of San Antonio in January and February at the small settlement of San Patricio, causing the start of civilian evacuations from there to the eastern parts of Texas as well. This too was related to the arrival of the Mexican army, although Santa Anna did not personally command the troops that marched on San Patricio. Instead, after the Texian forces had captured San Antonio in late 1835 from General Martin Perfecto de Cos, as many as one hundred

Anglo-American troops commanded by James C. Grant and Francis W. Johnson marched south towards Matamoros with the intention of capturing that Rio Grande town. This small force arrived at San Patricio, speedily taking the settlement from the small Mexican garrison that defended it. As a result, a second Mexican army led by General Jose Urrea entered Texas simultaneously with Santa Anna's larger force. Urrea and his men crossed the Rio Grande at Matamoros, bound for San Patricio and points to the north. The anticipated arrival of Urrea's army in the Anglo-American settlements motivated additional evacuations of men, women, and children that eventually joined with other families leaving San Antonio in February of 1836. Dilue Rose Harris later recalled: "By the 20th of February, the people of San Patricio and other western settlements were fleeing for their lives." Departures from the settlements lying to the southeast of San Antonio accelerated when the Anglo-American troops led by Johnson and Grant suffered a costly defeat on February 27. "The news brought this morning," one settler noted about this defeat, "alarmed our citizens to such a degree that by nine o'clock several of the families had left and by eleven all of them except two" were on the road.[9]

When Sam Houston reached Gonzales on March 11, he found the townsfolk there in consternation. Two Tejano men had arrived from Bexar with the news that the Alamo had fallen and the defenders had been martyred. The arrival soon thereafter of Susanna Dickinson, the lone Anglo-American female survivor of the Alamo, confirmed this tragedy to the people of the town. "News of the debacle," as historian Stephen L. Hardin has noted, "triggered a mass exodus of Texian families known as the Runaway Scrape." As Uncle Jeff Parsons, a slave at Gonzales later remembered of that day, "People and things were all mixed, and in confusion. The children were crying, the women praying, and the most cursing." News of the Alamo struck the residents of Gonzales unusually hard because just over thirty local men had recently ridden to its defense, and now all of them had been martyred. "Many of her best citizens," one of the men at Gonzalez noted that day, "some of them with large families to support, fell on this gloomy Sabbath." In particular, about two dozen Gonzales women became widows with the fall of the Alamo. One of Houston's officers later recalled: "In short, there was not a family in the once happy and flourishing settlement of Gonzales that did not mourn the death of some murdered relative. For several hours after the receipt of the intelligence, not a sound was heard, save the wild shrieks of the women, and the heart rending screams of the fatherless children."

Word also came from San Antonio that a large portion of the Mexican army was then marching on Gonzales. Houston thus decided to evacuate the town and move his army towards the east. He ordered the town burned as his men, along with most of the civilians, departed. This began the major movement eastward that would quickly become the main event of the Runaway Scrape, a mass flight which one of Houston's biographers has called "both a military withdrawal and a folk migration." Almost all of the women and children of Gonzales departed with Houston's army and, as the days passed, word of the Alamo massacre, coupled to Houston's march to the east, set additional families into motion as a larger and larger ring of evacuees extended out from the San Antonio River through the Guadalupe, Colorado, and Brazos valleys. The Juan N. Seguin family, already in Gonzalez, joined the general movement of the settlers eastward when Houston and his army decided to leave. "Within several weeks," one participant recalled, "all the country west of the Brazos was depopulated."[10]

The retreat of Houston's army soon became a controversial strategy. Even some of his own men questioned his motives at the time. What was Houston's purpose in fleeing from of the Mexican army? Was he planning to turn and fight? When would he stop retreating and take revenge for the Alamo and Goliad? Such questions were never fully put to rest, even after the victory at San Jacinto. Charges and countercharges surrounding Houston's motives in the Runaway Scrape lingered for years after the Texas Revolution and constituted a point of heated debate between his supporters and detractors for the rest of his career in public life. What was not a matter of debate at the time or later, however, was that the mass exodus of civilians from the Anglo-American settlements clearly occurred amidst great confusion, disorder, panic, and (in some cases) sheer terror, especially regarding the hardships experienced by Texas women and their children.

All across the region, people began packing and making ready to leave their homes. At Victoria, the local alcalde John Linn noted that "in my vehicle I placed a few articles of prime necessity, my wife with an infant but fifteen days old, and two poor women with two or three children who had no means of leaving the town." They then struck out for the east, leaving most of their household effects and possessions behind. Settlers repeated this scene by the hundreds all across the Anglo-American settlements. In some cases, those departing did so with determined and unusual haste. "We passed a house with all of the doors open," Mary A. Baylor observed. "The table had been set, all of the victuals on the table." In many cases, rationality gave way to pandemonium. Anne Fagan Teal recalled a horseman riding through the country yelling: "Run, run for your lives: Mexicans and Indians are coming, burning and killing as they come." [11]

At least initially, many of the families who left Gonzales with the army followed Sam Houston's men as they marched to the northeast. As Houston moved along the Gonzales–San Felipe Road, he delegated Juan N. Seguin and some of his men to provide rear guard coverage, assisting in evacuation of both Tejano and Anglo-American families who were spilling onto the road in the wake of the army. Seguin noted that marching through the heavy mud proved particularly hard on shoes and boots. He later remembered that, passing through San Felipe, he was able to purchase almost two dozen pairs of shoes "for the use of the company [under] at two dollars a pair." It was becoming increasingly clear by this time that several Mexican armies were moving through Texas. One force under the command of General Joaquín Ramírez y Sesma had left San Antonio after the fall of the Alamo, marching along the main road to the east that linked with the Brazos River and San Felipe, thus shadowing Houston's army.

A second Mexican force, commanded by José Urrea, had moved to the northeast after its victory at San Patricio towards Goliad where it was bearing down on the Anglo-American troops led by James Fannin. While Fannin began to dither, General Houston's initial plan in leaving Gonzales called for him to follow the old road that linked San Antonio with San Felipe by way of Gonzales, stopping to regroup where it crossed the Colorado River at a place known as Beeson's Crossing. At this point, near the modern city of Columbus, a man named Benjamin Beeson operated a ferry across the river while he kept a small inn nearby. This crossing was already choked with people. Houston and his army camped here from March 19 until March 26, while many of the civilians who at first traveled with him decided to continue their flight to the east. The impending arrival of the Mexican army under General Sesma, however, caused Houston to leave the Colorado River and press on toward the Brazos. This accelerated the number of families fleeing and brought the Runaway Scrape into the Brazos valley. William Fairfax Gray at San Felipe noted in his diary of March 18, 1836: "Many persons, moving eastward to escape the anticipated storm of war, came along with their families, some in wagons, some in carts, and some of foot, with mules and horses, packed with their moveables." All along the roads, new settlers arrived to replace those who kept moving as the roads began to fill to capacity. Juan N. Seguin noted: "The confusion and delay caused on the road by the immense, straggling column of fugitives were such that when my family was beginning to cross the Colorado with their livestock, the enemy was at their heels." Drenching rains made for steadily deteriorating travel conditions, making many avenues of escape nearly impossible. "It had been an usually wet winter," Kate Scurry Terrell recalled, "and the roads were long quagmires of bottomless mud, the prairies trackless sheets of water."[12]

Fear of the advancing Mexican armies had also spread to Bastrop, north of the San Antonio–San Felipe Road, where Noah Smithwick observed the local residents making preparations to join the exodus. "Families were gathering at Bastrop," he later recorded, "preparatory to a general hegira before the ruthless invaders, who were said to be waging a war of extermination, and we were ordered to cover their retreat, and afterwards join General Houston." In hopes of reassuring the locals and giving them more time to make preparations to leave, Smithwick posted several men outside of town on the road to San Antonio with instructions to sound an alarm if any Mexican forces appeared. None did. Later, after leaving Bastrop, Smithwick passed through areas that had been depopulated by families who had joined the scrape. He painted a poignant picture of what had been left behind: "Houses were standing open, the beds unmade, the breakfast things still on the tables, pans of milk moulding in the dairies. There were cribs full of corn, smoke houses full of bacon, yards full of chickens that ran after us for food, nests of eggs in every fence corner, young corn and garden truck rejoicing in the rain, cattle cropping the luxuriant grass, hogs, fat and lazy, wallowing in the mud, all abandoned." For the rest of his days, Smithwick vividly remembered the human pictures of hardship that he saw that month on the roads of Texas. On one occasion, he happened upon a young mother and her children traveling in a creaky, old wagon. They lacked proper grease for the wheels, which squeaked and smoked badly. The mother rode in the wagon with her smaller children while an older daughter walked alongside with a bucket of water, pouring it on the wheels and axel whenever they seemed on the brink of catching fire. The screeching of the dry wheels against the wooden axel, for Smithwick, became a sound that remained with him and it only added to what he called the horror of their situation.[13]

As evidenced by the small family in the dilapidated wagon whose path Noah Smithwick crossed, the Runaway Scrape proved to be a shining time of bravery for many Texas women, especially those who embraced their inner strengths and persevered. The various accounts complied by women who participated in this mass exodus are replete with stories of determination and resolve to save themselves, their children, and their families. For example, one fleeing woman tied a feather mattress to a pony and then lashed three of her children to it, walking alongside while she carried a baby in her arms. She eventually joined the company of several other women who assisted her with the four children. Another young mother who was ill from very recent childbirth decided to leave home with her nine-day-old infant. "While camping for the night," one of her female companions later remembered, "there came up a terrific rain storm, when the women in camp gathered around the sick woman and held blankets over her to keep her baby dry and warm." Illness took a general toll along the roads of Texas in March and April of 1836. "Soon hunger and sickness added to their gaunt forms," one of the women on the road later recalled about those moving eastward. "Women sank by the roadside from exhaustion," Kate Scurry Terrell reported, "and many little children died." There was, however, a spirit of humanity and common cause that sprung up among many of the women who traveled along under such difficult conditions. Kate took pride in the fact that "the stronger women became veritable Sisters of Mercy as they went about nursing, encouraging, and comforting the less fortunate."[14]

Rosa Kleberg, from whom a famous Texas ranching family later descended, proved to be one of these self-possessed women and she later wrote a fascinating memoir that included a recounting of her experiences during the Runaway Scrape. An immigrant to Texas from Germany, she lived west of San Felipe with her husband, children, and brothers. After discussion among the family members when news of the Alamo arrived at their home in March, the Klebergs decided that Rosa, the children, and her elderly father would flee eastward while her husband and brothers would join Houston's army. Rosa took several other people from the neighborhood with her. She remembered: "Having one big ox-wagon and being compelled to take in it four families and their baggage, we were compelled to leave behind much that was valuable." As well, she and her father herded along with them some of their cattle and pack horses. Rosa, however, did not ride in the wagon. Instead, she traveled on horseback to help with the cattle, carrying with her in the saddle her daughter Clara who was only a few months old. Mrs. Kleberg found driving the cattle "was attended with a good deal of difficulty," but everyone in her party persevered.[15]

Crossing the Brazos River proved to be a trying proposition for Rosa Kleberg and her family, in large part because they still had their cattle in train with them. Arriving on the west bank, they found forty to fifty families waiting to cross, many of them with cattle as well. Rosa noticed that "the noise and confusion were terrible." She also observed that many of the people waiting were on foot, hoping to board the small ferry boat that was still plying passengers to the east side in small groups, mostly a few women and children at a time. "The blockade continued from early morning until the late afternoon," Rosa recalled. The Klebergs, however, did not use the ferry, instead crossing as they forded their cattle to the other side.

Rosa Kleberg. From John Henry Brown, *Indian Wars and Pioneers of Texas*, 1896. Courtesy UNT Libraries, The Portal to Texas History, Denton, Texas.

Later, east of the river, Rosa and her party came upon a homestead belonging to a man named Cooper whose generosity helped many of the travelers that day. Rosa reported that he "told the people to help themselves to all the meat in his smokehouse, since he did not wish to have the Mexicans to have it." By this time, an unsettling phenomenon was also occurring along the roadways: deserters from the Texan army were mixing among the families as they too made their way east. The Klebergs understandably had a low opinion of these men since Rosa's husband, along with her brothers, had already departed to join Sam Houston's army. Her father and the other elderly men in the caravans had much fun calling after these deserters, yelling "Run! Run! Santa Anna is behind you!"[16]

Such taunts, however, were not entirely unfounded. On March 21 General Sesma and his force had arrived near Houston's encampment at Beeson's Crossing on the Colorado. Some of the officers under General Houston's command, especially Sidney Sherman, argued vociferously that the Texans should attack Sesma. Houston did not do so, but maintained his position on the east bank of the river while the raging flood tide of the river kept the Mexican army from crossing over from the west side. It was during this time that Houston received the astounding news about the massacre of Fannin and his men at Goliad. With Fannin's demise, Houston understood that his army represented the last hope for a Texan victory. He therefore decided to withdraw further to the east, pass through San Felipe, and make for the Brazos River in the hope of finding better ground upon which to meet the Mexican army in battle. On March 25 Houston and his army left the Colorado bound for San Felipe on the Brazos, arriving near there several days later. Turning south from there, Houston and his men continued down the Brazos River until March 31 when they reached the environs of Leonard Groce's plantation, Bernardo. Here Houston and his men remained for a full two weeks, regrouping and replenishing their supplies.[17]

Many of the settlers of the Brazos valley, especially along the lower reaches of the river, had been closely watching the movement of Houston's army and the growing escalation of the Runaway Scrape without yet becoming involved. While moving east from Gonzales, General Houston had sent word to the relatively populated settlements of the Brazos River plantations that there would be no need for them to evacuate. News of the Goliad massacre, coupled to Houston's appearance at Groce's plantation, made remaining in place an absolutely unacceptable proposition as the fevers of escape now spread down the Brazos all the way to Velasco at its mouth on the Gulf of Mexico.

Some warnings had already been sent to residents in that area, including Stephen F. Austin's family who resided at Peach Point Plantation. His sister Emily Bryan Perry and her husband James F. Perry resided here, along with their children and slaves. On March 5, Austin's cousin Henry had written to the Perrys from the town of Brazoria, urging them to evacuate. He told James Perry: "It would be judicious for you to send Emily and the younger children" away as soon as possible. The Perrys delayed until they received news of the depredations at Goliad and the arrival of Sam Houston on the Brazos, coupled to the news that Santa Anna was moving east himself to take command of General Sesma's army. The Perrys decided to evacuate, as did most of the other plantation families along the lower parts of the river. James and Emily packed a large wagon as full of supplies as they could manage. Along with their younger children and a group of slaves, they headed along the road to Velasco and to parts east. Emily's son from her first marriage, Guy M. Bryan, accompanied them and later recalled: "We joined the throng of fleeing people. As far as the eye could see, extended backward and forward, was an indiscriminate mass of human beings, walking, riding, and every kind of vehicle." The road was choked with "men, women, and children, walking, riding on horseback, in carts, sleds, wagon, and every kind of transportation known to Texas."[18]

Emily Bryan Perry. Courtesy Brazoria County Historical Museum, Angleton, Texas.

Emily Bryan Perry rode in the wagon, holding in her arms a recently born infant daughter. The group in the wagon also included slave women and children, along with three of the younger Perry sons and daughters. James Perry, along with Guy Bryan and several bondmen, either rode horses or walked. The roads were so thick with people that progress proved to be extremely slow. They sometimes measured the miles traveled in days rather than hours. Each stream and bayou presented a potentially insurmountable obstacle because hundreds of people waited to cross. At Cedar Bayou, the Perrys encountered a large group waiting to cross, everyone's progress blocked because a cart containing a woman and two small girls had become stuck in the shallow water halfway across the stream. Pulled by two oxen, this stranded cart filled the entire crossing, thus making it impossible for anyone else to ford the bayou. Emily Perry took stock of the situation as they waited to cross. Handing off her baby, she climbed down from her wagon and waded out to the stranded wagon. Mrs. Perry spoke tenderly yet firmly to the woman, encouraging her to once again try to spur the oxen into action. The woman responded, rising up and cracking her whip with renewed determination. "Up Buck! Up Ball! Do Your Duty!" she cried, continuing to yell the oxen's names as she cracked the whip above their heads. Emily also yelled encouragement. This worked, and the straining oxen pulled hard, freeing the wagon, and thus clearing the ford of the jam. The Perrys continued their travels east until they reached the plantation of William Scott on the San Jacinto River. Since things seemed to be secure for the time, James Perry left his family at the Scott Plantation and continued to Galveston with the males slaves in his party. There, he assisted in securing a shipment of provisions for the garrison there.[19]

By mid-April as the Perry family passed through, there were several thousand people waiting to cross the San Jacinto River. This was also true further to the west along the Trinity River. "At the mouth of the old river Trinity," William Fairfax Gray noted on April 17 as he waited to ford that river, "we found a great many fugitives. The wagons and tents look like the encampment of an army." There was great confusion, and it took Gray some four hours to cross, finally swimming his horses. "There were about seventy-five wagons in the company" waiting at one stream, as W. G. Dewees later remembered, "and on arriving at the river we found no way to cross; the river was up to the top of the banks and there was no ferry." A group of men in the waiting caravan eventually cut down two very large pine trees "so that their length might be sufficient to reach across the river . . . that we might place the wagons on them and pull them across … with a rope." Such difficult conditions continued all the way to the Sabine River and the Louisiana border. One traveler who made it all the way to the United States recalled: "The road from Nacogdoches to the Sabine is one unbroken line of women and children, on foot, with nothing but their clothes on their back."

By this time, hardship and suffering had taken their toll on many of the people moving east along the roads of Texas, some of whom had been traveling for several weeks. Lost children had become a very noticeable problem. Dilue Rose Harris recalled seeing "children falling from the wagons which still kept on leaving the children behind, till another wagon came along and picked them up." She noted "mothers in this manner have been separated from their children for days, and some for weeks, as the wagons would often take a different course; all seemed to look out for themselves alone, the fountain of benevolence seemed dried up." As William Fairfax Gray passed through Beaumont, he came upon a family that had found a small, unattended infant. "They have charge of the poor little lost baby," he recorded in his journal, "which each carried by turns. I took pleasure in carrying it a short distance to relieve the old man."[20]

News of Sam Houston's victory on the battlefield at San Jacinto had the net effect of stopping much of the exodus in place, although a considerable number of people had already crossed the Sabine River. Annie Fagan Teal and her family, for example, did go all the way to Louisiana, where they were met at the border by men who took their firearms from them. The Teals decided to remain there for a number of months because their "friends convinced them that it would be foolish to hasten home and find nothing to eat." Anne and her family therefore planted a corn crop that spring on land belonging to friends and raised other supplies to take back home to Texas with them later in the year. Rosa Kleberg too rejoiced in hearing news of Sam Houston's victory. "We learned the result of the Battle of San Jacinto," she recalled later, and "we did not believe the good news until she heard it confirmed by a young man whom we sent to ascertain the truth of the report." Like others, they too delayed their return home largely because of the lawlessness that reigned in many parts of Texas because of the breakdown of public order during the Runaway Scrape. Bands of robbers and brigands had terrorized a number of the deserted neighborhoods. "The robbers were still at work," Anne Fagan Teal observed several weeks after the victory at San Jacinto, and she "saw a load after load of elegant, richly carved Mahogany furniture taken from the deserted homes of rich Mexicans." Indeed, upon returning home after the scrape, Juan N. Seguin also found his ranch had been despoiled. He was not alone. Most of the other Tejano families who had participated in the exodus also suffered losses. "There was not one of them," Seguin later noted, "who did not lament the loss of a relative and, to crown their misfortunes, they found their houses in ruins, their fields laid waste, and the cattle destroyed or dispersed. I myself found my ranch despoiled; what little was spared by the retreating enemy had been wasted by our own army. Ruin and misery met me on my return to my unpretentious home." [21]

These conditions were not limited to Tejano families, as Anglo-Americans also experienced such losses. Dilue Rose Harris and her family returned home to find the floor boards of their house torn up by Mexican soldiers who had apparently been searching for valuables or foodstuffs. "As soon as it was light enough for us to see we went to the house," she later wrote in the reminiscences, "and the first things we saw was [sic] the hogs running out. Father's bookcase lay on the ground broken open, his books medicines, and other things scattered on the ground, and the hogs sleeping on them." Rather poignantly, young Dilue found broken toys belonging to her infant sister who had died during the Runaway Scrape. Like the Rose family, Emily Perry had also lost a daughter during the scrape. The infant she had carried across Texas, and whom Emily had handed off when she had helped free the oxen from the mires of Cedar Bayou, also succumbed to the rigors of harsh travel. The Perrys arrived back at Peach Point to find their entire plantation in disarray. Although no one had apparently robbed them or despoiled their property, chickens had found their way into the main house and taken roost in most of the rooms. "The hens had taken possession of beds, closet, bureaus," Emily's cousin Mary Austin Holley later wrote, and "every place was a nest." One side byproduct of this, however, was that everyone had lots of eggs to eat for days thereafter. In spite of the Perrys' experience with a house full of eggs, the Runaway Scrape did set back food production an entire season. "On account of being obliged to quit our homes," W. B. Dewees noted, "we were unable to cultivate our land and the consequence is a great scarcity of provisions."[22]

Although it took a number of months for most of the people who evacuated to return to their homes, by the summer of 1836 the rigors of the Runaway Scrape were quickly becoming a memory for most of the participants. It had proven to be a harsh and difficult time for many Texas women and their families. In retrospect, the Runaway

Scrape became for many women one of the most important events in their lives, having to rely on their own resources for survival. In that respect, it constituted an event that shaped their characters as frontier women, evidenced by the fact that a considerable number of accounts and reminiscences of it were written by women. The Runaway Scrape was in many respects a domestic event and one of the few chapters in the history of the Revolution of 1836 that explicitly involved them as participants.

Selected Bibliography

Callaway, Carolyn. "The Runaway Scrape: An Episode of the Texas Revolution." M.A. thesis, University of Texas, 1942.

Downs, Fane. "Tryels and Trubbles, Women in Early Nineteenth Century Texas." *Southwestern Historical Quarterly* 90 (July 1986).

Harris, Dilue Rose. "Reminiscences of Mrs. Dilue Harris." *The Quarterly of the Texas State Historical Association* 4 (1900–1901).

Kleberg, Rosa. "Some of My Early Experiences in Texas." *The Quarterly of the Texas State Historical Association* 1 (April, 1898).

O'Connor, Mrs. Thomas, ed. "Reminiscences of Anne Fagan Teal." *Southwestern Historical Quarterly* 34 (April 1931).

Endnotes

1   Carolyn Callaway, "The Runaway Scrape: An Episode of the Texas Revolution," M.A. thesis, University of Texas, 1942; Jo Ella Powell Exley, *Texas Tears Texas Sunshine: Voices of Frontier Women* (College Station: Texas A&M University Press, 1985), 53–74; Silk e-Katrin Kunze, *Experiences of Men and Women in Texas* (Norderstedt, Germany: Druck and Bindug, 2002), 10–13; Carmen Goldthwaite, "Emily D. West (Morgan): The Yellow Rose of Texas," in *Wild Women of the Old West*, ed. Glenda Riley and Richard W. Eutlain (Golden, CO: Fulcrum Publishing, 2003) 29–44; Adrienne Caughfield, *True Women and Westward Expansion* (College Station: Texas A&M University Press, 2005), 50–51; Fane Downs, "Tryels and Trubbles, Women in Early Nineteenth Century Texas," *Southwestern Historical Quarterly* 90 (July 1986): 35–56.

2   Mrs. Percy V. Pennybacker included a long excerpt from Harris's reminiscences in her best-selling history of Texas, a volume that served as the major history textbook in Texas from the 1890s to the 1920s. See Pennybacker, *A History of Texas for Schools* (Austin: Pennybacker, 1908), 179–181. See also: Evelyn M. Carrington, ed., *Women in Early Texas* (Austin: Pemberton Press, 1975). Ann Fears Crawford and Crystal Sasse Ragsdale, *Women in Texas* (Burnet, TX: Eakin Press, 1982); Vertical Files, Dolph Briscoe Center for American History, University of Texas at Austin.

3   Herbert C. Banks, ed., "Dilue Rose Harris," *Daughters of the Republic of Texas Patriot Ancestors Album* (Paducah, KY: 2001), 123–125; "Reminiscences of Mrs. Dilue Harris," *The Quarterly of the Texas State Historical Association* 4 (1900–1901): 85–127, 155–189.

4   Jesús de la Teja, *A Revolution Remembered: The Memoirs and Selected Correspondence of Juan N. Seguín* (Austin: State House Press, 1991), 89.

5   Randolph D. Campbell, *An Empire for Slavery, The Peculiar Institution in Texas, 1821–1865* (Baton Rouge: Louisiana State University Press, 1989), 43–44.

6   Stephen L. Hardin, *Texian Iliad: A Military History of the Texas Revolution* (Austin: University of Texas Press, 1994), 163.

7   Diana Everette, *The Texas Cherokees: A People Between Two Fires, 1819–1840* (Norman: University of Oklahoma Press, 1990), 79; Gregory and Susan Michno, *A Fate Worse than Death: Indian Captive in the West, 1830–1835* (Caldwell, ID: Caxton Press, 2007), 17; J. H. Kuykendall, *Reminiscences, The Quarterly of the Texas State Historical Association* 6 (January 1903): 302.

8   De la Teja, *A Revolution Remembered,* 88.

9   "Reminiscences of Mrs. Dilue Harris" (October 1900), 161; Callaway, "The Runaway Scrape," 6–7.

10   Hardin, *Texian Iliad,* 163; de la Teja, *A Revolution Remembered,* 88; John Hoyt Williams, *Sam Houston: Life and Times of the Liberator of Texas* (New York: Touchstone Books, 1993), 143; Mary A. Polley Baylor Reminiscences, Dolph Briscoe Center for American History, University of Texas at Austin, Box 2Q430.

11   Callaway, "Runaway Scrape," 12–13; Williams, *Sam Houston,* 144.

12   De la Teja, *A Revolution Remembered,* 88; Jesús de la Teja, "Rebellion on the Frontier," in *Tejano Journey, 1770–1850,* ed. Gerald E. Poyo (Austin: University of Texas Press, 1996), 59; William Fairfax Gray, *The Diary of William Fairfax Gray: From Virginia to Texas, 1835–1837,* ed. Paul D. Lack (Dallas: DeGolyer Library and William P. Clements Center for Southwest Studies, 1997), 126; "Reminiscences of Kate Scurry Terrell," *A*

Comprehensive History of Texas, 1685–1897, ed. Dudley Wooten (Dallas: W. G. Scarff, 1898), 669–671.

13 Noah Smithwick, *The Evolution of a State, or, Recollections of Old Texas Days* (1900; repr., Austin: University of Texas Press, 1983), 87–99.

14 "Reminiscences of Kate Scurry Terrell," 669–671.

15 Rosa Kleberg, "Some of My Early Experiences in Texas," *The Quarterly of the Texas State Historical Association* 1 (April 1898): 300.

16 Ibid., 300.

17 Hardin, *Texian Iliad*, 181–188.

18 Light Townsend Cummins, *Emily Austin of Texas, 1795–1851* (Fort Worth: Texas Christian University Press, 2009), 131–132.

19 Ibid., 132.

20 Callaway, "The Runaway Scrape," 43–33; "Reminiscences of Mrs. Dilue Harris," (October 1900), 204; Gray, "Diary of William Fairfax Gray," 167.

21 Kleberg, "Some of My Early Experiences in Texas," 302; Mrs. Thomas O'Connor, ed. "Reminiscences of Anne Fagan Teal," *Southwestern Historical Quarterly* 34 (April 1931): 325–326; de la Teja, *A Revolution Remembered*, 89.

22 Cummins, *Emily Austin of Texas*, 135; W. G. Dewees, *Letters from an Early Settler* (1853; repr., Waco: Texian Press, 1968), 203–209.

CHAPTER 7

"To the *Devil* with your Glorious History!"

Women and the Battle of San Jacinto

Jeffrey D. Dunn

On April 20–21, 1836, the battle of San Jacinto took place between the Texas army under General Sam Houston and a division of the Mexican army under General Antonio López de Santa Anna. During the afternoon of April 21, the Texans, numbering about 900 men, marched across a prairie separating the two armies and attacked the Mexicans, numbering about 1,300. In less than thirty minutes the Texans routed the Mexicans in their camp and spent the following hours indiscriminately slaughtering or capturing hundreds of Mexicans who were attempting to flee. Approximately 600 Mexican soldiers surrendered at dusk, ending the fight. Santa Anna fled west on horseback, but was captured the following day about eight miles from the battleground.[1]

The battle of San Jacinto ended the Texas Revolution, secured Texas independence, and became an iconic event in Texas history. There were no female combatants in either army, but it would be a mistake to assume that women were not involved or affected.

This chapter examines the stories of several women—Texans and Mexicans—whose lives were touched by the battle.

The area where the battle of San Jacinto was fought, near the junction of Buffalo Bayou and the San Jacinto River in what is now east Harris County, formed the eastern edge of Stephen F. Austin's colony during the period of Mexican sovereignty. Beginning in the early 1820s, families from the United States immigrated to this area, settling along both waterways. In 1836 this place was sparsely settled compared to other parts of Texas. [2]

The largest population center was at the town of Harrisburg, located where Brays Bayou meets Buffalo Bayou, less than a mile west of where the present Interstate 610 bridge crosses what is now the Houston Ship Channel. A visitor in March 1836 remarked that the town consisted of only twelve or fifteen houses, a steam saw, and a grist mill. One of these houses belonged to Jane Harris, the widow of the founder of the town, John R. Harris. When the Texan cabinet, including Interim President David G. Burnet, Vice President Lorenzo de Zavala, and others, established the temporary seat of government at Harrisburg in late March 1836, they made Mrs. Harris' home their headquarters. She boarded thirteen men, including officers, volunteers, and one prisoner during March and April.[3]

Many women in the region encompassing Harrisburg and the San Jacinto settlements used their skills to support the war effort. In September 1835 Captain Andrew Robinson organized a company of volunteers at Harrisburg. Sarah R. Dodson, the wife of Robinson's first lieutenant, Archelaus Dodson, made a flag out of calico, consisting of red, white, and blue squares, with a single white star in the blue square. The Dodson flag was the first Texas "tri-color lone star" flag.[4]

Another company of volunteers, organized on the San Jacinto River at the same time as Robinson's company, also commissioned a flag. William Scott, the company's captain, presented four yards of blue silk to one of his men, who painted a large white star in the center above the word "Independence." The soldiers then took the flag to the home of Frances Lynch, wife of Nathaniel Lynch, operator of Lynch's ferry on the San Jacinto River. Mrs. Lynch sewed a piece of domestic cloth to the flag to protect its edges and the flag was unfurled for the first time in late 1835 between the shore and Mrs. Lynch's house.[5]

Some women near San Jacinto aided the war effort by making bullets and clothes for the volunteers. Margaret Wells Rose, wife of Pleasant W. Rose, helped her brother James Wells prepare for the army when word arrived that the Alamo was under siege. The Rose family had come to Texas in 1833 and lived temporarily in Harrisburg before moving to Stafford Point about 20 miles southwest. Margaret's daughter, Dilue, recalled that she worked all day making bullets from molten lead while her mother stayed up all night sewing striped hickory shirts.[6]

When the Texas army reached the battleground on April 20, 1836, the men carried a flag featuring a defiant female, in the form of a goddess of liberty, with an outstretched arm holding a sword and a ribbon inscribed with "Liberty or Death." The ladies of Newport, Kentucky, had presented that flag to Sidney Sherman's company of Newport Volunteers before they left for Texas in December 1835. In August 1836 the government of Texas presented the flag to Sherman's wife, and it remained in the Sherman family until 1896 when descendants returned the flag to the state of Texas. The flag was later restored and today hangs behind the House speaker's podium in the Texas state capitol.[7]

In the weeks leading up to the battle—March and early April 1836—thousands of settlers from the Brazos River fled their homes in the episode known as the "Runaway Scrape." For those living in Harrisburg and along the San Jacinto River, the approach of the Texan and Mexican armies brought the full brunt of the war to

The restored San Jacinto battle flag. Courtesy The State Preservation Board, Austin, Texas.

their homes. One of the major escape routes for these refugees was through Harrisburg to Lynch's ferry on the road hugging the south bank of Buffalo Bayou. Dilue Rose and her family, with a group of fifty civilians, took this route and found "fully five thousand people" trying to cross the ferry at the San Jacinto River. She described the scene as "almost a riot." William Fairfax Gray arrived at the ferry on April 4 and found "large crowds, all seeking a passage across the same purpose, with their wives, children, negroes [*sic*], horses, cars, wagons, and droves of cattle." [8]

Widow Almyra McElroy, aged twenty-two with several children, lost four buildings and a large amount of furniture when a contingent of the Texas army burned San Felipe on March 29. Two weeks later she was at Lynch's ferry with a wagon and a yoke of oxen trying to cross with her family when Texan soldiers seized her property for the army's use. They took her wagon and team back to Harrisburg and never returned. After the war she made claims against the government of $1,173 for property destroyed at San Felipe and $325 for her wagon and oxen, but both claims were denied. [9]

Joseph and Elizabeth Atkins, natives of England, lived on the west side of the San Jacinto River near Lynch's ferry in a house rented from Dr. George Patrick. About April 5, while civilians were passing their home toward the ferry, Elizabeth, who was thirty-eight-years old, gave birth to her fourth son. Neighbors took Mrs. Atkins and her infant by an oxen-drawn sled to the San Jacinto River where they crossed over to Lynchburg. [10]

On April 15 the residents of Harrisburg evacuated the town after word arrived that Santa Anna was approaching. The Texan cabinet and most of the residents escaped on board the steamboat *Cayuga* down Buffalo Bayou toward Galveston. Santa Anna occupied Harrisburg that night and the following day sent fifty men on horseback under Col. Juan Almonte toward Lynch's ferry in an attempt to intercept the steamboat. Almonte arrived at the ferry landing

later the same day, April 16, just missing his opportunity to capture
the steamboat. The Texans had scuttled the ferry boat prior to his
arrival. [11]

By the time Santa Anna reached Harrisburg those who wanted
to cross at Lynch's ferry had made it across, and practically all of
the settlers in the area had abandoned their homes. But there was
one family who stayed behind. A woman named "Mrs. Brown" was
living at William Vince's home on Vince's Bayou, ten miles east of
Harrisburg on the road to Lynchburg. She was a native of Scotland
and a relative of the Atkins family. When Almonte's cavalry reached
her home on April 16, they seized her thirteen-year old son, James,
and a coal-black stallion he was trying to save. Mrs. Brown confronted the Mexicans and demanded protection as a subject of the
king of England. Almonte, who spoke fluent English, released her
son and assured her that she and her children would be safe, but
he kept the horse. Known as "Old Whip," the horse became famous
when he carried Santa Anna from the battleground after the battle
had been lost. [12]

Mrs. Lynch and her children were still at home on the east
bank of the San Jacinto River when Almonte arrived and called
to her from the opposite bank, in fluent English, to bring over a
boat. The frightened woman grabbed her children and a few supplies and rode east on horseback, warning other refugees: "The
Mexicans are upon us!" Among those who heard the alarm were
Vice President Lorenzo de Zavala, his wife Emily, and their three
children, all of whom were in a small skiff with two men at the
oars near the ferry crossing, but unseen by Almonte. The Zavalas
had abandoned their home on the north bank of Buffalo Bayou,
about one mile west of Lynchburg, the previous day, but were
returning to retrieve a trunk of silver left behind. After hearing
Mrs. Lynch's alarm, Lorenzo and Emily took the oars from their
frightened rowers, turned their boat around, and headed down

the river. The Zavalas met another family and together they were saved by the *Cayuga*.[13]

Almonte backtracked and turned south toward the settlement of New Washington, located on a peninsula separating the San Jacinto River from upper Galveston Bay. Now called Morgan's Point, this settlement was a real estate venture financed by New York capitalists and managed by their Texan agent, Col. James Morgan. Morgan was in Galveston on April 16 acting as commandant of the army post. But just prior to Almonte's arrival, Interim President Burnet and his family, along with many of Morgan's workers and slaves, hurriedly attempted to offload supplies for transport to Galveston. Burnet's servant soon warned them of the approaching Mexican cavalry. With only moments to spare, Burnet, his wife, their two young children, neighbor Frances Brooks, and Dr. George Patrick, jumped in a small skiff and with two servants at the oars managed to row far enough into the bay to avoid the Mexican cavalry as they arrived on the shore.[14]

According to Dr. Patrick's version of this incident, Burnet stood up in the boat and declared: "I will take the first shot!" His wife Hannah, thirty-six years old, frantically pulled on her husband's coat insisting that he sit down, but David refused. He vowed not to be taken alive, while Hannah said she would prefer to take a child under each arm and jump overboard rather than be taken herself. Somehow they managed to reach the schooner *Flash* and then Galveston. When Almonte became a prisoner after the battle, he told his captors he was close enough to have killed everyone in the skiff, "but would not let his men fire on them, because he saw ladies in the boat."[15]

Santa Anna joined Almonte at New Washington on April 18 after burning Harrisburg, including Jane Harris' home. The Texas army meanwhile arrived on Buffalo Bayou, opposite Harrisburg. From a captured Mexican courier, Houston learned that the main Mexican force was stationed on the Brazos River near present Richmond, while Santa Anna had marched ahead with only 750 men. The courier also told Houston that Santa Anna intended to cross the San Jacinto at Lynch's ferry. With this intelligence, Houston crossed Buffalo Bayou on April 19 and arrived at the ferry crossing the next day. His men found a defensive position in the timber along Buffalo Bayou and waited for the arrival of the Mexicans.[16]

Santa Anna took Morgan's workers as prisoners, burned New Washington on the morning of April 20, and marched north toward Lynchburg. The armies encountered each other near Lynch's ferry several hours later in the opening engagement of the battle. During the afternoon of the following day the Texans charged the Mexican camp and defeated Santa Anna's division. The pastoral scene where the engagement occurred would forever be known thereafter as San Jacinto battleground and, coincidentally, that ground happened to be owned by a woman named Margaret "Peggy" McCormick. [17]

Peggy McCormick was a native of Ireland and the widow of Arthur McCormick, one of Stephen F. Austin's colonists. Arthur received title to his property in 1824 and died only a few months later. As a widow McCormick continued to live on the land with her two sons, one of whom was serving as an army express rider in 1836. McCormick was a feisty lady who abandoned her home prior to the arrival of the armies, but returned soon after the battle to discover, to her horror, hundreds of Mexican corpses scattered near her home. In 1849 writer Samuel Hammett noted that she "achieved immortality by her dauntless courage, not at, but after the battle." She appeared before General Houston and imposed on him "the full weight and power of woman's first, best weapon of offensive or defensive war—her tongue." She demanded that Houston remove the bodies from her land. He replied: "Madam, your land will be famed in history as the classic spot upon which the glorious victory of San Jacinto was gained! Here was born, in the throes of revolution, and amid the strife of contending legions, the infant of Texan independence! Here that latest scourge of mankind, the arrogantly self-styled 'Napoleon of the West,' met his fate!" Unimpressed and furious, Mrs. McCormick replied: "To the *devil* with your glorious history! Take off your stinking Mexicans." He refused.[18]

Early in May 1836 the stench of decaying bodies was so strong that the Texan army was forced to abandon the battleground. They moved three miles up the bayou to Dr. Patrick's home, previously occupied by the Atkins family, taking the Mexican prisoners with them. The corpses decomposed before Mrs. McCormick and her neighbors began burying the bones. Visitors to the battleground for several years reported seeing skulls on the ground, and some were picked up as souvenirs. Mrs. McCormick also suffered the loss of over 230 livestock and 75 bushels of corn consumed by both armies. She tried three times—in 1836, 1843, and 1851—to receive compensation from the Texas government for this loss, but never received any payment. She lived on the battleground until 1859 when her home burned. She was found dead inside, a suspected victim of murder.[19]

Many of Peggy's neighbors also suffered losses as a result of the battle. The Texas army stripped the Zavala home of the family's carpenter tools, cooking utensils, shovels, spades, axes, and lead nails, and converted the home into a hospital. Many of the Mexican prisoners were kept on the grounds. Mrs. Zavala and her children were unable to move back into their home until late May when the wounded and the prisoners were relocated.[20]

Interim President David G. Burnet and his family lived a short distance east of Lynchburg. Although the Mexican army never reached their home, Texan refugees ransacked the place during their absence. Mrs. Burnet abandoned many of her personal belongings at New Washington in their escape. The Mexicans seized her dresses, which were recaptured by the Texans, and then auctioned to the Texas soldiers after the battle. The Burnets never received compensation for their losses, which were compounded by the death of their infant son in September 1836.[21]

In contrast to the experiences of Texan women who lived near the battleground, a handful of Mexican women accompanying the Mexican army, sometimes referred to as camp followers or *soldaderas,* became eyewitnesses to the battle. Some were the wives or sisters of soldiers. To ensure a fast approach to Harrisburg, Santa Anna left behind most of these women when he left the Brazos River on April 14. Mexican accounts of the battle do not mention any women with the army, but Col. George Hockley, who commanded the Texan artillery, reported that the Texans held six women among 600 Mexican prisoners. Stephen Sparks, a private in Col. Sidney Sherman's regiment, later wrote that he saved the lives of four of these women near the boggy bayou behind the Mexican camp. According to Mexican soldier Manuel Escalera, one of the few survivors of the battle who escaped the carnage and returned safely to Filisola's army on the Brazos River was a woman who was wounded in the thigh.[22]

Nearly a year after the battle, in April 1837, American naturalist John James Audubon arrived on Galveston Island and spotted three women, all of them Mexican prisoners. The whereabouts of the other three women prisoners, as seen by Hockley shortly after the battle, are lost to history. In August 1837, the Texas government commissioned the schooner *Harriet* to carry the remaining seventy-two prisoners from Galveston to Matamoros. When they arrived, the Matamoros newspaper reported that "tres mujeres mexicanos, que se hallaban prisioneros en Tejas," or that three Mexican women living as prisoners in Texas accompanied them. [23]

The eighth Mexican woman known to have been at the battle of San Jacinto died tragically during the slaughter that took place after the Texans took control of the Mexican camp, but prior to the final surrender at dusk. Colonel Sherman found her corpse near

Peggy's Lake, a body of water where many of the Mexican soldiers lost their lives. Sherman asked soldiers nearby: "Who killed her?" Several responded that Col. John Forbes, the army's quartermaster, was responsible.[24]

Forbes, born in Ireland to Scottish parents, had come to Nacogdoches by way of Ohio in 1835 and became one of Sam Houston's close friends. But despite his position, the rank and file taunted him for killing the woman. A few days after the battle Col. Alexander Somerville demanded that Houston discharge him from the army because "no honorable man can serve with him."[25]

Shaken by these accusations, Forbes asked Houston to call a "court of inquiry" to allow him to clear his name. Houston, "in a laughing mood," agreed and appointed Sherman to preside. While the army was still camped on the battleground, the court convened to determine if sufficient grounds existed for a court martial.[26]

During these proceedings Forbes admitted to killing the woman, but justified his action "for so doing in battle." He called one witness on his behalf. Ironically, it was one of the Mexican female prisoners, the wife of a muleteer. Sherman later wrote that "she testified to Col. Forbes' humanity and kindness extended to herself and other women made prisoners." No witnesses spoke against Forbes and the court ruled that no evidence supported his censure. On the contrary, the court found that his conduct during the battle was "characterized as that of a courageous as well as humane soldier."[27]

The incident did not appear in print until October 1858 when a memoir on the battle of San Jacinto prepared for the *Texas Almanac* appeared in the *Galveston Weekly News*. Galveston resident Dr. Nicholas Labadie, a surgeon at San Jacinto, wrote the narrative. In describing the closing scene of the battle, Labadie mentioned that "one or two women were killed by someone aiming at their heads," and that "Commissary Forbes, of Nacogdoches, was accused of the deed and arrested, but not tried, as his accusers were advised not to come forward."[28]

Labadie's narrative not only resurrected an embarrassing moment, but also misstated the facts and implied a cover-up. Newspapers in Texas circulated Labadie's "camp story." According to one paper, "Gentlemen in the army at the time accounted for it in this way: If a woman was killed in the *melee*, it was because she had on a soldier's *capote*, or overcoat, and was mistaken for a man." Despite this support, Forbes was not satisfied. In 1859 he filed a libel lawsuit against Labadie in Nacogdoches.[29]

Twenty-six veterans of the battle gave depositions in this lawsuit, including Sam Houston. The most incriminating testimony against Forbes came from Thomas F. Corry, a private who served in Captain William H. Patton's company. Corry, who knew Forbes when they both lived in Ohio, claimed to be an eyewitness to the killing and gave a graphic account of what happened. Corry stated that about an hour before sundown, near the timber skirting the San Jacinto River at the margin of the bay, he encountered Forbes walking toward him alone and holding a sword in his hand. They congratulated each other on the victory before seeing two Texan soldiers approaching with two prisoners: a man and a woman. Corry said he knew that one was a woman because of "her form, her hair, her features and her dress." He recalled that she was about twenty-five or thirty years old. An officer riding by yelled at the soldiers: "Kill them, God damn them. Remember the Alamo." The soldiers turned on the male prisoner and killed him with their bayonets. According to Corry, Forbes then "thrust his sword into the woman's breast." The sword passed through her body and she immediately fell dead. Corry claimed to have said to Forbes: "Damn you; you have killed a woman."[30]

The lawsuit was dormant during the Civil War, but on November 20, 1866, Labadie and Forbes agreed to end the case before trial.

Labadie entered a statement disclaiming any intent to prejudice Forbes' reputation or charge him "with any conduct unworthy of a soldier or a man of honor." In return, Forbes withdrew his lawsuit. Following this settlement, no published account of the battle mentioned this incident again during Forbes' lifetime.[31]

In addition to the Texas women whose lives were upended by the battle and the experiences of the Mexican *soldaderas*, one "mulatto" female taken prisoner by the Mexicans shortly before the battle became a late twentieth-century phenomenon. The story surrounding this woman places her in Santa Anna's tent at the precise moment the Texans attacked the Mexican camp. A passport record from the Texas State Library and an employment contract discovered in 1991 indicate that her name was Emily D. West and she was a house worker for Col. James Morgan at New Washington. The late Dr. Margaret Henson claimed that Emily's story was told around camp fires and bar rooms in the nineteenth century, but no evidence exists to substantiate this claim or that the story was widely known in either Texas or Mexico. The anecdote of Emily in Santa Anna's tent may not be true, but it is not a legend or myth. To fully appreciate and understand what is fact and fiction, the historiography of the anecdote and how it has been interpreted and misinterpreted is itself an important part of the story.[32]

The source of the anecdote comes from *one sentence* inserted in an unpublished essay, written about 1850 by an Englishman named William Bollaert. He was visiting Texas in 1842 when he learned of the event and recorded it in his notes. The story was told in Bollaert's unpublished essay as follows:

> Much has been written relative to this celebrated battle in which the flower of the Mexican army perished and when Santana was made prisoner, but I beg to introduce the following as given to me by an officer who was engaged in it—given in his own words

"The battle of San Jacinto was probably lost to the Mexicans,
owing to the influence of a Mulatta Girl (Emily) belonging to
Col. Morgan who was closeted in the Tent with G'l Santana,
at the time the cry was made "the Enemy! they come!
they come! & detained Santana so long, that order could
not be restored readily again."[33]

Marked to the side of the quoted sentence was the word "private,"
underlined three times.[34]

Bollaert apparently wrote this essay about 1850, six years after
returning to England in 1844. He was a prolific writer and published
ten articles about Texas, but never once mentioned this anecdote
in any of them. His unpublished essays and journals survived his
death in 1876 and Edward Ayer, a businessman and avid collector
of American literature, bought them in 1902 at a London auction.
Ayer donated the papers to Chicago's Newberry Library in 1911
where they remain today.[35]

Bollaert's papers became a treasure trove for historians interested
in life in the Republic of Texas, but the anecdote about Emily was
either ignored or overlooked for decades. The story finally made its
inaugural publication in 1951, as a footnote, when Texas historian
Joe Frantz published his biography of early Texas dairyman Gail
Borden. In 1956 western historian Eugene Hollon edited and published Bollaert's papers and inserted the anecdote about Emily, again
as a footnote. Without any corroborating evidence to rely upon,
early commentators assumed the mixed-race female known only
as "Emily" was Morgan's slave and for this reason she was initially
assigned the name "Emily Morgan."[36]

The anecdote might have become nothing more than an academic
curiosity except for the efforts of Texas A&M publicist and amateur
historian Henderson Shuffler, who turned the story into a public
sensation. In a private letter written in 1959 to musical historian John

The sole source of the story of the mulatto girl Emily in Santa Anna's tent comes from this quote preserved in William Bollaert's handwriting from an unpublished manuscript circa 1850. The manuscript was written in ink, but the left margin (not clearly shown here) includes the word "private" written in pencil and underlined three times. Courtesy William Bollaert Papers, the Newberry Library, Chicago, Illinois.

A. Lomax, Jr., Shuffler wrote that he had a "hunch" that the song, "The Yellow Rose of Texas," grew up around the stories of Emily, but he had no evidence to prove it. In 1960, in another letter to Lomax, Shuffler expressed frustration that Emily's story has "flitted through the footnotes of history," but still no direct evidence linked the story to the famous song. Nonetheless, he wrote, "if there is not, as I still suspect, a remote connection between the story of Emily and the original folk version of 'The Yellow Rose,' there should be. Surely, such a genuine heroine of the battle for Texas freedom should not go unsung." Both Shuffler and Lomax communicated their "hunch" to Frank X. Tolbert, a popular Texas history writer for the *Dallas Morning News*, and in 1961 Tolbert wrote about the song's association with Emily, the first time this connection found its way into print. In *An Informal History of Texas*, Tolbert wrote that Emily:

> lived to tell her story to her master, Colonel Morgan, and to in-spire a wonderful song. Musical historians seem to agree that the folk song "The Yellow Rose of Texas" was inspired by a good-looking mulatto slave girl. And in one set of original lyrics—not the ones popularized by Mitch Miller—the girl of the song is called "Emily, the Maid of Morgan's Point."[37]

Martha Anne Turner, an English teacher at Sam Houston State University, attempted to substantiate the legitimacy of this connection in her book, *The Yellow Rose of Texas: Her Saga and Her Song*, published in 1976, but a consensus of scholars has long since refuted Turner's analysis and any authentic association between the story and the song. Texan folklorist F. E. Abernethy published a remarkable article in 2001 concerning how this story's association with the song evolved into bad history, placing much of the blame on himself. But fifty years after Shuffler's "hunch," his vision of taking Emily from the ranks of unsung heroines has been resilient. Regardless of evidence to the contrary, Emily's association with "The Yellow Rose of Texas" has likely become an enduring part of her legacy.[38]

The absence of an authentic connection between the story and the song is not an excuse for dismissing the credibility of the story. No eyewitness accounts of the battle have surfaced to either confirm or refute the story, but there are intriguing clues that suggest the story was not merely a figment of someone's imagination. Three clues to Emily's identity can be found in the anecdote itself, as related by Bollaert: her given name ("Emily"), her mixed racial ethnicity ("mulatto"), and an association with Col. James Morgan ("belonging to Col. Morgan"). Emily's relationship with Morgan provides the context for the time and place of her presumed capture on April 17 when Almonte's cavalry seized New Washington. Dr. George M. Patrick, who escaped from Almonte in Burnet's skiff, stated in an affidavit signed in 1850 that "the incursion of the Mexicans was so sudden and unexpected that all the servants together with several other individuals were taken prisoners." Among those known to have been captured was a thirteen-year-old free African-American from New Haven, Connecticut, named George Cooper. Cooper later stated that after his capture he witnessed the burning of New Washington on April 20, was with the Mexicans when they encountered Houston's army later that day, and was released and returned to New Washington after the battle the following day. Cooper's account of his experiences does not mention Emily or the names of any other prisoners or servants taken at New Washington, but his story and Dr. Patrick's comments provide corroborating evidence for the Bollaert anecdote. [39]

Bollaert's unpublished essay introduces the anecdote as a story that came from an officer in the army, but he does not name that officer. Archivist James Lutzweiler, in an analysis of Bollaert's manuscripts as a graduate student in the 1990s at the Newberry Library in Chicago, Illinois, discovered from another manuscript in the

collection that the officer was Sam Houston and that the source
of the story came from a letter that Houston wrote to a friend.
This "friend" was most likely Judge John M. Dor, one of Houston's
former law partners who was living in Galveston in 1842. Bollaert's
journal entry for July 3 indicates that he spent the morning with
Dor reviewing letters Houston had written to Dor.[40]

Despite her much criticized attempt to link the story to "The Yellow Rose of Texas" song, Martha Anne Turner nonetheless became
the first writer to connect the story to a passport record preserved
in the Texas State Library in Austin. This remarkable document
reads as follows:

> Capitol, Thursday Morning
> To the Hon. Dr. Irion,
> The bearer of this—Emily D West has been, since my first ac-
> quaintance with her, in April of -36 a free woman—she emigrated
> to this Country with Col. Jas. Morgan from the state of N. York
> in September of -35 and is now anxious to return and wishes a
> passport.
> I believe myself, that she is entitled to one and has requested me
> to give her this note to you. Your Obt servt,
>
> I N Moreland [signed]
> Her free papers were lost at San Jacinto as I am informed and
> believe in April of -36
>
> Moreland[41]

This letter not only placed a woman named "Emily" at the battle of San Jacinto, but described her ethnicity in a manner that is
consistent with Bollaert's reference to her as a "mulatto." In this
letter, Emily is not Anglo-American, but a "free woman" who had
"free papers" with her at the battle of San Jacinto. The letter also

corroborated her connection with James Morgan and established that their relationship was not master and slave, both of which were consistent with Bollaert's anecdote. The letter, however, described Emily as having a middle initial "D" and surname "West," additional details that are missing from Bollaert's account of her story. The revelation of this document meant that the assigned name "Emily Morgan" was wrong.

The letter was also significant because it corroborated Emily's presence at the battle of San Jacinto. The author was Isaac N. Moreland, a Texan artillery officer who participated in the battle. He left the army in early 1837 and wrote this letter as her lawyer. By confirming his personal acquaintance with her and vouching for the truth of her statements, Moreland gave credibility to her passport request.

Moreland did not date his letter, but its date can be inferred. The letter was addressed to Dr. Robert Irion, who was appointed Secretary of State on June 13, 1837. Irion had not worked for the Department of State prior to his appointment. His office was in the "capitol" building erected in Houston in 1837 and first used in early May. Moreland's notation at the top of the letter showed that he wrote the letter in this building. A copy of the letter was recorded in the Department of State's Letter Book in July 1837, indicating that the letter was addressed to Irion in his capacity as Secretary of State, the department that issued passports in 1837. Thus, Moreland wrote the letter to Irion sometime after June 13 and prior to the end of July 1837.[42]

In 1991 a third document emerged that shed additional light on Emily's identity. This new evidence was an employment contract between "Emily D. West" of New Haven, Connecticut, and "James Morgan" of Texas. The contract, signed in New York City on October 28, 1835, obligated West to go to Texas in Morgan's vessel and work for Morgan "at any kind of house work she, said West is qualified to do and to industriously pursue the same from the time she commences until the end of twelve months." She was to be paid $100 for the year's work, payable every three months if requested.[43]

The contract was one of six agreements between Morgan and workers hired in New York during October 1835 and found in a private collection of Texana documents pledged to a Houston bank. This collection was acquired by Houston businessman David M. Smith in the early 1970s from the estate of Texas autograph collector William A. Philpott, Jr. Smith sold about 730 of these documents in an auction 1986, but another 215 documents from this collection, including 12 letters to Philpott and a Philpott photo, were not included in that sale. Instead, they remained pledged to the bank. Approximately 60 of these 215 documents relate to James Morgan's business affairs in Texas. In 1991 this author found the Emily D. West employment contract among these 60 documents.[44]

The contract corroborates Emily's first name, middle initial, and surname, her relationship with Morgan as an employee and not a slave, and that she came to Texas from New York in 1835, facts that are consistent with her passport request prepared in 1837. The passport request stated that she immigrated to Texas in September 1835, one month prior to the date of the employment contract, but the reference to the September date may be a reference to the time when she left New Haven, or it could simply be an error in her recollection. Whether her departure for Texas occurred in September, October, or November 1835 was not critical to her request for a passport in 1837.

The employment contract does not mention Emily's race or color, but it was witnessed by Simeon Jocelyn, a prominent Anglo-American abolitionist and preacher at an all-black church in New Haven in the early 1830s. The twelve-month term of employment was also significant because it provided the reason for Emily's request for a passport to return home in 1837—her employment term had ended.[45]

Both the passport record and employment contract, after surfacing from independent collections, are consistent with the anecdote recorded by Bollaert. Together they suggest that the story of Emily in Santa Anna's tent cannot be dismissed as folklore, legend, or myth. But is there any evidence from the Mexican army's perspective?

Santa Anna never mentioned in his writings whether he had a woman in his tent, but in two letters written shortly after he returned to Mexico in 1837, he admitted that he was sleeping when the battle commenced. In one letter he said that he was sleeping "under a tree," but Corporal Juan Reyes stated in a deposition in July 1836 that Santa Anna retired to "*su chosa*" (his hut) about an hour before the battle started, indicating that he was in his tent. Furthermore, Santa Anna apparently enjoyed female companionship when the opportunity arose. Henry Brewster, a Texan soldier at San Jacinto and private secretary to Sam Houston, interviewed Santa Anna after the battle. He wrote that Santa Anna "professed a warm admiration of female character, and said women were the 'gravy of society.'"[46]

Both Colonel Pedro Delgado and Santa Anna's secretary, Ramón Martínez Caro, saw Santa Anna as the battle unfolded, but neither mentioned this incident in the accounts they later wrote. Both were severely critical of Santa Anna's conduct preceding the battle. If Emily's story were true, why would these accounts be silent? Likewise, if Bollaert really did copy the anecdote from a letter written by Sam Houston, why did neither Houston nor any other Texan who may have heard about the story mention it or give a hint of it in any publication or private letter, so far as we know? Although their silence is frustrating for modern historians, the lack of direct evidence corroborating the story is not evidence that the story was not or could not have been true. When Bollaert wrote "private" and underlined the word three times in the margin next to where he wrote the anecdote, the notation may have been a reminder from his source not to reveal the anecdote publicly. And that notation may have ultimately convinced Bollaert not to publish his essay.[47]

There is one additional curiosity and coincidence worth mentioning. Emily D. West's name was strikingly similar to Mrs. Lorenzo de Zavala's maiden name, "Emily West." The late historian Margaret S. Henson in the 1980s and 1990s attempted to link the two women in some manner, but no document has surfaced to indicate that they had a master-servant or other relationship, or that they even knew each other. Furthermore, government and other records refute speculation that these women were one and the same. Mrs. Zavala received a passport from the Department of State on December 10, 1836, in the name of "Mrs. Emily Zavala" and left Texas for New York City under that name with her three children on March 4, 1837, on the schooner *Flash*. Thus, Mrs. Zavala left Texas more than three months before Emily D. West delivered her request for a passport to the Texas Department of State in late June or July 1837, arriving in New York at the same time Emily D. West was seeking her passport to leave Texas. One of the mysteries of this intriguing story is that Department of State records do not indicate if Emily D. West's request for a passport was granted or denied, and no documents have surfaced thus far to indicate what happened to her after July 1837.[48]

The battle of San Jacinto directly affected a relatively small number of women and it is regrettable that only a few left written accounts of their experiences. Many other incidents involved women, including African-American female slaves who lived in the vicinity of the battleground. But in the absence of records, their names and experiences likely will never be known. The surviving stories of the women of San Jacinto, even though most are limited in scope and come largely from the writings of men, are compelling and in some instances riveting. They provide a dramatic backdrop to this singular event in Texas history.

Selected Bibliography

Abernethy, F. E. "The Elusive Emily D. West, Folksong's Fabled 'Yellow Rose of Texas'" in *2001: A Texas Folklore Odyssey*. Denton: University of North Texas Press, 2001, 319–329.

Blake, R. B. comp. *The San Jacinto Campaign of 1836 as given by Depositions in theCase of John Forbes vs. Nicholas D. Labadie, District Court of Nacogdoches County, Texas*, 2 vols., typescript, n.d.

Castañeda, Carlos. *The Mexican Side of the Texan Revolution*. 2nd ed. Austin: Graphic Ideas Incorporated, 1970.

Gray, William Fairfax. *Diary of Col. Wm. Fairfax Gray: From Virginia to Texas 1835–36*. Houston: The Fletcher Young Pub. Co., reprint 1965.

Harris, Dilue Rose. "Reminiscences of Mrs. Dilue Harris, II." *The Quarterly of the Texas State Historical Association* 4 (January 1901).

Hollon, W. Eugene, and Ruth Lapham Butler, eds. *William Bollaert's Texas*. Norman: University of Oklahoma Press, 1956.

Jenkins. John H., ed. *The Papers of the Texas Revolution 1835–1836*. 10 vols. Austin: Presidial Press, 1973.

Labadie, N. D. "San Jacinto Campaign." *The Texas Almanac 1857–1873*. Compiled by James M. Day. Waco, TX: Texian Press, 1967.

Looscan, Adele B. "Harris County, 1822–1845." *Southwestern Historical Quarterly* Part 1, 18 (Oct. 1914) and Part 2 (Jan. 1915).

Maberry, Jr., Robert. *Texas Flags*. College Station: Texas A&M Press, 2001.

Muir, Andrew Forest, ed. *Texas in 1837*. Austin: University of Texas Press, 1958.

Perry, Carmen, trans. *With Santa Anna in Texas: A Personal Narrative of the Revolution by José Enrique de la Peña*. College Station: Texas A&M University Press, 1975.

"Recollections of S. F. Sparks," *The Quarterly of the Texas State Historical Association* (July 1908).

Endnotes

1   Houston's computation of the number of participants and casualties can be found in his report of the battle. See Sam Houston to David G. Burnet, Apr. 25, 1836, in John H. Jenkins, ed., *The Papers of the Texas Revolution 1835–1836* (Austin: Presidial Press, 1973), 6: 72 (#2871). José Enrique de la Peña, who was with the Mexican army on the Brazos River, reported that one wounded officer and "a few soldiers and domestics" arrived

from the battleground on April 24, and four additional soldiers arrived the following day. See Carmen Perry, trans., *With Santa Anna in Texas: A Personal Narrative of the Revolution by José Enrique de la Peña* (College Station: Texas A&M University Press, 1975), 125–127.

2   Adele B. Looscan, "Harris County, 1822–1845" (part 1), *Southwestern Historical Quarterly* 18 (Oct. 1914).

3   Ibid.; *Richmond Enquirer*, June 7, 1836; Jane Harris, June 18, 1836, Audited Claim #487, Texas State Library, Austin, Texas.

4   Adele B. Looscan, "Harris County, 1822–1845" (part 2), *Southwestern Historical Quarterly* 18 (Jan. 1915): 273–274; Robert Maberry, Jr., *Texas Flags* (College Station: Texas A&M Press, 2001), 24; Mamie Wynne Cox, *The Romantic Flags of Texas* (Dallas: Banks Upshaw and Company, 1936), 158.

5   Looscan, "Harris County, 1822–1845" (part 2), 271–273; Maberry, *Texas Flags*, 23–24; Cox, *The Romantic Flags of Texas*, 172.

6   "Reminiscences of Mrs. Dilue Harris, II," *The Quarterly of the Texas State Historical Association* 4 (January 1901): 160; Herbert H. Lang, "Harris, Dilue Rose," *Handbook of Texas Online*, http://www.tshaonline.org/handbook/online/articles/fha89 [accessed May 1, 2011].

7   Mrs. M. Looscan, "The History and Evolution of the Texas Flag," in *A Comprehensive History of Texas*, ed. Dudley Goodall Wooten (Dallas: William G. Scarff, 1898; repr., Austin: Texas State Historical Association, 1986), 1:695–696; *Daily News* (Galveston), Sept. 6, 1896; Edward Miles to Miss Sherman, Nov. 2, 1885, Carrie Menard to H. A. McArdle, Nov. 22, [1891], and Carrie Sherman Menard to H. A. McArdle, Mar. 16, 1894, in H. A. McArdle, *The McArdle Notebooks: The Battle of San Jacinto* (Archives Division, Texas State Library, Austin, Texas); "Treasured Artworks at the Texas Capitol," http://www.tfaoi.com/aa/1aa/1aa4g.htm [accessed Mar. 17, 2011].

8   Andrew Forest Muir, "The Municipality of Harrisburg," *Southwestern Historical Quarterly* (July 1952): 45–46; "Reminiscences of Mrs. Dilue Harris, II," 160–171; William Fairfax Gray, *Diary of Col. Wm. Fairfax Gray: From Virginia to Texas 1835–36* (Repr., Houston: The Fletcher Young Pub. Co., 1965), 151, 152.

9   Almyra McElroy, Apr. 27, 1839, Unpaid Claims, Texas State Library, Austin, Texas.

10 *History of Texas, Together With a Biographical History of the Cities of Houston and Galveston* (Chicago: The Lewis Publishing Co.,1895), 701; Joseph O. Dyer, *The Early History of Galveston, by Dr. J. O. Dyer* (Galveston: Oscar Springer Print, 1916), 21; 1850 US Census, Galveston County, page 282 ("Joseph Adkins" [sic]); "Reminiscences of Mrs. Dilue Harris,

II," 176; Adele B. Looscan, "Harris County, 1822–1845," *Southwestern Historical Quarterly* 18 (Oct. 1914): 206; Gray, *Diary of Col. Wm. Fairfax Gray*, 144, 146, 152, 161; Joseph Atkins, Sept. 17, 1874, Pension Claim, Texas State Library, Austin, Texas.

11 Gray, *Diary of Col. Wm. Fairfax Gray*, 144, 161; Carlos Castañeda, *The Mexican Side of the Texan Revolution*, 2nd ed. (Austin: Graphic Ideas Incorporated, 1970), 74-75.

12 Mrs. Brown may have been the widow of James Brown. "Reminiscences of Mrs. Dilue Harris, II," 175, 176; 1850 US Census, Galveston County, Series M432, roll 910, page 242 ("James K. Brown"); A. J. Sowell, "'Old Whip'—The Horse That Santa Anna Rode at San Jacinto," *History of Fort Bend County* (Houston: W.H. Coyle & Co., 1904), 155–158; Jesse A. Ziegler, "Old Whip—Black Stallion of Santa Anna," *Wave of the Gulf* (San Antonio: The Naylor Co., 1938), 190–193; N. D. Labadie, "San Jacinto Campaign," in *The Texas Almanac 1857–1873*, comp. James M. Day (Waco, TX: Texian Press, 1967), 170.

13 After Nathaniel Lynch died in late 1836, Frances married Martin Hardin, who moved into the Lynch home. They were still living at the Lynch ferry house in 1850. US Census, Harris County, Series M432, Roll 911, page 252. "The Private Journal of Juan Nepomuceno Almonte, February 1–April 16, 1836," *Southwestern Historical Quarterly* 48 (July 1944): 32; Castañeda, *Mexican Side of the Texan Revolution*, 75; Andrew Forest Muir, ed., *Texas in 1837* (Austin: University of Texas Press, 1958), 20; Charles Adams Gulick, Jr., Harriet Smither, et al., eds., *The Papers of Mirabeau Buonaparte Lamar*. 6 vols. (Austin: Texas State Library, 1920–27), 1:522, 4: pt. 1, 124-125, and 5: 384; "Journal of Lewis Birdsall Harris, 1836–1842," *Southwestern Historical Quarterly* 25 (Oct. 1921): 136; Gray, *Diary of Col. Wm. Fairfax Gray*, 161.

14 Castañeda, *The Mexican Side of the Texan Revolution*, 75; *Daily News* (Galveston), June 4, 1889; *Daily News* (Galveston), June 4, 1889; *Morning News* (Dallas), Oct. 10, 1899; *Telegraph and Texas Register* (Houston), Apr. 7, 1838, Aug. 4, 1841, Aug. 25, 1841.

15 In 1889, a newspaper article stated that Captain Luke Falvel, of the schooner *Flash*, claimed that he took Mrs. Burnet and one son on board the *Flash* at New Washington and that David Burnet insisted on staying behind, but that he reached the *Flash* later in a small boat before the schooner arrived at Galveston. *Daily News* (Galveston), June 4, 1889; *Morning News* (Dallas), Oct. 10, 1899. See also *Telegraph and Texas Register* (Houston), Apr. 7, 1838, Aug. 4, 1841, Aug. 25, 1841; Wooten, *A Comprehensive History of Texas*, 1:277–278; Edward E. Este to Joseph

C. Clopper, June 5, 1836, in Edward N. Clopper, *An American Family* (Huntington, WV: Standard Printing & Publishing, 1950), 265.

16 "Journal of Lewis Birdsall Harris, 1836–1842," 139; Harris; Houston to Burnet, Apr. 25, 1836, *Papers of the Texas Revolution*, VI, 72 (#2871).

17 James Morgan, affidavit, Jan. 26, 1850, John A. Rockwell Papers (Dolph Briscoe Center for American History, University of Texas at Austin); Castañeda, *The Mexican Side of the Texan Revolution*, 75–76; Margaret Swett Henson, "McCormick, Margaret, *Handbook of Texas Online*, http://www.tshaonline.org/handbook/online/articles/fmcbs [accessed May 1, 2011].

18 Philip Paxton (psued. Samuel A. Hammett), *A Stray Yankee in Texas* (New York: Redfield, 1853), 247; John J. Linn, *Reminiscences of Fifty Years in Texas* (New York: D. & J. Saddlier & Co., 1883), 264; *The Narrative of Robert Hancock Hunter* (Austin: The Encino Press, 1966), 17; Henson, "McCormick, Margaret," *Handbook of Texas Online*.

19 Jeffrey D. Dunn, "The Mexican Soldier Skulls of San Jacinto Battleground," https://www.friendsofsanjacinto.com/sites/default/files/uploads/MexicanSkulls4-1-10.pdf [Accessed Feb 8, 2011]; Margaret McCormick, Dec 16, 1836, Dec. 13, 1843, Dec. 30, 1851, Memorials and Petitions, Texas State Library, Austin, Texas; *Daily Evening Bulletin* (San Francisco, Calif.), Aug. 15, 1859; Henson, "McCormick, Margaret," *Handbook of Texas Online*.

20 Perkins Island is now called Alexander Island. Clopper, *An American Family*, 265; "Journal of Lewis Birdsall Harris, 1836–1842," 137–138; Lorenzo de Zavala, Jr., Jan. 15, 1841, Memorials and Petitions, Texas State Library, Austin, Texas; S. B. Raymond to James Morgan, May 14, 1836, *Papers of the Texas Revolution*, 6, 271 (#3051); Mirabeau Lamar to James Morgan, May 19, 1836, *Papers of the Texas Revolution*, 6, 338 (#3108); Labadie, "San Jacinto Campaign," in Day, *The Texas Almanac 1857–1873*, 165, 170–171, 174-175; Louis E. Brister, "The Journal of Col. Eduard Harkort, Captain of Engineers, Texas Army, February 8–July 17, 1836," *Southwestern Historical Quarterly* 102 (January 1999): 372.

21 Clopper, *An American Family*, 265; *Texas Centinel* (Austin), August 12, 1841; *Telegraph and Texas Register* (Houston), Oct. 4, 1836.

22 Wallace Woolsey, trans., *Memoirs For the History of the War in Texas by Don Vicente Filisola* (Austin: Eakin Press, 1987), 2: 124–125, n.1; Carmen Perry, trans., *With Santa Anna in Texas: A Personal Narrative of the Revolution by José Enrique de la Peña* (College Station: Texas A&M University Press, 1975): 22, 111, 113; *The Gloucester Telegraph* (Gloucester, Massachusetts), May 28, 1836; Linn, *Reminiscences of Fifty Years in Texas*, 285; Gregg J. Dimmick, *Sea of Mud* (Austin: The Texas State Historical Association, 2004), 36–40, 122; "Recollections of S. F.

Sparks," *The Quarterly of the Texas State Historical Association* (July 1908): 71–72.

23   *Gazette* (Alexandria), June 25, 1836; Robert Buchanan, *Life and Adventures of Audubon, the Naturalist* (London: J. M. Dent and Sons, Ltd., 1869): 307; *Telegraph and Texas Register* (Houston), Aug. 14, 1837; *Mercurio del Puerto de Matamoros* (Matamoros, Tamp.), Sept. 8, 1837, Matamoros Archives 24, 82 (Dolph Briscoe Center for American History, University of Texas at Austin, Austin, Texas); Lewis Williams, May 6, 1851, Pubic Debt Claim #873, Texas State Library, Austin, Texas; Margaret S. Henson, "Politics and the Treatment of the Mexican Prisoners After the Battle of San Jacinto," *The Southwestern Historical Quarterly* (Oct. 1990): 220.

24   "Second Deposition of Sidney Sherman," Dec. 27, 1859, in *The San Jacinto Campaign of 1836 as given by Depositions in the case of John Forbes vs. Nicholas D. Labadie, District Court of Nacogdoches County, Texas*, comp. R. B. Blake; typescript, n.d., 1: 56-57.

25   "John Forbes," Louis Wiltz Kemp San Jacinto Biographies (San Jacinto Museum of History), http://www.sanjacintomuseum.org/Herzstein_Library/Veteran_Biographies/San_Jacinto_Bios/biographies/default.asp?action=bio&id=3134 [accessed Mar. 1, 2011]; "Deposition of Joel W. Robison," Blake, *The San Jacinto Campaign*, 79; "Deposition of James Gillaspie, Blake, *The San Jacinto Campaign*, 87; A. Somervell to Sam Houston, Apr. 24, 1836, in Jenkins, *Papers of the Texas Revolution*, 6, 51–52 (#2860).

26   John Forbes to Sam Houston, Apr. 26, 1836, *Papers of the Texas Revolution*, 6, 85 (#2880); "Second Deposition of Sidney Sherman," *San Jacinto Campaign*, 58–59.

27   "Second Deposition of Sidney Sherman," *San Jacinto Campaign*, 58, 60; Sidney Sherman to Lt. Tinsley, Apr. 28, 1836, *Papers of the Texas Revolution*, 6, 112 (#2914); Sam Houston to Geo. W. Hockley, Apr. 29, 1836, *Papers of the Texas Revolution*, 6, 119 (#2922).

28   Labadie, "San Jacinto Campaign," in Day, *The Texas Almanac 1857–1873*, 163.

29   *The Rambler* (Austin), Nov. 9, 1858; John Forbes to Editors of the Galveston News and Publishers of Texas Almanac, 1859, Oct. 18, 1859, in Day, *The Texas Almanac 1857–1873*, 339–341; *John Forbes vs. N. D. Labadie*, In the District Court of Nacogdoches County, Texas, January Term, 1859, No. 2509, in Blake, *The San Jacinto Campaign of 1836*, 1: 1–9 (Original Petition), and 1: 10–19 (Amended Answer of Defendant).

30   "Deposition of Thomas F. Corry," Dec. 12, 1859, in *Sidelights on the Battle of San Jacinto*, comp. R. B. Blake , typescript, n.d., 2: 7, 16–17.

31   Blake, *Sidelights on the Battle of San Jacinto*, 2: 185–190.

32 Margaret Swett Henson, "West, Emily D.," *Handbook of Texas Online* http://www.tshaonline.org/handbook/online/articles/fwe41 [accessed Apr. 9, 2011]; Ann Fears Crawford, ed., *The Eagle: The Autobiography of Santa Anna* (Austin: The Pemberton Press, 1967), 265, n.25. See generally James E. Crisp, *Sleuthing the Alamo: Davy Crockett's Last Stand and Other Mysteries of the Texas Revolution* (New York: Oxford Univ. Press, 2005), 193–194.

33 For a biography of Bollaert, see Stanley Pargellis's introduction in Hollon and Butler, *William Bollaert's Texas*, xi–xx; and Sir Rutherford Alcock, "Address to the Royal Geographical Society," *Proceedings of the Royal Geographical Society of London* (1876–1877), 21: 422–424; William Bollaert, "Texas in 1842—By a Traveller," William Bollaert Papers, Ayer MS 83d (Newberry Library, Chicago, Illinois).

34 Bollaert, "Texas in 1842—By a Traveller."

35 See W. Eugene Hollon and Ruth Lapham Butler, eds., *William Bollaert's Texas* (Norman: University of Oklahoma Press, 1956).

36 Hollon and Butler, *William Bollaert's Texas*, ix, xviii–xix, 108, n.24; Joe B. Frantz, *Gail Borden: Dairyman to a Nation* (Norman: University of Oklahoma Press, 1951), 110, n.9; Crawford, *The Eagle: The Autobiography of Santa Anna*, 265, n.25.

37 Frank X. Tolbert, *An Informal History of Texas From Cabeza de Vaca to Temple Houston* (New York: Harper & Brothers, 1961), 96–97; Henderson Shuffler to John A. Lomax, Jr., July 6, 1959, and Feb. 20, 1960, in "Lomax (John Avery) Family Papers," (Dolph Briscoe Center for American History, University of Texas at Austin, Austin, Texas); *Morning News* (Dallas), Apr. 14, 1968; Sept. 20, 1970.

38 Martha Anne Turner, *The Yellow Rose of Texas: Her Saga and Her Song* (Austin: Shoal Creek Publishers, 1976), 36; F. E. Abernethy, "The Elusive Emily D. West, Folksong's Fabled 'Yellow Rose of Texas,'" in *2001: A Texas Folklore Odyssey* (Denton: University of North Texas Press, 2001), 319–329. Tolbert's book on the battle of San Jacinto, published two years before his *Informal History of Texas*, mentions Emily as part of the battle narrative, but does not link her to the song. Frank X. Tolbert, *The Day of San Jacinto* (New York: McGraw-Hill Book Co., 1959), 147.

39 George M. Patrick, affidavit, June 26, 1850, and George Cooper, affidavit, June 20, 1850, John N. Haggerty et al. claim, Commission on Claims Against Mexico, National Archives, Washington, D.C.

40 William Bollaert, "Personal Narrative of a Residence and Travels in the Republic of Texas by W. B. During the years 1842–1844," William Bollaert Papers, Ayer MS83e (Newberry Library, Chicago, Illinois); James Lutzweiler, "Emily D. West and the Yellow Prose of Texas: A Primer on

Some Primary Documents and their Doctoring," *2001: A Texas Folklore Odyssey*, 295–315; William Bollaert, *Private Journals, 1841–1849*, William Bollaert Papers, Ayer MS 83b (Newberry Library, Chicago, Illinois); John M. Dor Deposition, Galveston County, Sept. 25, 1839, in Gulick, et. al., *The Papers of Mirabeau Buonaparte Lamar*, 3, 117.

41 I[saac] N. Moreland to Dr. R. A. Irion, Papers of the Secretary of State, RG 307, Passports issued by the Department of State, Republic of Texas, 1836–1845 (West, Emily D.), Texas State Library, Austin, Texas, http://www.tsl.state.tx.us/arc/passports/west.pdf [accessed Apr. 8, 2011]; Turner, *The Yellow Rose of Texas*, 35, citing Andrew Forest Muir, "The Free Negro in Harris County Texas," *Southwestern Historical Quarterly*, 46 (Jan. 1943): 218.

42 Papers of the Secretary of State, Letter Book of the Department of State, II, 47-48, Texas State Library, Austin, Texas; *Telegraph and Texas Register* (Houston), June 24, 1837; James Glass to Jeff Dunn, April 28, 2006. See also Thomas W. Cutrer, "Moreland, Isaac N.," *Handbook of Texas Online* (http://www.tshaonline.org/handbook/online/articles/fmo43), accessed March 19, 2011.

43 Emily D. West agreement, Folder 926, William A. Philpott, Jr. Collection, University of Texas at Arlington, Arlington, Texas; Jeffrey D. Dunn, "Known Provenance and Description of the William A. Philpott, Jr. Collection of Texana Documents Held by Wells Fargo Bank Texas, National Association," June 30, 2003, University of Texas at Arlington Library, Arlington, Texas.

44 Dunn, "Known Provenance and Description of the William A. Philpott, Jr. Collection of Texana Documents Held by Wells Fargo Bank Texas, National Association." See also Jeff Dunn, "One More Piece of the Puzzle: Emily West in Special Collections," *The Compass Rose* 19 (Spring 2005), http://libraries.uta.edu/speccoll/crose05/Compass_Rose_Spring_2005%20%282%29.pdf.

45 In *Sleuthing the Alamo*, James E. Crisp suggests that Emily D. West might be the free female of color shown living in Jocelyn's household in the 1830 census, but subsequent research by Tim Niesen, of Lancaster, Pennsylvania, indicated that the free colored female was a black teenager named Harriet Lanson, who died in New Haven in early November 1835. Crisp, *Sleuthing the Alamo*, 193–194. Information on Simeon Jocelyn can be found in *New York Evangelist*, Sept. 5, 1835; obituary in *Brooklyn Eagle*, Aug. 20, 1879, *The American Missionary* (Oct. 1879), and Mary McQueeney, "Simeon Jocelyn, New Haven Reformer," *Journal of the New Haven Colony Historical Society*, 19:3, 66; (letter of S. S. Jocelyn) *Liberator*, Dec. 19, 1835, and (Harriet Lanson obituary by S. S. Jocelyn) Apr. 2, 1836.

46 Santa Anna to Ministry of War and Marine, Mar. 11, 1837, and May 10, 1837, in Castañeda, *The Mexican Side of the Texan Revolution*, 24, 32, 77; Juan Reyes, deposition, Transcripts of Archivo General de Mexico, Book 335, 14, Dolph Briscoe Center for American History, University of Texas at Austin, Austin, Texas; Henry Stuart Foote, *Texas and The Texans*, II (Philadelphia: Thomas, Cowperthwaite & Co., 1841), 315.

47 *Morning News* (Dallas), Nov. 17, 1985; Ramon Martinez Caro, "A True Account of the First Texas Campaign and the Events Subsequent to the Battle of San Jacinto," in Castañeda, *The Mexican Side of the Texan Revolution*, 117; Pedro Delgado, "Mexican Account of the Battle of San Jacinto," in Linn, *Reminiscences of Fifty Years in Texas*, 232.

48 *Morning News* (Dallas), Nov. 17, 1985; *Chronicle* (Houston), Feb. 2, 1986; *Morning News* (Dallas), Apr. 26, 1987; Jeff Dunn, "Emily West de Zavala and Emily D. West: Two Women or One?" *The Compass Rose* 20 (Spring 2006), http://www.tamu.edu/ccbn/dewitt/images/texforum/drose06.pdf [accessed Mar. 30, 2011]; Margaret Swett Henson, "West, Emily D.," *Handbook of Texas Online* http://www.tshaonline.org/handbook/online/articles/fwe41 [accessed Apr. 9, 2011].

CHAPTER 8

Women and the Texas Revolution in History and Memory

Laura Lyons McLemore

"Sentimentalism is a cluster of ostensibly private feelings which
always attains public and conspicuous expression."
Ann Douglas, *The Feminization of American Culture.*[1]

Browsing through DeWitt Clinton Baker's *Texas Scrap-Book* (1875),
a compendium of primary documents, memoirs, and biographical
sketches, it is striking to note how completely masculine it is, except
for a handful of poems by women, one of whom turned out to be
an African black man, "Forestina," Moses Evans' "Wild Woman of
the Woods." Even an article on "The Archive War" by George Gray
mentioned Angelina Eberly, who fired the cannon to prevent the
state archives from being moved, only twice and only as the pro-
prietress of the boarding house where the records were deposited
until the reopening of the Land Office. Women were essentially not
part of the narrative. Any wonder, then, that they would become
the memorializers of Texas revolutionary heroes? That was the only
way they could claim their own place in the Texas Revolution. They

may not have been able to fight on the battlefield or sign the Texas Declaration of Independence, and their activities may have been omitted from or marginalized in the historical record, but by putting themselves in charge of its memory, they secured a role in it for themselves.[2]

In fact a case could be made that women were in some sense the real heroes of the Texas Revolution. Women participated in the revolution—like Dilue Rose Harris, Jane Birdsall Harris, and Jane Wilkinson Long—who made bullets for the Alamo, took part in the Runaway Scrape, and hosted the provisional Texan government, respectively. Women were affected by it. They had to manage during the conflict and afterward, many times alone, maintaining property and sustaining families. Like Mary Jane Briscoe, many of them were widows who had to support themselves and their children in a frontier setting. Furthermore, women shaped the memory of it with great energy, determination, and purpose. They were the ones who worked to make the Texas Revolution memorable. They saved battle sites like San Jacinto and the Alamo and erected monuments. They preserved the documents, celebrated the veterans, wrote the stories, and made sure that Texas history was taught in schools and made available in libraries. While Stephen F. Austin, Davy Crockett, Jim Bowie, William B. Travis, and Sam Houston might be names most associated with the historical origins of the "Texas State of Mind," and while historians John Henry Brown, George P. Garrison, Eugene C. Barker, Walter Prescott Webb, J. Frank Dobie, and T. R. Fehrenbach might be names most popularly associated with its written history, the women of Texas had more to do with the public memory of Texas and the "Texas State of Mind" than the veterans of the Texas Revolution themselves. It was Texas women who nurtured, preserved, and promoted the memory of Texas' veterans and their victorious revolution.

The impulse to memorialize Texas heroes and historic sites was not a spontaneous reaction in the aftermath of the revolution. The Alamo did not become a site of public culture soon after the battle nor were the veterans of the Texas Revolution particularly celebrated. Many spent decades just trying to secure their bounty land grants. The Texas Veterans Association did not hold its first meeting until 1873, and not until the late 1890s did two women, Adina de Zavala and Clara Driscoll, collaborate (or some would say compete) to preserve the Alamo, which had fallen into such disrepair that little of it remained. [3]

The sentimentalization and memorialization of the Texas Revolution and its heroes came out of a flurry of groups organized after Texas emerged from Reconstruction (post-1870) and coincided with a national trend of sentimentalizing and memorializing the momentous places and events of American history following the Civil War (1861–1865). During this period, not only the Texas Veterans Association, but also women's clubs (notably the Daughters of the Republic of Texas [DRT], and the Texas Woman's Press Association) turned their attention to Texas' creation story. These organizations brought historical preservation into the political consciousness of the era. Because of their success, it is commonly and understandably assumed that Texans' collective memory was a product of group activity, motivated by a reverence for the past and the desire to benefit posterity. But the motivations may have been much more complex and personal than that and as much about the present as the future and more about the future than the past. The efforts of the women who championed the cause of Texas' veterans and memory-places may often have had as much to do with the women themselves as with the causes they promoted. The compulsion to enshrine the places and persons involved in Texas independence stemmed at least in part from the psychological and social needs of the survivors and their descendants. Leading figures in the movement to promote the

memory of the Texas Revolution, Mary Jane Harris Briscoe, Adina
de Zavala, and Clara Driscoll, exemplified this premise. They show
that personal experiences, backgrounds, and motivations do not
have to be similar to make common cause and that personal visions
produce public memory.[4]

Mary Jane Harris was born in 1819 in St. Genevieve, Missouri, the
daughter of John Richardson Harris, founder of Harrisburg, Texas,
and Jane Birdsall Harris of Seneca Falls, New York. As fortune would
have it, the Harris' neighbors in St. Genevieve were Moses Austin
and his family. In short order Austin convinced Harris to embark
upon the colonization enterprise he was planning. So, Harris sent
his family back to New York, and he went with Moses Austin "to
explore the resources of Texas." It was a long overland journey from
St. Genevieve, Missouri, to Cayuga, New York, and all the responsibility throughout the trip rested upon the wife. At the time Mary
Jane was eleven months old and she never saw her father again.[5]

In 1826 John Harris obtained a land grant and laid out the town
of Harrisburg at the junction of Buffalo and Bray's bayous near
present-day Houston where he erected a steam sawmill. On a trip
to New Orleans in August 1829 to procure equipment, he contracted
yellow fever and died. By this time Mary Jane was ten years old. Her
brothers, DeWitt Clinton, Lewis, and John were fifteen, thirteen,
and eight, respectively. In 1833 when the Harris boys at last attained
enough maturity to be of some help, the widow Harris (nee Jane
Birdsall) traveled to Texas with the eldest, DeWitt Clinton, to claim
her husband's interests. She opened a farm and built a house, but due
to tension between the colonists and the Mexican government, the
situation remained unsafe. Not until October 1836 did Mrs. Harris
send for her only daughter.

Mary Jane Harris, now seventeen, traveled to Texas in the company of her grandfather and some other male relatives. After arriving in New Orleans, they traveled to Quintana where she was

introduced to many of the men who had "lately made their names famous in heroic action." At Brazoria, the travelers stayed for two weeks at the boarding house of Mrs. Jane Long, "whose romantic history was listened to with unflagging interest by all." Less than a year later, on her eighteenth birthday, Mary Jane Harris married her brother Dewitt's business partner, Andrew Briscoe, a veteran of the battle of San Jacinto and nine years her senior.[6]

The couple went to live in Houston for two years where Captain Briscoe had been elected chief justice of the county court. Accounts of the Anahuac disturbance in 1835 and some of his own correspondence hint that Briscoe was something of a hothead. According to the *Memoirs* of Francis R. Lubbock, an early Texas immigrant and future Confederate Texas governor, Briscoe rather distrusted his own abilities to discharge his legal responsibilities. At the end of his two-year term, the Briscoes therefore returned to Harrisburg, built a brick house, went into the cattle business, and ostensibly enjoyed ten years of prosperity and wedded bliss, during which time they had five children, four of whom survived to adulthood.

Everything, however, did not go all that well. Briscoe seemed to be one of those restless individuals full of money-making schemes that never seemed to work out. In 1839 he planned a railroad from Harrisburg to the Brazos River, but the project was abandoned in 1840 with only about two miles of road laid. That same year Briscoe drew up a plan for building a railroad from Harrisburg to San Diego, and in 1841 he secured a charter from the Republic of Texas for the Harrisburg Railroad and Trading Company, of which he was president. In 1847 the Harrisburg Town Company transferred all unsold lots and lands to Sidney Sherman. By early 1849 Briscoe was involved in a lawsuit against Sidney Sherman and spoke to his brother, James, of a plan to go to California, acknowledging that should he die there, his family "would probably be left with very little active means on which to live." Meanwhile, he moved his wife and children to New Orleans with the idea of going into a different line of work, this time banking and finance. In July 1849, he confided to his father: "My rents come enormously heavy, but if I can obtain the business, that will not make much difference. Here I am, and here I mean to stay till [*sic*] I have just means enough left to transport myself and family to California." Briscoe's father responded with concern and skepticism: "I am fearful that you may suffer by sickness. I am also fearful that you may not succeed in your line of business to your hopes & expectations." On October 4, 1849, Andrew Briscoe died, most likely from malaria as he had been sick on and off for several months, leaving Mary Jane with four small children and no means of support.[7]

As so many other women had done on the frontier, Mary Jane Briscoe rose to the challenge. Of necessity, she followed her head more than her heart, and she had a very good head on her shoulders. She accepted the shelter and support of her father-in-law in Port Gibson, Mississippi, primarily for the sake of her children. When General Briscoe joined the rush westward in search of California gold and then drowned in a storm on the return journey in 1851, Mary Jane found herself once again without a home or support for her family. Relying on the advice of her brother-in-law, James M. Briscoe, family friends Charles Babcock and Francis R. Lubbock, and a cousin, Thomas Carothers, she converted her husband's fallow real estate and land grant certificates in Texas into revenue-producing property. She returned to Texas, first to Grimes County where Briscoe owned property, and later to Galveston, Harrisburg, and finally to Houston in 1874.

By the time Mary Jane Briscoe returned to Houston, both sons had served in and survived the Civil War; two of her children were married and settled; the other two had completed their educations and the eldest, Parmenas, was gainfully employed. Her mother, Jane Harris, had died in 1869. Many friends and neighbors from her early years in Harrisburg had migrated to Houston or Galveston, but she retained a deep emotional tie to that time and place. As founding DRT member and biographer Adele Looscan stated in an article about Mary Jane Briscoe, she cherished "an ardent love for everything connected with the first years of her life in Texas" and felt "great pride in her father's and mother's association with its early history." She further noted that, "one of the happiest occasions of her advanced life" was the annual reunion of the Texas Veterans Association, of which she became an honorary member on March 3, 1884. Mary Jane's own journal bears out Looscan's assessment. On New Year's Eve, 1885, she reminisced about her days in Harrisburg: "I did my first dancing on a puncheon floor in a room with 3 beds in it: Old Matthew's fiddle strings often reduced to one, but what cared I; I was young and carried away with excitement." She fondly remembered "the gay and happy hours of the winter where we all lived in one room [and] cooked out of doors."[8]

Mary Jane Briscoe's life experience explains her sentimentality, dedication to the Texas Veterans Association, and commitment to the preservation of memory-places such as the San Jacinto battle-ground. She had never known her own father except through family lore and the accounts of his acquaintances and business associates in Texas. She could remember her husband positively within the context of his participation—and by extension, success—in the Battle of San Jacinto; those friends to whom she looked for business advice and with whom she socialized and grew old shared the same memory-places and lived experiences. Associating intimately with the Texas veterans enabled her to relate to the two most important men in her life in a way that elevated her feelings both about them and about herself. An entry in her journal describing the veterans' reunion in Sherman on April 21, 1885, as "the greatest day in Texas History" illustrates this clearly: "The vets met at the Court house. All the school children with bouquets marched before the vets, then they opened their ranks and the veterans marched down between the rows of children and they strewed flowers in our paths. It was a 'very beautiful sight.'"[9]

In addition to the personal comfort and sense of pride and belonging to something momentous, Briscoe's involvement with the Texas Veterans Association provided socialization with those who shared her memories and lived experiences. Although she was very socially active in Houston, the annual reunion afforded her the opportunity to travel, always a favorite pastime, and to see old friends from all over the state. Her account of the reunion and trip to Dallas in 1886 had the tone of a giddy young girl describing a sleepover, even though she was going on sixty-seven at the time. She wrote on April 20, 1886, that she "did not sleep much for somebody was being serenaded" and the music kept her awake. The next day she excitedly reported that she had a carriage ride around the celebration grounds with speeches and singing along the way. She also visited with "so many old friends, I cannot enumerate" and enjoyed "ice cream & oranges also champagne."[10]

Old friendships, thus, were a powerful factor in Mary Jane Briscoe's dedication to Texas veterans. One of her greatest achievements on behalf of Texas veterans was her role in effecting the purchase and designation of the San Jacinto battleground property as a state park. When credit was given to "agitation by the Texas Veterans Association" for the appropriation of funds for the purchase of portions of the battle site, Briscoe was among the leading agitators. She carried the cause of the San Jacinto battle site into her association with the Daughters of the Republic of Texas in the 1890s. Earlier, Briscoe and her daughter, Adele, Hally Bryan, and Betty Ballinger had established the Daughters of the Republic of Texas, one of the oldest patriotic women's organizations in the nation, in her parlor on November 6, 1891. Together they formed an association of women who were the direct descendants of the men and women who established the Republic of Texas. Hally Bryan's father, Guy M. Bryan, a member of the Texas Veterans Association, encouraged their efforts. As individual women they may have had little power, but as a group these Texas women were able to accomplish what the veterans had not. A letter from Dr. L. D. Hill, state representative from Travis County, in 1897 attests: "Honored Lady, Permit me to congratulate you and your co-workers on the final passage of the bill appropriating ten thousand Dollars for the purchase of the San Jacinto Battle ground. We in the coming future may have to explain many of our votes in the 25th Legislature to our constituency but the vote for the San Jacinto Bill will stand approved for all time, by all patriotic Texans." Hill then credited the women for the success of "the first appropriation bill to purchase the ground where Texas liberty was won by the grandest set of Patriots in human history." He then thanked God that "the women of Texas can always be trusted to lead in all great reforms and patriotic movements. God bless them and aid them in all their efforts to elevate our race."[11]

Of course Mary Jane Briscoe, the widow of a signer of the Texas Declaration of Independence and participant in the Battle of San Jacinto, had a vested interest, financially, in the Texas Veterans Association for which she received her husband's land grant certificate. From her journal it appeared that Briscoe was not particularly engaged with Texas or United States politics, though she possessed a lively curiosity and was exceptionally well-read, reinforcing the impression that the memorialization of Texas heroes had a personal meaning for her. The fact that her husband and most of her oldest friends were part of that revolutionary era stimulated her devotion to Texas veterans and Texas shrines. This shared experience provided not only a means of defining herself, but maintaining social contacts with her contemporaries as well.

Texas veterans and Texas shrines also had great personal meaning for Adina de Zavala, granddaughter of Lorenzo de Zavala, the first

Military Plaza, San Antonio, Texas, circa 1875. Courtesy Library of Congress Prints and Photographs Division.

vice president of the provisional government of the Republic of Texas. Her motives, however, differed from those of the revolutionary generation. To de Zavala, the Texas Revolution represented a multi-historical past, evidenced by her vision for the old San Antonio de Valero mission, better known as the Alamo. For her, it was a site influenced and constituted by the presence of Indians, Spaniards, Mexicans, and Anglo-Americans. Her attention to historical detail and her effort to highlight the Alamo's occupation by Spanish and Mexican soldiers exemplified this vision. As Virginia Taylor, Spanish archivist at the Texas General Land Office noted, her grandfather's career provided de Zavala with an abiding interest in Texas history and a lifelong desire to preserve not only the spirit, but the physical evidence of the historical drama in which he had participated. Significantly, he had participated as a Mexican Texian.[12]

Adina de Zavala was born at de Zavala Point on Buffalo Bayou in Harris County November 28, 1861. She was of a different generation than Mary Jane Briscoe, and her personal motivations were different as well. But her zeal for the preservation of Texas' heritage and historical sites surpassed even that of the survivors of the revolutionary era. Like Mary Jane Briscoe, she understood the power of collective effort and marshaled even more volunteer groups for these purposes. The results were prodigious. She spearheaded the preservation of four former Franciscan missions and the Spanish governor's palace in San Antonio and encouraged the recognition of March 2 as Texas Independence Day. She suggested that Texas public schools be named for state heroes, and she facilitated the marking of almost forty major sites as places of historical significance. But the campaign that brought her the greatest notoriety by far was her personal battle for the Alamo.[13]

As early as 1887, while teaching school in San Antonio, de Zavala began her lifelong efforts to preserve Texas' historic places and patriotic traditions. In 1889 she and other San Antonio women

founded one of the first societies of Texas women organized for
patriotic purposes. By that time the mission of San Antonio de
Valero had changed hands many times. It had been used as an army
depot during the Mexican War and again during the Civil War. In
1877 Honoré Grenet, a local merchant, purchased the convent and
added wooden porticoes to it. When Grenet died in 1882, the state
acquired his lease to the mission church and placed it in the hands
of the city of San Antonio. City officials then sought a new owner
for the business and mission convent (long barracks) and in 1886 the
Hugo-Schmeltzer Company, a wholesale grocery firm, acquired the
property. Commercial success and modernization then became the
primary function of the Alamo and its significance as a historical
site was secondary.

The attention of de Zavala and her group of preservation-minded
San Antonio ladies inevitably turned to the Alamo, and in 1892 she
extracted a promise from the Hugo-Schmeltzer Company to give
her group first chance at buying the property should they decide
to sell it. In 1893 de Zavala's group affiliated with the Daughters of
the Republic of Texas, which had organized in 1891 in the home of
Mary Jane Briscoe in Houston. The de Zavala chapter immediately
became a vibrant asset to the DRT. They assisted in the projects
of other chapters, such as the naming of public schools for Texas
heroes and the purchasing of the San Jacinto battleground by the
state. Furthermore, they sought with impressive success to repair,
preserve, and mark historical sites, particularly the missions in the
San Antonio vicinity. By 1902 de Zavala's leadership had earned
her a place on the DRT executive board. She wasted no time in
proposing that the DRT formulate a plan to preserve the mission
and began to investigate the possibility of the state purchasing the
Texas missions. She also proposed that the Daughters ask the state
to transfer control of the Alamo to the DRT. The group decided to
leave the matter with the mayor of San Antonio with the request

that a member of the de Zavala chapter be placed on the committee to appoint a custodian for the property. There the situation stood when Clara Driscoll joined the DRT in 1903.[14]

That same year commercial enterprises in the eastern United States expressed interest in acquiring the Hugo-Schmeltzer property. For a while it seemed likely they would do so because the DRT had not been able to raise enough money to purchase it and their option was about to expire. Through a series of somewhat serendipitous events, de Zavala encountered Clara Driscoll, the daughter of a wealthy, elite Corpus Christi family, who had recently returned to Texas from Europe. De Zavala made her case to Driscoll, who had previously expressed concern about the condition of the Alamo. However, de Zavala and her cohort, sculptor Pompeo Coppini, enlisted her aid by appealing not so much to Driscoll's patriotism as to her egoism, explaining "how she could become famous all over the nation by saving that sacred spot." Ultimately, Clara Driscoll did advance the money necessary to acquire the Hugo-Schmeltzer property, but the outcome of this collaboration underscored the differences in the personal motivations of the two women. De Zavala's vision depicted all inhabitants of Texas in 1836 as members of the same social order. The Alamo represented to her the shared sacrifices of Mexican and Anglo Texians fighting for common cause. What motivated de Zavala and her supporters, even after the chapter was expelled from the DRT in 1910, was this inclusive vision of the Texas creation narrative in which the fall of the Alamo represented only one chapter, but one in which their own heritage held a stake. Adele Looscan attempted to explain this, writing:

The great tragedy that occurred within its walls seventy years ago last March in a manner obliterated from the minds of the general public the recollection of any other history connected with this venerable relic of old Spanish dominion . . . . In the course of years, the truth of history has become so obscured, that the tale must be told anew and not only told but insisted upon. It is easy to account for this strange amolition, for it has arisen from false teaching right in the old Alamo Church—It made the old church more interesting to tell visitors that Travis fell here, Crockett there, Bowie yet in another place, that 178 men, nearly the whole force, was after ten days siege, slaughtered right there in the church. The great public, who do not read history, accord these statements as history, and [they] grew to believe that the small church which sheltered not only the whole garrison but a number of Mexican families, all the munitions, and provisions, including about thirty beeves, was, in short, all of the Alamo. No wonder that the public believed what they learned by books and placards as well as by word of mouth from those in charge of the old Church. But false teaching cannot reverse the facts of history.[15]

The history of the mission impelled the women of the de Zavala chapter to invoke the power of group effort to preserve Texas' cultural heritage. For de Zavala and her followers, however, group association was secondary in importance to the original goal. This distinction pointed to the divergence between the motivations and visions of Adina de Zavala and Clara Driscoll, who ostensibly were both working toward the same purpose, that is, the preservation of a Texas shrine. Inspired by de Zavala's vision, the DRT chapter sought to restore the unity of experience and vision that animated the revolutionary generation. They wanted to reestablish a link with a past in which heroes were identified as neither Mexican nor American, but as "the whole people of her beloved Texas land," one of Spanish and Mexican making, but now a social and cultural world lost. While legally disaffiliated from the DRT, de Zavala and her followers still played a major role concerning the structure of the Hugo-Schmeltzer building (the long barracks). From her initial inception, de Zavala envisioned preserving the Alamo as it stood in its mission days, as well as a landmark to the heroes of the 1836 battle. To this end her own research produced plats, maps, and early narrative accounts of the mission in its early years. As researcher Susan Schoelwer wrote: "De Zavala hoped to emphasize its mission background, restoring the main building (convent) to its original arcaded appearance. The Driscoll faction, in contrast, focused primarily on the revolutionary battle and considered the church to be the main feature of the site, which could be better emphasized if the convent was removed."[16]

Driscoll's personal vision of the Alamo as a public place, like Clara Driscoll herself, came out of a different background and a different perspective on both the past and future than that of Adina de Zavala. If de Zavala saw the Alamo in light of a romantic past, Driscoll's romanticism had more in common with a Harlequin novel. In effect, their very public clash over the preservation of the Alamo was a turning point in Texas history and memory. As anthropologist Richard Flores has pointed out, their differences coincided with the divergence between historical Texas and modern Texas. "Adina De Zavala was much more likely to define the Alamo in terms of all those who tread through its historical doors; Clara Driscoll, on the other hand, was intent on interpreting it as a place that legitimated the ensuing social transformation and economic development."[17]

For Driscoll social life was disengaged from commonplace history and the conditions from which it emerged, providing, as Flores has noted, "a self-absorbed reading of both the past and the present." The past was not the entirety of all previous occurrences, but a single incident made to represent all prior events. Her collection of short stories, *In the Shadow of the Alamo*, published in 1906, showcased this perspective. Driscoll's narrative made no attempt to engage the forces and conditions of its historical setting but, instead, valorized her present social milieu. The complex factors that brought Anglo Americans to Texas, influenced Mexico's acceptance of them, and impelled Mexican Texans to join forces against Santa Anna were entirely absent. Driscoll depicted the events of 1836 as a sentimental narrative that denied the hidden "dynamics of development." Her private vision reconfigured the social scene as a place where Texans reigned supreme over those "swarthy-skinned neighbors" from south of the border. This vision of the Alamo served the interests of Driscoll and her milieu far better. The preservation of the Alamo, then, coincided with capitalist expansion and emergent modernization in South Texas. Developments in both railroads and large-scale commercial agriculture eroded the traditional, family-based, cattle ranching society of South Texas and reshaped it to meet the needs and logic of a market economy.[18]

Clara Driscoll was born April 2, 1881, in St. Mary's, Texas, the daughter of Robert Driscoll, Sr., who had amassed a fortune in railroads, ranching, banking, and commercial developments in the Corpus Christi area. The Driscolls were deeply involved in the social and economic restructuring of South Texas. Their business interests in railroads were partially responsible for the economic displacement of Mexicans in South Texas. To see Mexicans as injured by the socioeconomic reorganization to which her family contributed would imply her responsibility for it in some measure. Instead, her vision of an Alamo "theme park" excised the remnants of its Spanish and Mexican origins as surely as her romantic fiction marginalized the Mexican characters in her stories about the Alamo. In every narrative Driscoll depicted Mexicans as deeply flawed. Driscoll's Mexican figures were not whole persons, either psychologically or socially, but individuals who were skewed, off-balance, and lacking. Her Mexican characters were flawed due to their romantic failures and, by extension, personally responsible for their beleaguered condition, stemming from their cultural inadequacy and way of life. By perceiving Mexicans as personally responsible for their own social demise, Driscoll could absolve herself and others of her class of any responsibility.[19]

The conflicting visions of de Zavala and Driscoll with regard to the preservation of the Alamo touched off a battle within the DRT as destructive as any that had occurred within the walls of the old mission. In some ways it was symbolic of the pain and divisiveness accompanying the social and economic transition of Texas from a rural to a modern state. Driscoll became the figure head (and later the president) of the DRT. Her vision of the official Alamo narrative continues to infuse the public presentation of history even today though the "new Texas historians" have made inroads. In her own words she made clear that the preservation of the Alamo was less about the past than about the future of the chosen few: "By the honoring of a glorious past we strengthen our present, and by the care of our eloquent but voiceless monuments we are preparing a noble inspiration for our future."[20]

To her credit, Clara Driscoll devoted the rest of her life to making the Alamo "a symbol of courage and sacrifice that transcended time, space, and ethnicity," not just for Texans, but for all Americans. The stamp of her personality and dramatic flair continued to be evident in that effort. During the centennial celebrations in 1936, she orchestrated an interfaith service at the Alamo featuring a Jewish choir chanting Kaddish to honor the dead.[21]

The women of the DRT continue to this day as faithful custodians of that physical symbol. Adina de Zavala fought valiantly (if in vain) for the restoration of the Alamo's convent until her death in 1955. Her many contributions to the history of Texas and its revolution are well documented. In 1912 she organized the Texas Historical and Landmarks Association, which admitted both male and female members ineligible to join the DRT. She probably did more than any other one person to spur preservation of the Spanish governors' palace in San Antonio, which was purchased by the city 1928 and restored. She was one of the original members of the Committee of One Hundred appointed to plan a state centennial and served on

Plaque at the Alamo historic site honoring two opposing visions that helped preserve the Alamo. Courtesy Dreanna L. Belden, photographer, May 4, 2005, UNT Libraries, The Portal to Texas History, Denton, Texas.

the advisory board of the Texas Centennial Committee. De Zavala, too, authored a book, *History and Legends of the Alamo and Other Missions in and Around San Antonio* (1917), pamphlets, including *The Story of the Siege and Fall of the Alamo: A Résumé* (1911), and contributed to the *Handbook of Texas* (1952). Time has proven that Adina de Zavala was correct in most of her historical contentions concerning the mission.[22]

The women of Texas nurtured, preserved, and promoted the history of the Texas Revolution, but they did more, as the examples of Mary Jane Briscoe, Adina de Zavala, and Clara Driscoll show. Each generation shaped the public memory of that event in its own way and for its own reasons. They demonstrated that the motivations behind public perceptions of the Texas Revolution and the "Texas Myth" were much more complex than many revisionists have assumed. That women's groups have been primarily responsible for preserving and shaping the public memory of the Texas Revolution is now well-recognized. The key question with regard to women, history, and the memory of the Texas Revolution is not what or how but, as Richard Flores observed, why? Although devoted to a common cause, these women were motivated by different factors and varying personal visions of its meaning. It is ironic that the sentimentalization of the Texas Revolution, by Clara Driscoll and others, in many ways does a disservice to genuine heroism. As Columbia University professor Ann Douglas has argued: "Sentimentalism . . . always borders on dishonesty, but it is a dishonesty for which there is no known substitute in a capitalist country." In the end the efforts of Adina de Zavala and her cohorts, while honoring the heroism of the Texas Revolution by insisting on accuracy, were left figuratively "In the Shadow of the Alamo," displaced by the new socio-economic order that accompanied modernization and "progress" in Texas.[23]

Selected Bibliography

Ables, L. Robert. "The Second Battle of the Alamo." *Southwestern Historical Quarterly* 70 (January 1967): 372–413.

Baker, D. W. C., ed. *A Texas Scrap-Book Made Up of the History, Biography, and Miscellany of Texas and Its People*. New York: A. S. Barnes and Co., 1875; repr., Austin: Texas State Historical Association, 1991.

Douglas, Ann. *The Feminization of American Culture*. New York: Alfred A. Knopf, 1977.

Driscoll, Clara. *In the Shadow of the Alamo*. New York: Putnam & Sons, 1906.

Flores, Richard R. "Memory-Place, Meaning, and the Alamo," *American Literary History* 10 (Autumn 1998): 428–445.

———. "Private Visions, Public Culture: The Making of the Alamo." *Cultural Anthropology* 10 (February 1995): 99–115.

Kammen, Michael. *Mystic Chords of Memory*. New York: Vintage Books, 1991.

Looscan. Adele B. "Mrs. Mary Jane Briscoe." *Quarterly of the Texas State Historical Association* 7 (July 1903): 65–71.

Lubbock, Francis R. *Six Decades in Texas, The Memoirs of Francis R. Lubbock, Confederate Governor of Texas*. Edited by C. W. Raines. Austin: The Pemberton Press, 1968.

Salvucci, Linda K. " 'Everybody's Alamo': Revolution in the Revolution, Texas Style." *Reviews in American History* 30 (June 2002).

Schoelwer, Susan Pendergast, ed. *Alamo Images: Changing Perceptions of a Texas Experience*. Dallas: De-Golyer Library and Southern Methodist University Press, 1985.

Zavala, Adina de. *History and Legends of the Alamo and Other Missions in and around San Antonio*. San Antonio: Adina De Zavala, 1917.

Endnotes

1 Ann Douglas, *The Feminization of American Culture* (New York: Alfred A. Knopf, 1977), 254.

2 Forestina, "To the Wild Man of the Woods" in *A Texas Scrap-Book Made Up of the History, Biography, and Miscellany of Texas and Its People,* ed. D. W. C. Baker (New York: A. S. Barnes and Co., 1875; repr., Austin: Texas State Historical Association, 1991), 361, 365; Baker, *A Texas Scrapbook,* 142–143.

3 L. W. Kemp, "Texas Veterans Association," *Handbook of Texas Online,* http://www.tshaonline.org/handbook/online/articles/vot01, accessed

January 23, 2011; Richard R. Flores, "Private Visions, Public Culture: The Making of the Alamo," *Cultural Anthropology* 10 (Feb. 1995): 99.

4 Michael Kammen, "The Enhancement of Retrospective Vision," *Mystic Chords of Memory* (New York: Vintage Books, 1991), 93–100.

5 Adele B. Looscan, "Mrs. Mary Jane Briscoe," *The Quarterly of the Texas State Historical Association* 7 (July 1903): 65.

6 Looscan, "Mrs. Mary Jane Briscoe," 67–68.

7 Lubbock gives the following extract from a letter of Briscoe's in the office of the Secretary of State: "You must be aware that none but lawyers can pretend to do law business correctly. It is extremely awkward to undertake a kind of business of which one is entirely ignorant of the rules and form of proceedings. I believe I am a good soldier; but I shall make a very indifferent probate judge or notary public." Francis R. Lubbock, *Six Decades in Texas, The Memoirs of Francis R. Lubbock, Confederate Governor of Texas*, ed. C. W. Raines (Austin: The Pemberton Press, 1968), 48; A. Briscoe to James M. Briscoe, Feb. 5, 1849; Andrew Briscoe Papers, MC055, San Jacinto Museum of History, Houston, Texas; A. Briscoe to Gen. Parmenas Briscoe; July 9, 1849. Andrew Briscoe Papers, MC055; Parmenas Briscoe to Andrew Briscoe, August 26, 1849, Andrew Briscoe papers, MC055.

8 Looscan, "Mrs. Mary Jane Briscoe," 70; George W. Grover to Mrs. M. J. Briscoe, Mary Jane Harris Briscoe Papers, MC056, San Jacinto Museum of History, Houston, Texas; Mary Jane Briscoe, journal, December 31, 1885, Mary Jane Harris Briscoe Papers, MC056.

9 Ibid., April 21, 1885.

10 Mary Jane Briscoe, journal, April 20–23, 1886.

11 D. L. Hill to Mrs. Briscoe, Daughters of the Republic of Texas, May 10, 1897, Mary Jane Harris Briscoe Papers, MC056.

12 Flores, "Private Visions, Public Culture," 112. http://www.jstor.org/stable/656233. 22/01/2011 17:02; Virginia H. Taylor, "Adina de Zavala," *Women of Early Texas*, ed. Evelyn M. Carrington, (Austin: Jenkins Publishing Company-Pemberton Press, 1975), 301.

13 Frank W. Jennings and Rosemary Williams, "Adina de Zavala: Alamo Crusader," *Texas Highways Magazine* (March 1995): 14–21. http://www.tamu.edu/faculty/ccbn/dewitt/adp/history/bios/zavala/zavala.html. Accessed 21 April 2011.

14 L. Robert Ables, "The Second Battle of the Alamo," *Southwestern Historical Quarterly* 70 (January 1967): 378.

15 Ibid., 381; Adele B. Looscan, "A History of the Purchase of the Alamo Mission by the State of Texas," manuscript, Adele Briscoe Looscan Papers, MC041, n.d. There is no date on this manuscript and no clue as to where

it might have been published, but specific reference to the anniversary of the battle suggests this was delivered either in print or in person in 1906 or 1907, which would correspond with the controversy in the DRT. Pieces of it appeared in "The Work of the Daughters of the Republic of Texas in Behalf of the Alamo," *Quarterly of the Texas State Historical Association* 8 (July 1904): 79–80.

16 Adina de Zavala, *History and Legends of the Alamo and Other Missions in and around San Antonio* (San Antonio: Adina De Zavala, 1917), 62, quoted in Flores, "Private Visions, Public Culture," 110; Flores, "Private Visions, Public Culture," 109; Susan Pendergast Schoelwer, ed., *Alamo Images: Changing Perceptions of a Texas Experience* (Dallas: De-Golyer Library and Southern Methodist University Press, 1985), 47–48, quoted in Flores, "Private Visions, Public Culture," 103.

17 Flores, "Private Visions, Public Culture,"104.

18 Flores, "Private Visions, Public History," 105; Clara Driscoll, *In the Shadow of the Alamo* (New York: Putnam & Sons, 1906), 5; Ann Douglas, *The Feminization of American Culture*, 13; Flores, "Private Visions, Public History," 105–106, 111; Driscoll, *In the Shadow of the Alamo*, 5.

19 Ibid., 107.

20 Linda Salvucci praises Randy Roberts and James Olson's *A Line in the Sand: The Alamo in Blood and Memory* (New York: The Free Press, 2001) for presenting a story that "starts in Mexico, with Lopez de Santa Anna front and center." Linda K. Salvucci, " 'Everybody's Alamo:' Revolution in the Revolution, Texas Style," *Reviews in American History* 30 (June 2002): 239; Driscoll, *In the Shadow of the Alamo*, 25.

21 Roberts and Olson, *A Line in the Sand: The Alamo in Blood and Memory*, 223, quoted in Salvucci, "Everybody's Alamo," 242.

22 L. Robert Ables, "Zavala, Adina Emilia de," *Handbook of Texas Online*, http://www.tshaonline.org/handbook/online/articles/fzafg, accessed April 21, 2011. Published by the Texas State Historical Association.

23 Douglas, *The Feminization of American Culture*, 12.

Contributors

Angela Boswell: Dr. Boswell is a professor of history at Henderson State University in Arkadelphia, Arkansas. She earned her Ph.D. from Rice University and her research focuses on Texas and southern women's history. She has published *Her Act and Deed: Women's Lives in a Rural Southern County, 1837–1873*, and has edited two collections of essays in the *Southern Women Lives* series for the Southern Association for Women's Historians.

Light Townsend Cummins: Guy M. Bryan Professor of History at Austin College, Dr. Cummins served as the Texas State Historian from 2009 to 2011. He is a Minnie Stevens Piper Professor, belongs to the Texas Institute of Letters, and is a member of the Philosophical Society of Texas. He is the author or editor of eleven books and several dozen historical articles. His book, *Emily Austin of Texas, 1795–1851*, won the Liz Carpenter Award from the Texas State Historical Association.

Jeffery D. Dunn: As a practicing banking and finance lawyer in Dallas, Jeff Dunn received his master's degree from the LBJ School of Public Affairs at the University of Texas at Austin and a law degree from Southern Methodist University. He is a former chairman of the San Jacinto Historical Advisory Board and both a co-founder and board member of the Friends of the San Jacinto Battleground Association. Mr. Dunn is also a board member of the Texas State

Historical Associaton, former president of the Texas Map Society, and former chairman of the Dallas County Historical Commission.

William L. (Lindy) Eakin: Dr. Eakin received his Ph.D. in history from the University of Kansas. He has spent the past 30 years in university administration, mostly at the University of Kansas. His 1997 dissertation was on the Hasinai Indians of Texas during the seventeenth and eighteenth centuries. He has taught courses on the Spanish Borderlands, Native American history, and Kansas history since 1998. He is currently the Director of Fiscal Affairs at Kansas State University at Olathe.

Dora Elizondo Guerra: Head of Rare Books and Special Collections at the University of Texas at San Antonio for twenty years, Dora Guerra was the curator for the John Peace Texana Collection that included the Jose Enriqué de la Peña Diary. Other important collections she curated were first edition books about Texas and an extensive collection of Spanish colonial manuscripts. Guerra also worked at the Daughters of the Republic of Texas Library at the Alamo, where she was a translator for their Spanish language manuscript collection and a reference librarian.

Laura Lyons McLemore: Head Archivist at LSU-Shreveport, Dr. McLemore received her PhD. from the University of North Texas. She is a member of the Louisiana Historical Association, Texas State Historical Association, Louisiana Archives and Manuscripts Association, Society of Southwest Archivists, Society of American Archivists, and the Academy of Certified Archivists. She is the author of *Inventing Texas: Early Historians of the Lone Star State*, which was published by Texas A&M University Press in 2004.

Mary L. Scheer: As editor of this volume, Dr. Scheer is an associate professor and chair of the Lamar University history department. In 2004 she was a Fulbright Scholar to Germany. Dr. Scheer authored *Foundations of Texan Philanthropy* (2004), co-edited with John W. Storey *Twentieth-Century Texas: A Social and Cultural History* (2008), and has written several scholarly articles. She is a board member of the Texas State Historical Association and in 2009 received the Ottis Lock Award as educator of the year from the East Texas Historical Association.

Jean A. Stuntz: Dr. Stuntz is an associate professor of History at West Texas A&M University in Canyon, Texas. She is past-president of H-Net:Humanities and Social Sciences Online and book review editor for the West Texas Historical Association Yearbook. She is the author of the award-winning book, *Hers, His, and Theirs:Community Property Law in Spain and Early Texas*.

Index